D0064882

Milton's Epic Process

Milton's Epic Process

Paradise Lost and Its Miltonic Background

CHRISTOPHER GROSE

New Haven and London, Yale University Press, 1973

Library of Congress catalog card number: 73-77151
International standard book number: 0-300-01574-7

Designed by Sally Sullivan
and set in Linotype Baskerville type.
Printed in the United States of America by
Vail-Ballou Press, Inc., Binghamton, N.Y.

Published in Great Britain, Europe, and Africa by
Yale University Press, Ltd., London.
Distributed in Latin America by Kaiman & Polon,
Inc., New York City; in Australasia and Southeast
Asia by John Wiley & Sons Australasia Pty. Ltd.,
Sydney; in India by UBS Publishers' Distributors Pvt.,
Ltd., Delhi; in Japan by John Weatherhill, Inc., Tokyo.

For Eleanor and Minot Grose

Contents

Acknowledgments

It is a pleasure to acknowledge the assistance and encouragement I have received at every stage in the preparation of this book. I am grateful for generous support from the Humanities Institute of the University of California and for fellowships from the Folger Shakespeare and William Andrews Clark libraries that enabled me to read and write in good company and the best of scholarly surroundings. At various times, parts of this book were read and improved by Arthur Marotti, Earl Miner, and H. T. Swedenberg, Jr. I owe a great deal to conversations with Boyd Berry, Milton Crane, William Haller, Merritt Hughes, Lee Jacobus, David Miller, Stella Revard, John Steadman, and Edward Weismiller. Among my colleagues at the University of California, Los Angeles, Paul Sellin and Paul Sheats have been especially encouraging and helpful. My greatest debts are to the writing, teaching, and friendship of Joseph H. Summers; and to my wife, who has listened patiently and critically to almost every page.

Parts of chapters 4, 5, and 6 have appeared in different form in *Journal of English and Germanic Philology, Huntington Library Quarterly,* and in *Seventeenth Century Imagery,* ed. Earl Miner (Berkeley and Los Angeles: University of California Press, 1971). They are included here with the permission of the editors and of the Regents of the University of California.

All citations to the works of Milton, with exceptions recorded in the footnotes, are to the edition of Merritt Y. Hughes, *John Milton: Complete Poems and Major Prose* (New York: Odyssey, 1957); the present publishers of this edition, The Bobbs-Merrill Company, Inc., Indianapolis, have kindly granted permission to quote.

C. G.

Santa Monica, California
March 1973

Abbreviations

Anatomy	Robert Burton. *The Anatomy of Melancholy*. Edited by Floyd Dell and Paul Jordan-Smith. New York: Tudor, 1927.
AP	*An Apology against a Pamphlet*
CD	*De Doctrina Christiana*
CE	Columbia edition of *The Works of John Milton*. Edited by F. A. Patterson et al. 18 vols. New York: Columbia University Press, 1931–38.
CPW	*Complete Prose Works of John Milton*. Edited by Don M. Wolfe et al. 6 vols. to date. New Haven: Yale University Press, 1953–.
Educ	*Of Education*
EL VI	*Elegia Sexta*
Hughes	*John Milton: Complete Poems and Major Prose*. Edited by Merritt Y. Hughes. New York: Odyssey, 1957.
L	*Lycidas*
Mask	*A Mask Presented at Ludlow Castle* (*Comus*)
N	*On the Morning of Christ's Nativity*
PL	*Paradise Lost*
Prol 1, etc.	Prolusions 1, etc.
RCG	*The Reason of Church Government Urg'd against Prelaty*
Ref	*Of Reformation Touching Church-Discipline in England*

PART ONE

1

Introduction

If an expanding divergence of critical approaches is any indication, Milton is even more alive than he was during the primary phases of his "controversy." By 1945 it was relatively safe to say, as did Douglas Bush, that "he still stands there, 'like Teneriff or Atlas unremov'd.' "[1] The controversial defensiveness has now largely disappeared from the critical arguments of Milton's readers, and in general our attention has been shifted from the poetry (and its implicit connections with the author's sensibility) to the poem, its wholeness and its parts. But the terminology of the Milton controversy remains historically interesting, influential, and even critically useful—if for no other reason, because Milton was himself obliquely responsible for much of T. S. Eliot's critical vocabulary.

The writers and educators who followed Eliot's lead in questioning the epic poet's stature also shared his assumption that in Milton's verse poetry and what they called rhetoric are radical enemies (as real poetry and rhetoric always were for these readers). Another way of saying this was to claim that Milton was a "dissociated" poet, to argue from a deficiency in imagination presumably implicit in Milton's blindness to the conclusion that Milton "writes English like a dead language."[2] To Milton (and thus to a Miltonic tradition in English poetry), Eliot and his followers opposed a *precise* tradition, that of Shakespeare, the metaphysical poets, and Henry James. The language of this superior tradition, Eliot believed, gives us the impression of "being in a particular place at a particular time" (p. 140). James, for

1. Douglas Bush, *English Literature in the Earlier Seventeenth Century,* rev. ed. (Oxford: Clarendon, 1962), p. 377.

2. T. S. Eliot, *Of Poetry and Poets* (London: Faber & Faber, 1957), p. 141, hereafter cited as Eliot. The succeeding quotations from Eliot, in this paragraph and the next, are from the same work.

example, is like Milton in being complicated in style. But James's style reveals "a determination not to simplify, and in that simplification lose any of the real intricacies and by-paths of mental movement"; while Milton's, perversely, is an "active complication, a complication deliberately introduced into what was a *previously* simplified and abstract thought" (p. 142; my italics).

The disadvantage of "the rhetorical style," in Eliot's view, thus sprang from the "hypertrophy of the auditory imagination at the expense of the visual and tactile," with the result that the reader experiences a "dislocation" of the following sort: "The inner meaning is separated from the surface, and tends to become something occult, or at least without effect upon the reader until fully understood" (p. 143). For Eliot and his followers, it seems quite clear, there is a kind of speech (at least ideally) which *is* thought; [3] and there is also a verbal art which can follow it. This form of speech is great poetry, this kind of poetry makes up the great tradition. At the source, Shakespeare's language embodies a fusion of "the auditory imagination and the imagination of the other senses" (p. 142). Writing later at the time of the great dissociation —indeed largely creating it—Milton exploits the rhetorical tradition, while Dryden is nurtured in a more healthy linguistic milieu and preserves conversational language in poetry.

What linked the styles of James, Shakespeare, and the metaphysicals in the minds of these readers was a sensed quality (presumably present in Eliot's own verse) which pretends to be antecedent both to "thought' and to formal distinctions (which were lost on many of these critics): the quality of sensuous immediacy which gives no illusion of a literary or rhetorical medium and which reproduces the processes of a sensibility submerged in experience. This style is the appropriate "surface" for virtually any dramatic mode, whether it be the novel of central perspective or the dramatic lyric or monologue. In other words, the only real genre or mode which emerges from their discussion—and from

3. The precision of Eliot's prose here is revealing. Milton becomes the Arnoldian "critic" who abstracts and then ornaments, while Eliot's poetry presumably seeks to crystallize metaphoric processes which *precede* thought in the usual sense; thus the wording in the account of Milton's complication, which (Eliot believes) is artificially introduced into what is "a previously *simplified* [not just simple] and abstract thought."

their rewriting of literary history—is a peculiarly modern one, a mode which Robert Langbaum has called "the poetry of experience." [4]

What seems odd about the judgments of Milton's twentieth-century antagonists, and what makes the vocabulary of the Milton controversy particularly interesting, I believe, is partly that "sensuous immediacy" is a term of only limited value in reading and assessing Milton's verse—despite the unquestionable presence and use of sensuous immediacy in *Paradise Lost.* One might even conjecture that Milton himself might have taken an unexpected part in the controversy. As Frank Kermode has said, "He was the main sufferer in the great experiment of projecting onto an historical scale a developed Romantic-Symbolist theory of the Image [the historical effort of which] has been to identify a period happily ignorant of the war between Image and discourse, an undissociated age." [5] To state the problem in another way, the grounds of the Milton controversy, and of the metaphysical revival, though depending upon such Miltonic words as "sensuous," have distorted some primary Miltonic attitudes.

In general, these attitudes have to do with what is usually thought of as the mere "binding-matter" of poetry, the rhetorical mode of procedure pragmatically necessary within the long, public poem. For Milton as for others in the Renaissance, the discursive demands of such a poem as *Paradise Lost*—themselves an integral product, historically speaking, of his very subject—were self-evident and even a potential asset. Furthermore, they do not imply a dissociation from vision, or even from concrete visualization in the poem. Near the beginning of *Paradise Lost,* the poet prays that he may *both* see and tell (III. 54). As students of Re-

4. Robert Langbaum, *The Poetry of Experience* (1957; rpt. New York: Norton, 1963); see also Frank Kermode, *Romantic Image* (1957; rpt. London: Routledge and Kegan Paul, 1961), especially chap. 8, "'Dissociation of Sensibility': Modern Symbolist Readings of Literary History."

5. Kermode, discussing Eliot's wish for either an illiterate audience or a cultivated one preferring "unified" art, mentions the irony that "Milton, rather exceptionally, believed and argued for the unity of the soul (a continuum of mind and sense), allowed his insistence on the inseparability of form and matter to lead him into heresy; and believed that poetry took precedence over other activities of the soul because it was simple (undissociated by intellect), sensuous, and passionate" (*Romantic Image,* p. 150).

naissance curricula have abundantly demonstrated, the arts of discourse were virtually a mental habit at the grammar school level, whether in poetry or oratory; the purest poetry was potentially a mode of argument at some level of appeal. Neither rhetoric nor logic, moreover, would have seemed incompatible with Milton's primary intention in *Paradise Lost* (e.g., I. 6, 13), which is to sing, or to join in singing.

Still, together with other critics, the anti-Miltonists assumed that this linguistic medium could not be integral, that it was at best a verbal vehicle for "poetry," whose essence was somewhere else, closer to the "*real* intricacies and by-paths of mental movement" (Eliot, p. 142; my italics). And to some extent, we still lack formulations of how poem and poetry actually relate. The best of the many recent studies of *Paradise Lost* have been concerned in some way with Milton's structure. Several have focused on single elements in the poem's manner of presentation: for example, the narrator, the reader.[6] Generally, we may say that while, during the Milton controversy, the question was in effect, Where is the *poetry* of *Paradise Lost?* the liveliest recent books have asked, Where is the essence of the *poem?* And even allowing for polemic hyperbole, the answers tend toward one or another of two extremes, as proposed in two challenging and helpful books: (1) that essence lies in what might be called the poem's dialectical process, that is, on the poetry's surface, conceived as a kind of running argument with the reader, whose mind is the poem's "scene"; and (2) that essence resides in a poetic "core," distinct from the poem's mere rind, in what Jackson Cope calls its "metaphoric structure." [7]

Clearly, these are two quite different answers, each of which is provided with telling argument, evidence, and background. Yet an examination of another kind of background, which I shall call Miltonic intention in one of its aspects, suggests a third and mid-

6. See Anne Davidson Ferry, *Milton's Epic Voice: The Narrator in "Paradise Lost"* (Cambridge: Harvard University Press, 1963), and Stanley Eugene Fish, *Surprised by Sin: The Reader in "Paradise Lost"* (London and New York: St. Martin's, 1967).

7. Fish, *Surprised by Sin,* p. 1; Jackson I. Cope, *The Metaphoric Structure of "Paradise Lost"* (Baltimore: Johns Hopkins University Press, 1962) hereafter cited as Cope. See below, chap. 5, for a brief discussion.

dle course: that we further study the *articulation* of metaphor in *Paradise Lost,* with a view to granting a functional significance to the poem's discourse, its necessarily temporal process of speech. Indeed, it is the poem which suggests this recourse to an examination of its own intentionalism. Among the difficulties of *Paradise Lost* for its modern readers, perhaps the greatest is the impression (to which the most helpful annotation unwittingly contributes) that the poem itself represents an ideology, or that it is a series of references to that ideology. The earlier discontent of the anti-Miltonists was directed in like manner at an undeniable and paradoxical fact which we may find it difficult to believe Milton missed: this is a poem which ultimately abjures poetry. In its opening lines, *Paradise Lost* complicates a most delicate critical question by announcing that the *poem,* the "advent'rous Song" itself, "*intends* to soar / Above th'Aonian Mount, *while it pursues* / Things unattempted yet in Prose or Rhyme" (I. 13–16; my italics). Indeed, with its persistent hint that the real poem is somewhere behind or above the one we are reading—inherent in the argument to which *Paradise Lost* itself is only potentially answerable—Milton's epic seems even at the outset to entangle us in the very categories with which we presume to clarify the ways of art. How are we to talk about a poem so self-conscious about its own status, origins, "success," even its mere communication?

Milton was modern in thinking that poetry was intimately associated with images; and along with some modern theorists, he associated images in turn with "corporal forms" whether verbal or plastic. But for a reforming poet of the seventeenth century this was not necessarily a cause for celebration; and the problem lay with both audience and poet. Language somehow became opaque in becoming merely verbal, and the result, in Milton's view, was a paralyzing formalism likely to cause a kind of delusion in the reader, "so that he wretchedly thinks he is blind, where there is nothing for him to see." [8] Moreover, the

8. Prol III, Hughes, p. 606A; CE 12 : 167. All quotations from the Prolusions are taken from the translations of Bromley Smith in CE 12, and I refer to Hughes chiefly for the reader's convenience. The dangers in translating Milton's Latin are obvious; where verbal alignment with his English poetry

reader to whom Milton referred in this passage was most cooperative, a passenger actually traveling in search of Truth by torchlight. Milton likens him to Ceres in quest of Proserpina, thus employing a mythological parallel he shortly afterward applied to his own pursuit of Beauty (see below, pp. 23–26). As Milton's writing frequently suggests, the trouble with images was their tendency to become self-sufficient, their almost corpuscular discreteness as "things." To adapt the pregnant word he later used to describe the condition of our parents' primal liberty, they were not clearly enough "placed." Their status as parts of an argumentative design was insufficiently evident, and the irrational admiration they invited could too easily blend with a literary form of worship or even idolatry. Where did they come from? To what were they related? Such questions become more urgent if we recall Satan's general impulse to *abstract* in *Paradise Lost.* As a manipulator of images, he urges Eve to "Look on mee," while providing her with one of the poem's mirrors to her vanity. Ultimately, like the innumerable sons of the poem's mythological allusions, Satan wishes to reign "usurping," himself a self-originated "center." Moved by the sense of his exclusion from the divine joy and from the decorous ascent to light and spirit to be more narrowly missed by Adam and Eve, Satan thus ironically dissociates himself from the only kind of liberty, political or psychological, that the poem offers. His doom, like that of James's Jonathan Marcher in "The Beast in the Jungle," is to be made a mere spectator of the divine argument; and it is finely epitomized in the moment when he views "askance" the situation of Adam and Eve "in true filial freedom plac't" (IV. 294 ff. and I. 507 ff.).

Preoccupied though Milton seems to have been with becoming his nation's epic poet, another immediately pertinent strain in his thinking was thus the problem of how actually to write "true" poetry, a problem Milton himself usually confused by identifying the poet *with* the true poem. The very words, written in 1642, make us painfully aware of how biographical literary theory can be, of how imperceptibly the materials of the psychologist or

---

and prose is an immediate danger I quote the Latin. Milton's choice of "these British isles" as "my world" must be measured against the studied and successful Latin translucence of his epic's English.

historian of thought become the materials of the literary critic. At times the prose seems quite more than half-formed poetry.[9] On the other hand, the purest theory Milton wrote, in the preface to the second book of *The Reason of Church Government,* is both the speech of a biblical prophet and a specific "politick" proposal. Thus it is important to emphasize here that in the prose works we are not dealing with a theory of literary art as such. I believe that Milton's writing in nearly any context was to a degree always potentially practical, in the sense that, besides exploiting the same vocabulary, it had strategic implications for particular poems. We may even claim, perhaps, that a close reading of Milton's prose dispels the notion that there were really two careers for Milton, or that the one was felt to exclude the other. And it is the way in which Milton conceives of the poet and the true poem that forces us to revise these conceptions, conditioned as they are by romantic and postromantic views of the artist. Milton anticipated and greatly influenced his nineteenth-century successors in thinking of the artist as a prophet. But the relation of prophet to society as he viewed it was a complicated one which seems to have changed after 1644; and we need its details. My "history" here is the evolving self-consciousness of a poet who consistently thought of his art in social terms.

To be more specific, the question which underlies Part One of this study is only secondarily a critical question: What did Milton mean—practically—by a "true" poem? and, further, What technical aspects could we reasonably associate with the phrase? Clearly, it is a question Milton probably never asked, at least in this form. In asking it, I am attempting quite artificially to pull the vague realm of the poet's intention closer to what Milton called "the very critical art of composition." But my use of "intention" here is specific and in a way Miltonic.[10] Poetry for Mil-

9. Eliot, p. 175.

10. Hughes, p. 669B. In a difficult moment during the period of his divorce pamphlets, Milton found it necessary to reconcile the two conflicting texts on divorce, Deut. 24 : 1–2 and Matt. 19 : 3–9, a task made difficult by the fact that the New Testament in this case explicitly forbids divorce "except it be for fornication." Milton's strategy was an appeal to the "intention" of an obscure scriptural text, to be established by "considering upon what occasion every thing is set down: and by comparing other texts"—texts found, need-

ton was by itself a "device," and a prime feature of his own verse is a dramatization of the "process" or "procedure" which we often assign to the discussion of a literary background.[11] What we are concerned with in asking about the "truth" of *Paradise Lost* is an attempt to account for a *poem's* intentionalism—the ascribing or pretending to ascribe purposefulness to a process which is itself also a poem. Thus, in simplest terms, the purpose of this book is to discuss several epic conventions or devices in *Paradise Lost* in the light of certain issues raised persistently in Milton's earlier prose and confronted artistically in some of the early poems.

My inquiry is divided into two parts, dealing respectively with backgrounds, at once biographical and historical, and with conventional devices in the structure of *Paradise Lost.* But as I have suggested, my point is ultimately historical in this sense: that Milton's first epic—subtitled in the first editions merely "A Poem"—can be seen as the fullest artistic solution to a problem which for Milton was more than technical in nature. It is not the first such solution in Milton's career; and he did not repeat it, very obviously at any rate, in *Paradise Regained* or *Samson Agonistes.* For reasons I shall clarify below and in chapter 4, I believe *Lycidas* may well mark the moment of its discovery—or "moments," since the survival of the Trinity Manuscript allows us to observe that poem in process of emergence from its poetry.

Briefly, the problem solved—preeminently in these two poems—may be described at this point as a radical (though quite traditional) skepticism concerning the value of poetry per se, as a mode of discourse. By this I do not mean the question posed in

less to say, in the same book he assumed to be single and "whole" (*The Doctrine and Disciple of Divorce,* Hughes, p. 713A). That intention of the Gospel was what Milton had somewhat earlier called "her own authentic hand-writing and command"; it was to be sharply distinguished from a critical literalism with which he ultimately associated mere literary technique in *Paradise Lost*—"from the borrowed manuscript of a subservient scroll, by way of imitating" (*RCG,* Hughes, p. 648B).

11. Both are Milton's terms, and Raphael's phrase "process of speech" (*PL* VII. 178) appears to be a conscious play on the common usage "process of time"; even Milton's pronunciation (pro*cess*) may be idiosyncratic here. On the critical uses of "process" see Ralph Cohen, *The Art of Discrimination* (Berkeley and Los Angeles: University of California Press, 1964), pp. 12–72.

Lycidas (lines 64–65), "What boots it . . . / To tend the homely slighted Shepherd's trade?" although the most cursory glance at *Ad Patrem*, for example, makes it clear that the question occurred to Milton in less mediated forms. Milton's skepticism had much to do with his vocational crisis, and even with his decision to "be" a poet at once national, Christian, and epic. But I am referring specifically to a limited kind of rationalism that in effect seems to "deny" so much of Milton's fine poetry, resulting at times in such bitter "truths" as the following:

> Bid *Amaranthus* all his beauty shed,
> And Daffadillies fill their cups with tears,
> To strew the Laureate Hearse where *Lycid* lies.
> For so to interpose a little ease,
> Let our frail thoughts dally with false surmise.
>
> [*L*, 149–53]

Or the conditional qualifications of these lines:

> For if such holy Song
> Enwrap our fancy long,
>   Time will run back, and fetch the age of gold.
>
> [*N*, 133–35]

Like *Paradise Lost*, both these examples exhibit a controlled use of such skepticism, and they thus imply a willingness to deploy the fancy's "frail thoughts" strategically, as part of a poetic structure whose argument ultimately transcends them. Both, of course, are taken from serious, even religious poems, one dealing centrally with the poet's identity. But another poem, a well-advertised poetic failure which Milton displayed only in 1645 as being "above his years" makes it clear that such doubts could appear in other contexts, too. Milton's prose similarly reveals them, attaching them (as we might expect) to the aesthetic dimensions of the prelatical controversy. Indeed, we shall see that from the Prolusions onward, Milton's theoretic discussion of poetry is remarkably consistent, and notably pejorative.

Milton's solution to the skepticism we have mentioned was in part vocational and related directly to abuses of imagery in the Church; it was, in short, to *be* a poet—and even in some sense *the* poet—in England. But it was also at least potentially artistic, I believe; and it is with the artistic confrontation of imagery's dangers that I am primarily concerned here. Generally, we may say that if poetry tended to become a mere image, or verbal icon, Milton exploited—paradoxically, and in true warfaring fashion—its virtual opposite in modern critical debate, that "process" which alone could articulate the poem or image with its several matrices—including the Holy Light, the imagination, myth, in general the common experience of poet and reader. To stage the poem's origins, and, so to speak, its emergence from them, would provide the poet's equivalent of the preacher's logical scaffolding, and thus the process of speech—including the speaker—which could somehow validate whatever acts the true poem might effect. More particularly, and much more daringly, Milton could in effect split his poems into petition and answer, subject and answerable object, in such a way as to stage the definitive results of his poet's words, giving them the literary equivalent of the Son's powers as Logos—within the poem's quite frankly secondary microcosm.

Thus, in simplest terms, the thesis of the following chapters points less to the mind of the reader, or to a metaphoric core for the poem, than to the figure of the poet and to our frequently shifting relations with his images. While the poet—virtually dramatized and essentially fictional—narrates the Fall, he emphasizes its epistemological dimensions in doing so. It is that epistemological fall which is to a great extent responsible for the poem's oddly "dissociated" texture and hence for the relative inaccessibility of its metaphoric or paradoxical center.[12] To put it another way, the Fall's linguistic and logical results are dramatized most clearly in that part of the poem which in a sense constitutes the *apprehension* of the plot, not in the plot itself; in what Eliot called the rhetorical action of the poem's language. It is with good reason that the narrator has emerged as a central problem in recent critical commentary, notably in the work of Anne Ferry; for we are never allowed to forget his difficulties as well as his triumphs. Both are ours as well. But it is specifically the act of a

12. It is the poet's and audience's, as distinct from Milton's, dissociation, and the poet's at least is not consistently present or operative throughout.

poet's mind in speaking for our own less unified ones that is a primary experience in most readings of *Paradise Lost.* The important point to stress is that to a great extent this activity was strategic, even "intended," and that its use in the first of Milton's epics is the culmination of thought, experience, and of somewhat similar projections in Milton's earlier work.

In the modest or at any rate disguised form appropriate to pastoral, this strategic uncouthness is displayed in *Lycidas,* the subject of chapter 4. In turning to *Paradise Lost,* we must be more selective, and I have chosen to examine the ways in which its conventional epic features function. Compared with other epics, *Paradise Lost* is "placed" or "situated" with extraordinary care within the ken of its audience; in particular its fable seems almost secondary to the way in which our relation to it, even our apprehension of it, is scrupulously established and controlled. The poet too is somehow "within" the poem, as recent studies have shown; and we must speak of his presence somewhat differently from the way in which we speak of the "implied author" of most fiction. He is more fully realized—even as a speaker he is more of a participant or celebrant—than the relatively neutral medium of conventional narrative. Together with us—though his relation to poem's audience and fable varies considerably—he stands beneath or outside the poem's unexpressive mysteries, to which our human notion, and this poem, can perhaps ultimately be answerable.

Ironically enough, it is the most conventional epic devices which give us this sense that *Paradise Lost* "builds in" so much of the apparatus normally supplied by the critical reader. Though they unmistakably establish the poem's relation to epic tradition, and its famous epic "magnificence," the invocations serve to dramatize the poet as well, sometimes in relatively "low" postures. They serve as the poem's frame as well, we might say, in the sense that they represent the poem's emergence from its various sources; and only at times do they merely "internalize" the poem. But clearly it is a mistake to take them at their word, for *Paradise Lost* includes them, regardless of those unattempted things they claim only to pursue. Though they apologize, the relation they bear to a wondrous confirming narrative only pretends to be accidental.

Though the invocations occasionally refer to another "contingency" Milton decided to include within his poem, the reader of *Paradise Lost* is located in a way more than merely implied, and most significantly, I believe, in the epic similes, where once again we find ourselves at the poem's margins. Without question, the similes give the poem its well-known density, its epic loftiness. But they are also, paradoxically, moments of relation, in which the poet pretends to clarify a difficulty. Like the invocations these may well seem to be moments when the poem threatens to "refer," to take us beyond its confines for more ultimate meanings; but again, we should not mistake the similes' emblematic microcosms (designed strategically to include us within the poem) for an actual crisis, merely referring, for example, to a lingering seventeenth-century belief in "faery elves."

Theoretically and historically too, the similes prove to be a useful focus for analysis. As chapter 5 illustrates, "argument" by similitude is a useful theoretic epitome, if we can include within that vague category the handbook on logic which Milton published between the first two editions of *Paradise Lost*. Beyond describing an area of discourse in which logic and poetry converge with peculiar clarity, Milton's twenty-first chapter reveals one of the few instances in which we can be rather precise about his "Ramism" and about the bearing this background, so controversial in recent scholarship, may have had on the poetry.

During the period when a prime critical concern was to isolate for appreciation the quintessentially "Miltonic" passages of *Paradise Lost,* readers who did not insist that Milton's best poetry was contained in the first two books of the epic were likely to agree that the similes, somewhat scattered, were a reliable focus of "poetry" in the poem. Because they were conventional formal devices in epic poetry, they were considered to afford poets (as distinguished from mere storytellers) the rest we all need from the rigors of our business, in particular the demands of the poet's fable. They gave the poet a chance to show off, to display epic bravura, or at the very least to call attention more closely to the *presentation* of his fable. But because *Paradise Lost* seems largely to *assume* the dissociation it has been accused of having caused (among other things, a dissociation between "meanings" and "names"), and because it deals with settings and insights in some sense unknown to human notion (Hell, Heaven, and Eden, divine "causes," the "ways of God"), there is additional pressure on similes and invocations to serve functionally as a guide to apprehension. To a great extent, indeed, the similes of the poem may be said to embody its "normal mode of procedure." [13] Because they present as well as dramatize a presenter in difficulty, because even in the matter of their location they are patently more than the ornaments of Statius's *Thebaid*,[14] it is more than ordinarily helpful to describe the complex ways in which, simultaneously, they make part of a poem's procedure and its structure; in the case of Milton, as I have suggested, it is also necessary to describe the ways in which they articulate and serve to place that structure, potentially so dangerous in itself. This structure is my general subject in Part Three of this book.

More specifically, chapter 6, the first of three chapters on *Paradise Lost,* deals with the poem's similes from two separate points of view.

1. Regarded as "references," the formal similes call attention to the poem's presentation and necessarily to its presenter, its audience, and the material of its fiction. They open out the fiction in the sense that they articulate it with the reader's experience; in this sense they are "appeals" taking us ostensibly outside the poem. But in concentrating thus on their form we call attention to them as modes of argument and thus to the poem itself as one kind of logical discourse. In the terminology of Milton's handbook, the similes thus epitomize a speaker's effort at secondary definition—through description and through words, they reveal the speaker as poet verging on definer.

2. As containers of a body of material, the similes also serve to establish or place the reader's world within the poem's mythic coordinates. In them we come to see that we *are* dealing with an

13. On the War in Heaven as a departure from the poem's normal mode of procedure, see John Peter, *A Critique of "Paradise Lost"* (New York: Columbia University Press, 1960), pp. 63–84.

14. See James Whaler, "Grammatical *Nexus* of the Miltonic Simile," *Journal of English and Germanic Philology* 30 (1931): 327–34.

external "world"; but it is of the utmost importance to readers of *Paradise Lost* as a poem that the similes only pretend to take us outside the poem. For the world they reveal in such moments of rhetorical appeal is itself originated, and mythically explained, on the more definitive level of the poem's fictional narrative. Two early segments reveal this origin with special clarity: the epic catalogue, which reveals the origin of "human names" and divinities; and Chaos, the description of which in a context of unqualified or "metaphoric" description reveals the "base originals" of what we can call the poem's emblematic norm of reference. Chaos itself is closely associated with Satan's, and other, voyages—it *is* the archetypal "Illimitable Ocean." Comprised of a metaphoric cluster of associated references—including chivalry, fortuitous astronomical phenomena, royalism, a universal hubbub wild, it is the source of the poem's "anticreation." Within the poem's context, it is opposed to *Paradise Lost*'s author and in general to the source of his authority: the poem's matrix, so evidently built-in (perhaps originally, as in the *Nativity*, for "protective" purposes), its origins in the Holy Light of divine wisdom.

In chapter 7, I argue that the world revealed as a norm of reference in the similes and "originated" in the catalogue, and during the portrayal of Chaos, also has a kind of verification on the definitive narrative level—there is a real eclipse to fulfill the figurative one. *Paradise Lost* thus contains a general movement, mirrored by the similes in little, in the direction of things "not Mystic" and, too, in the direction of an area which Frank Kermode has recently suggested is usually *outside* the worlds adumbrated in literary works—the "midst."[15] While the ending to the poem's fabled history is portrayed precisely in the poem's apocalyptic middle section, and portrayed "darkly," as a kind of *beginning* (it appears again, properly placed, in book XII), the

15. Frank Kermode, *The Sense of an Ending* (New York: Oxford University Press, 1967). This is a provocative and illuminating discussion of time in fiction. See especially "Fictions" (pp. 35–64) for the distinctions pertinent to our study between *kairos* and *chronos*. Kermode quotes Sidney's *Apology for Poetry* as follows: "a Poet thrusteth into the middest, even where it most concerneth him, and there recoursing to the thinges forpast and divining of things to come, maketh a pleasing analysis of all" (p. 181).

poem's ending actually converges with the reader's experience. As a whole, then, in causing the two Adams to meet again in both speaker and reader, the poem itself also opens out.

In discussing the poem's "structure" we thus find ourselves speaking inevitably of things also "beyond" the poem—"in thir own dimensions like themselves" (*PL* 1. 793). The ending to book 1 appeals finally to a sphere of definition beyond poetic description, to a world of meanings, not names, in which "essences" are not accessible to ordinary perception. Only the forms of things artificial are visible, Milton tells us in the *Art of Logic* (see below, p. 131). Similarly, the poem as a whole must transcend the secular. Its attempt to do so is emphasized most clearly perhaps in the ninth book's opening assault on our metaphoric cluster, where in a satiric "burst" the poet appears to transcend the very world we have previously viewed as our own. This point—that Milton calls attention to his poem and poetry alike as descriptive and "secondary," thus making both his poem "sincere" and his words lucky, dramatizing both the origins and results of the poet's words—leads into the final chapter, which discusses the poet of *Paradise Lost,* and what I believe is, in its extent, an unusual bifurcation of the poem into narrative and drama or rhetoric. It is this poetic Manichaeism, so to speak, which makes the poem's words lucky in a manner relating to what Milton called "the very critical art of composition." The implications are provocative, conjectural and "extrinsic" though they may be. We might say that the *Passion* and *Nativity* reveal gestures partly autobiographical in nature, those of a poet to whom sincerity and decorum—both vocational and artistic—were matters of infinite importance. To some extent they remained so, as the recurrent theme of the decorous son testifies, from the *Passion* above the young poet's years to the theological "subordinationism" of *De Doctrina Christiana.* If we read *Lycidas* in this light, as the first semipublic staging of an artistically "successful" solution, in which a public poem's words are lucky in more than the conventional sense used by appreciative readers, then *Paradise Lost* can be said to implement more profoundly the same, partly technical, discovery.

Taken together, the conventional epic devices on which I am focusing here can epitomize what we may call the poem's process of speech. Within the poem, the phrase is Raphael's; it is used to call attention to the difficulties in presenting to a time-bound human sense any such material as the "immediate" acts of God (see *PL* VII. 178, and n. 11 above).

> Immediate are the Acts of God, more swift
> Than time or motion, but to human ears
> Cannot without procèss of speech be told,
> So told as earthly notion can receive.
>
> [VII. 176–79]

To the best of my knowledge, the phrase is unique; and we must distinguish Raphael's attitude toward his methods from Milton's own. I believe Milton regarded his own process of speech as a literary equivalent of the trial through which alone we can "repair the ruins of our first parents," as he put it in the tract *Of Education*. Its function in *Paradise Lost*—its relation to the central mystery of the poem—is analogous to Michael's amplification provided in books XI and XII. Near the end of the poem, Michael describes the purpose of his role as an explicator of that "mysterious" doom provided in Gen. 3 : 15 (and in *Paradise Lost* at X. 175–81). The meaning of that passage has now been illuminated, "The Woman's seed, obscurely then foretold, / Now amplier known thy Saviour and thy Lord" (XII. 543–44). I believe we have taken too literally Milton's own pretended apology for this discursive manner, and it is for this reason that we shall turn first to the biography and some of the earlier poems, to see (if we can) the pretense evolve as a strategy. For plainly enough, in Milton's earliest—and until 1645 unpublished—poems, the hesitancy later to be exploited artistically, as the mere human articulation of things in some way mystic, was intimately involved in biography, and in Milton's search for an identity and poetic vocation "beside the office of a pulpit."

Himself a True Poem

When Milton discusses the poet, the uses or "powers" of the poet/prophet, or the place of poetry in a proper school curriculum, the skepticism to which I have alluded above is notably absent. I shall take somewhat for granted his own "vocational" relation to that important figure in discussing the prose of the 1640s, which mentions it with an assurance at times disarming. But because the autobiographical passages of that prose refer pointedly to the late 1630s, it may be appropriate here to make sense of Milton's work during the decade in large measure responsible for his most frustrating theoretic conjunction, between poet and poem. The passage from *An Apology against a Pamphlet* is as follows:

> And long it was not after, when I was confirmed in this opinion, that he who would not be frustrate of his hope to write well hereafter in laudable things, ought himself to be a true poem, that is, a composition and pattern of the best and honorablest things—not presuming to sing high praises of heroic men or famous cities, unless he have in himself the experience and the practice of all that which is praiseworthy. These reasonings, together with a certain niceness of nature, an honest haughtiness and self-esteem either of what I was or what I might be (which let envy call pride), and lastly that modesty whereof, though not in the title-page, yet here I may be excused to make some beseeming profession; all these uniting the supply of their natural aid together, kept me still above those low descents of mind beneath which he must deject and plunge himself that can agree to saleable and unlawful prostitutions.[16]

Milton does not say what (or who) "confirmed" him in his opinion, though the context may support the connection of the moment with a particular poem, and (perhaps) its favorable reception. It is not even clear to what period this fascinating paragraph refers, though, again, the context points most clearly, perhaps, to the months following his return from Italy. We should remember that whatever confirmed Milton in his opinion, what he was strengthened in was a moral (and perhaps sexual) discipline; and the only possible allusion to his actual poetry of the period refers merely to writing "hereafter in laudable things."

16. Hughes, p. 694A. For the fuller annotation of Frederick Taft, see *CPW*, 1 : 890.

The evidence is sketchy at best, and it may be helpful to begin with Arthur Barker's suggestion in 1941 that in the ode *On the Morning of Christ's Nativity* Milton "recorded" an experience which was "partly religious, partly literary"; and that the ode consequently expresses "Milton's first clear apprehension of the office and the qualifications of the divinely inspired poet." [17] Barker thus saw the ode as completing a process of purification, begun in *O Nightingale* and the series of Italian sonnets (1630?) in response to suggestions of immorality in the earlier Latin elegies.

Milton's own comments on his ode rather complicate the picture, at least, of any simple experience underlying the *Nativity*. In the relatively intimate closing of *Elegia Sexta*, addressed to his intimate friend Charles Diodati, he refers rather diffidently to the *pressa meditata*—the "measures meditated" on native pipes (*patriis cicutis*), which await the private consideration of his friend—"when I recite them to you," he adds (*El* VI, 89–90; Hughes, p. 53). There can be no doubt that Milton was rightly proud of this poem. It may have suggested the quasiliturgical cycle of which *On the Circumcision* is the last composition. In one poem of this group, the abortive *Passion*, Milton looked *back* to the Christmas poem (rather than ahead toward any literary career laudable or otherwise in a "hereafter," for instance) in the first-person singulars which so clearly distinguish it from the earlier "success." He likens his shift in theme, oddly enough, to ordinary emotional fluctuations and in his fourth and fifth lines suggests quite precisely the technical accomplishment of the *Nativity:*

> Erewhile of Music and Ethereal mirth,
> Wherewith the stage of Air and Earth did ring,
> And joyous news of heav'nly Infant's birth,
> My muse with Angels did divide to sing;
> But headlong joy is ever on the wing,
>   In Wintry solstice like the short'n'd light
>   Soon swallow'd up in dark and long outlivng night.
>
> [*Passion*, 1–7; see *N*, 26–27]

17. Arthur Barker, *Milton and the Puritan Dilemma* (Toronto: University of Toronto Press, 1942), p. 6; idem, "The Pattern of Milton's Nativity Ode," *University of Toronto Quarterly* 10 (1941) : 167–81.

Elegia Sexta, moreover, extends such observations to the point of distinguishing, quite specifically, the gifts which a collective *we* gave to the infant Christ (*Dona quidem dedimus*) from the more informal memorial context provided in the ode's framing proem: "Illa sub auroram lux mihi prima tulit," "the first light of the dawn brought me these gifts" (*EL* VI, 87–88). Parker is surely right in saying that there is a trace of reproach in this poem toward the good friend inquiring about what Milton was doing—it was an embarrassing question often asked, and with similar results, during this critical decade.[18] But Milton is quite precisely describing "the critical art of composition" in his poem, not necessarily invoking an experience behind it.

Whatever the private significance of the poem for Milton or Charles Diodati, however, the poem cannot be simply identified with the critical moment which confirmed Milton in a poetic vocation, and this for two further reasons. The "autobiographical" preface to book II of *The Reason of Church Government* apparently refers to a critical moment following Milton's return from Italy, when certain thoughts "possessed" the poet. The emphasis in the preface is on vernacular verse, and specifically on England as "my world," a public theater for a poet avowedly *prophetic.* The only vernacular religious poem of that period whose continuing effects or reception might confirm the hopes mentioned in *An Apology* also deals explicitly (however conventionally) with that vocation. And it does so in a manner definitely pointing to "hereafters" both literary and apocalyptic.

Furthermore, two fascinating letters of 1633 and 1637 have survived to reveal a Milton obsessed with time and frankly addressing himself to the possibility that the poet, perhaps for Milton a "negative identity," does indeed have access to "the forms of things divine."[19] The letters illuminate the vocational discussions of 1642; the tone of Milton's autobiography in that year and the finality of the remark that he had been "Church-outed" by the prelates, indeed, suggest that *The Reason of Church Government* and *An Apology* can serve as a convenient

18. William R. Parker, *Milton: A Biography* (Oxford: Clarendon, 1968), 1 : 69, hereafter cited as Parker.

19. On the conception of "negative identity," see Erik Erikson, *Young Man Luther* (New York: Norton, 1962), pp. 51–54, hereafter cited as Erikson.

terminus ad quem for a Miltonic vocational crisis—if we can separate autobiography from rhetoric in the two pamphlets.[20] In neither of these letters does Milton speak as one settled on a vocation. But in each case, context suggests a felt antithesis between poet and preacher; and Milton is both less settled, and less defensive about "not preaching," in 1637.

Sometime in 1633 Milton met an older acquaintance, who seems to have chastised him for his procrastination in entering the ministry. The letter he wrote the following day is preserved in two drafts and constitutes the original "setting" for the sonnet beginning "How soon hath Time . . ." (VII). The editors of the *Complete Prose Works* are certainly right in calling this a most revealing letter, and it is unfortunate that retrospective biographers seeking the beginnings of Milton's poetic career have made it necessary to stress so unequivocally the view that "it says nothing about poetic ambitions, and it implies throughout that the writer will eventually become a clergyman" (Parker, 1 : 122). For in its flexibility of argument and in the humorous self-confidence with which Milton offers his "nightward thoughts," there are all the earmarks of an effective counterattack which Milton perhaps could not manage face-to-face the day before. Confronted by a criticism he is bound to respect (the letter indicates it has previously occurred to Milton himself, and not merely at the instigation of the friend, from whom he has heard it before), he defends his own "tardie moving," the decision "wth a sacred reverence & religious advisement how *best* to undergoe" (my italics), rather than merely how soonest (*CPW,* 1 : 320). He is particularly concerned, indeed, that his love of learning be distinguished from the "unprofitable" sin of curiosity "wherby a man cutts himselfe off from all action & becomes the most helplesse, pusilanimous & unweapon'd creature in the word, the most unfit & unable to doe that wch all mortals most aspire to, either to defend & be usefull to his freinds, or to offend his enimies."[21] And he marshals argument after argument to dis-

20. See the brief discussion of the problem by Ernest Sirluck, *CPW,* 2 : 1–2, and the admirable introduction to *Areopagitica,* pp. 158–83.

21. *CPW,* 1 : 319, but I have retained the reading of the Trinity MS, draft 2, emended to "world" by the editor of *CPW*. Though a law of parsimony

sociate himself from "this *affected* solitariness," concluding with a distinction between his own scrupulous and "tymely" obedience to "that command in the gospell set out by the terrible seasing of him that hid the talent" and what he conceives to be the usual purpose of such moratoriums, namely, "the emptie fantastick chase of shadows and notions." [22]

The letter strikes us as undoubtedly genuine in its articulation of scruples. For all this, however, Milton's arguments are patently artificial or at least hypothetical in nature; if they are not the very "set apology" Milton says he will avoid in favor of "what my mynd shall have at any tyme to declare her selfe at her best ease" (*CPW,* 1 : 319), at the very least they indicate that Milton's mind at her best ease was during this time preoccupied with such self-defense. At most, Milton's letter with all its arguments amounts only to a plea for continued trust in a "true and unfained friend." Indeed, the best reason Milton can offer "to keepe me as I am"—in the very procrastination for which he was scolded—is framed in language at once conceding genuine self-doubt and expressing sharp and humorous self-confidence, especially if we note the flip way in which Milton answers his friend's appeal to the imminent night of John 9 : 4 with his own "nightward thoughts": [23]

> Yet that you may see that I am something suspicious of my selfe, & doe take notice of a certaine belatednesse in me I am the bolder to send you some of my nightward thoughts some while since (because they com in not altogether unfitly) made up in a Petrarchian stanza. wch I told you of
>
> after ye stanza [Sonnet VII]
>
> by this I beleeve you may well repent of having made mention at all of this matter, for if I have not all this while won you to this, I have certainly wearied you to it. This therefore alone may be a sufficient reason for me to keepe me as I am

---

would seem to apply here, I am assured more by the context of the present discussion.

22. *CPW,* 1 : 320. See Hughes, p. 632B, and below, p. 34. On the "moratorium," see Erikson, pp. 100–04.

23. For additional implications of "nightward thoughts," see Hughes, p. 635B.

> least having thus tired you singly, I should deale worse with a whole congregation, & spoyle all the patience of a Parish. [*CPW*, 1 : 320–21]

The Latin letter written to Charles Diodati in 1637 is more straightforward in the sections which concern us. After writing at some length on the friendship, which continues despite Diodati's occupation in what Milton calls "the tyrannical citadel of Medicine," Milton admits the following, referring again, it would seem, to his own ecclesiastical destiny.:

> Do not try to terrorize me, now that you hold that tyrannical citadel of Medicine ["arcem illam Medicinae tyrannicam nactus"], as if you would take back your six hindred healths, withdrawing them little by little, to the last one, should I by chance desert friendship, which God forbid. And so remove that terrible battery which you seem to have trained on me, forbidding me to be sick without your permission. For lest you threaten too much, know that I cannot help loving people like you. For though I do not know what else God may have decreed for me, this certainly is true: He has instilled into me, if into anyone, a vehement love of the beautiful. Not so diligently is Ceres, according to the Fables, said to have sought her daughter Proserpina, as I seek for this idea of the beautiful, as if for some glorious image, throughout all the shapes and forms of things ("for many are the shapes of things divine"); day and night I search and follow its lead eagerly as if by certain clear traces.[24]

In answer to previous correspondence (again, not extant), Milton writes that he contemplates "So help me God, an immortality of fame."

> What am I doing? Growing my wings and practising flight.
> But my Pegasus still raises himself on very tender wings.
> Let me be wise on my humble level.
>
> [*CPW*, 1 : 327]

24. *CPW*, 1 : 326–27, with the Latin text of CE 12 : 24. Milton's choice of *nanciscor* for Diodati's manner of possessing this stronghold suggests less that his friend has taken it as in a military siege (Masson's translation, as used in CE) than that he has either stumbled upon it or held it virtually from birth. See also the translation and commentary of John T. Shawcross in *The Prose*

He plans to move shortly to the Inns of Court and reports of his studies in Greek and Italian history, "to the time when liberty was granted them by Rudolph, King of Germany." From there, he concludes his itinerary, "it will be better to read separately about what each State did by its own Effort" (*CPW,* 1 : 327).

Even if we allow for the considerable differences owing to the age and the "function" of each recipient, the two letters, so widely separated in time, show a remarkable likeness in tone and stance. Between poetry and preaching in both letters there is the uneasiest of partnerships. In the earlier, which implies that he *will* eventually preach, Milton both defends himself with a Petrarchan medium and humorously equates preaching, or at least the prospect of his own premature preaching, with the boredom he now inflicts "singly" on the unknown friend. In the letter to his good friend Diodati, he is far more serious, not perhaps about *being* a poet but about his "practising" and the purposes disclaimed in 1633 and perhaps requiring secrecy here. The most striking difference lies elsewhere, however. In concluding he speaks clearly as a "free man," and one of a society of men, looking back jestingly (and not altogether considerately) at a good friend apparently imprisoned within his family as well as the tyrannical citadel of Medicine. We need not decide here whether at this point Milton thought of himself as actually being a poet, though the question of what he was, and would become, evidently grows crucial in these years. It is somewhat clearer as to that other antithetic destiny. Milton admits that he does not know "what *else* God may have decreed" ("Nam de caetero quidem quid de me statuerit Deus nescio") in a manner almost joyful in its implied shrug. It seems likely that divine poetry is a possible tenor for the cryptic mention from Euripides, concerning the variety in "shapes of things divine"—on the whole, much clearer than in 1633. But decorous though he may be in beginning on tender wings, Milton gives the distinct impression of a joyous freedom from such prisons and citadels which immure his friend Diodati. And it may not be altogether fortuitous that his facile plea for Diodati to join "us" in London

of John Milton, ed. J. Max Patrick (New York: New York University Press, 1968), pp. 591 ff. Irene Samuel discusses this letter from a related point of view in *Plato and Milton* (Ithaca: Cornell University Press, 1947), p. 9.

before winter follows the account of his studies in history, specifically the history of political liberty.[25]

It is not far from this position of 1637 to the view, expressed in his retrospections of 1642, that poetic "abilities"—Milton does not mention poems, even at this late date—possess a power *"besides* the office of a pulpit" (Hughes, p. 669B; see below, pp. 61–68.) But Milton spoke in *An Apology* of a specific confirmation of hopes, and *The Reason of Church Government* seems to suggest that the consolidation of identities which resulted in an epic poet without a poem took place after the rather leisurely return from Italy. The central text responsible for this consolidation is, I believe, *Lycidas;* but more specifically, I would point to whatever experience confirmed its words between its composition (and initial publication, 1637–38) and the "autobiography" of 1642, the experience resulting ultimately in the headnote prefixed to the elegy in the 1645 *Poems of Mr. John Milton.* That experience was by no means exclusively political. The death of Charles Diodati in 1638 removed the correspondent who uniquely provoked Milton's innermost writing—less than a year after the letter we have just quoted. But by the end of 1641 and early in 1642 —when the bishops' votes in the House of Lords diminished even as Milton wrote *The Reason of Church Government Urg'd against Prelaty*—the lines which publicly announced the imminence of the "two-handed engine" might well have acquired the local application responsible for Milton's misleading headnote of three years later. It need hardly be added that Milton was by then "the Author" engaged in the display of juvenilia and not the mere poet practicing—or the nearly anonymous J. M. who signed *Lycidas* in 1638. It is in this volume, indeed, that the *Nativity*—and its "unsuccessful" complement—made its first public appearance, along with the poem marking the English pamphleteer's poetic reunion with society. If the pamphlets had not already made it clear, the headnote to *Lycidas* underlined the vengeance, and the presumed allies, with which he made his return.[26]

25. For Milton's curriculum and its place for this study, see Hughes, p. 636A.

26. For a discussion focused somewhat differently, see Michael Fixler, *Milton and the Kingdoms of God* (London: Faber & Faber, 1964), pp. 46–75.

2

The Greatest Decency: Poetry, Images, and Discourse in Milton's Prose

> The worship of God singly in it selfe, the very act of prayer and thanksgiving with those free and unimpos'd expressions which from a sincere heart unbidden come into the outward gesture, is the greatest decency that can be imagin'd.
>
> *An Apology against a Pamphlet,* 1642

As long as *Paradise Lost* continues to be read, the chances are good that it will be read rather self-consciously, as a poem. In the twentieth century—and in Milton studies this means following Raleigh and subsequent to the Milton controversy—to read any literary work "as a poem" has often implied an effort with a largely negative purpose. Descriptions of the "real" poem excluded a great deal of *Paradise Lost* as being irrelevant or even antithetic to the values of *real* poetry. The poem's theology (or its ideas) was the first to be thus discarded. More recently, discourse itself has suffered a similar fate. If we take the crucial terms of distinctions even from the most sensitive readers of *Paradise Lost,* we still emerge with what is clearly a polemic contrast; vision, myth, and metaphor (or simply image) on one side are opposed to the furniture of dissociated sensibility, rhetoric, and discourse. As self-conscious as recent readers of the poem have been, the very bulk, if not indeed the *nature,* of the poem often appears to force a kind of critical Manichaeism, in which the "poem" is viewed to some extent as an essence that's not seen, a core somehow integrally related to the first set of terms and merely *opposed* to the second. The unfortunate result is that the poem's mere length combines with an unquestioned assumption that discourse itself is poetically insignificant. Given such circumstances, is it any wonder that Milton was on the devil's side without knowing it, that the best poetry was to be found in the first two books, while books XI and XII were "weak"? [1] Needless to say, the picture of the author which emerged from such discussions—where it emerged at all—was of a figure who lacked the craftsman's ability to make aesthetic decisions.

In the face of these difficulties, a good place to begin the amphibious task of reading *Paradise Lost* at once historically and critically is at the title page of the first editions. Milton's epic proclaims its ties to generic tradition throughout its length, and its relation to the epic has been fully explored. But the title page of *Paradise Lost,* like that of *Paradise Regained,* calls it merely "A Poem," and it is useful to ask about the Miltonic implications of this label. Indeed, with even a minimal consideration of Milton's biography, we may well find that the decorum implied by the terms *poem* and *poetry*—though difficult to establish —is fully as relevant to our reading of *Paradise Lost* as such well-explored backgrounds as epic or hexameral commentary. An appeal to the background of an author's own critical terminology can be particularly helpful in providing, at the very least, a salutary resistance to our latent or militant postromanticism— our own ingrained views of the poet, of poems, and, in particular, of poetry's images. To an extent, as I am aware, such an appeal is a form of intentionalism; and we should clearly not attempt easy connections between poetry and prose. I would claim, however, that given a circumscribed and relevant field of inquiry, a reading of the prose can be helpful, as a kind of ballast in our efforts to describe the nature of *this* poem's image. It can even confirm our impressions of what is actually *within* the poem and thus a legitimate focus of criticism. If a poem is an object, as Milton partly agreed it might be, to what extent is the nature of its contemplation controllable? To what degree can a reader of poetry be anticipated? At the very least, we can profit by know-

1. For a recent version of this judgment, see Louis L. Martz, *The Paradise Within: Studies in Vaughan, Traherne, and Milton* (New Haven: Yale University Press, 1964), pp. 141–67. The most convincing replies include those of F. T. Prince ("On the Last Two Books of *Paradise Lost,*" *Essays and Studies* 11 [1958] : 38–52) and Joseph H. Summers ("The Final Vision," *The Muse's Method* [London: Chatto & Windus, 1962], pp. 186–224).

ing that Milton thought about aesthetic contemplation with some concern, and even alarm—for both audience and artist. At best, it can increase the significance of some passages in *Paradise Lost,* and even the number of significant passages, to know what may be involved in the claim that *Paradise Lost* is, throughout its great length, conceived as "A Poem."

Soft and Delicious Temper: The Uses of Poetry

Milton's most influential statement on poetry appears in the informal letter to the Comenian educator Samuel Hartlib.[2] Published as an anonymous pamphlet without a title page in 1644, it was later included (with some changes) in *Poems etc. upon Several Occasions* . . . (1673). The combination is only apparently incongruous, for throughout his writings in prose and verse Milton conceives of poetry as integrally related with wisdom, and with the sage's "perfection" through the articulation of that wisdom. In *Of Education* it is discussed as part of a liberal curriculum, the values of which seem more Greek than Puritan or Comenian. But Milton appears to make poetry crucial *within* his scheme merely by worrying the formulation of its relevance. The "organic arts" (poetry, logic, and rhetoric) are the culmination of this course of studies, which begins with grammar and proceeds from personal to "economical" and political arts. Milton is particularly concerned to correct the scholastic error of presenting "young unmatriculated novices at first coming with the most intellective abstractions of logic and metaphysics," the effect of which is a merely verbal wisdom, "ragged notions and babblements," the products of "unballasted wits" (Hughes, p. 632A). Indeed poetry's increased prominence seems part of Milton's desire to avoid abstraction altogether in the educational process. The proper place of the organic arts is thus last, since they enable men to "discourse and write perspicuously, elegantly, and according to the fitted style of lofty, mean, or lowly":

> Logic, therefore, so much as is useful, is to be referred to this due place with all her well-couched heads and topics, until it

2. See the valuable introduction by Ernest Sirluck, *CPW,* 2 : 184–216.

> be time to open her contracted palm into a graceful and ornate rhetoric, taught out of the rules of Plato, Aristotle, Phalereus, Cicero, Hermogenes, Longinus. To which poetry would be made subsequent, or indeed rather precedent, as being less subtle and fine, but more simple, sensuous, and passionate. I mean not here the prosody of a verse, which they could not but have hit on before among the rudiments of grammar; but that sublime art which in Aristotle's *Poetics,* in Horace, and the Italian commentaries of Castelvetro, Tasso, Mazzoni, and others, teaches what the laws are of a true epic poem, what of a dramatic, what of a lyric, what decorum is, which is the grand masterpiece to observe. This would make them soon perceive what despicable creatures our common rhymers and playwriters be, and show them what religious, what glorious and magnificent use might be made of poetry, both in divine and human things.[3]

The proper reading of this formulation is clearly essential to any complete understanding of Milton's theory of poetry; and I have quoted more fully than is customary in studies of the passage, primarily to show how large poetry does indeed bulk in Milton's scheme. Since we are concerned here only with one strand in the development of that theory, from the Prolusions (1628?–1632) to the treatise *Of Education,* we may emphasize only the *utility* Milton's definition discovers in poetry: B. Rajan, whose masterly exposition of "Simple, Sensuous, and Passionate" remains the most useful of the commentaries, makes it plain that in Milton's general rationale for poetry, the relevant backgrounds are Renaissance education—particularly the fascinating figure of the Orphean prophet—and contemporary interpretations of the Great Chain of Being.[4] Milton clearly accepts the traditional inner correlatives of the scale; but its graduations are also associated with the limitations of fallen perception:

3. Hughes, pp. 636B–37A. A somewhat similar passage in *RCG* (Hughes, p. 670A) is discussed below.

4. B. Rajan, "Simple, Sensuous, and Passionate," *Review of English Studies* 21 (1945): 289–301; reprinted in Arthur E. Barker, ed., *Milton: Modern Essays in Criticism* (New York: Oxford University Press, 1965), pp. 3–19, hereafter cited as *Modern Essays.*

> But because our understanding cannot in this body found itself but on sensible things, nor arrive so clearly to the knowledge of God and things invisible, as by orderly conning over the visible and inferior creature, the same method is necessarily to be followed in all discreet teaching.[5]

As we have observed, the position of the organic arts in this scheme is last. Their study is subsequent to the analysis of matter in general, to the study of single and collective man, to the literary genres appropriate to each subject and each degree of psychological elevation—in effect, subsequent to the entire curriculum proper. As Milton stressed in his *Art of Logic,* the arts of discourse are the most general; they occupy that crucial position which allows the sage to "discourse and write." Clearly enough, poetry is placed in such a plan. And Rajan shows how Milton's hierarchical conceptions inform even the apparently narrowed focus of the famous definition. Milton's poet is indeed the sage (and the Greek poet / statesman); the products of Milton's educational plan are primarily "able writers and composers in every excellent matter"—though only "when they shall be thus fraught with an universal insight into things" (Hughes, p. 637A). It is thus evident that Milton's emphasis shifts somewhat in this important passage. He is discussing the reading (and presumably the performance) of the organic arts—poetics (for example) and not the poetry already absorbed in abundance from pastoral lyric to tragedy—when he pinpoints "poetry" as the means for the sage's "return" to a discursive community; and he dwells, perhaps somewhat confusingly, given this context, upon its properties. The entire discussion, in fact, places an enormous and double burden on poetry. It is the prime vehicle in the sage's "perfection," the articulation of his wisdom—something it is easy to miss in the often matter-of-fact tone of Milton's curriculum. Secondly—and not inconsistently, it would seem—precisely because poetry is simple, sensuous, and passionate, it is a radical instrument in perfecting a *collective* understanding, which "cannot in this body found itself but on sensible things." Both parts of this burden assume the reality and immediate relevance of

5. Quoted by Rajan in *Modern Essays,* p. 5.

original sin. The very existence of the curriculum and its place for poetry, in fact, have the effect of defining the Fall in this context as an event at once perceptual and social, an epistemological emphasis also notable in *Paradise Lost* (see below, Part Three, and especially chaps. 6–7).

Thus, in the successful completion of Milton's curriculum, poetry will have served an essential function, without doubt, but for whom? Milton is writing educational theory, we must recall, for the benefit of "our noble and gentle youth." Still, his failure here to distinguish between poet / sage and an *audience* for those organic arts is most interesting for the student of Milton's poetic theory and its history. The very concept of audience, of course, seems totally alien to the drift of Milton's discussion; poetry in this account renders the wisdom of sage and society at once. To a limited extent, the audience seems to *become* the poet, in the manner of the Greek social and literary situation as described by Werner Jaeger:

> The great men of Greece came forward . . . to teach the people what they themselves knew, to give shape to their ideals. . . . The Greek trinity of poet, statesman and sage (*poietas, politikos, sophos*) embodied the nation's highest ideal of leadership, bound by deep knowledge (as if by a divine law) to the service of the community.[6]

Milton's theoretic stress on poetry takes on a different light, however, when we turn to the "uses" of his curriculum, particularly if we recall our discussion of Milton's vocation. As Ernest

6. Werner Jaeger, *Paideia: The Ideals of Greek Culture,* trans. Gilbert Highet (New York: Oxford University Press, 1939), 1 : xxvi. An interesting comparison is the theory of Wordsworth, who was unusual among his contemporaries in wishing to include scientific truth as part of poetry's province. Wordsworth defined the poet's ambiguous social position in similar but somewhat more normative terms; he is a man speaking to men. "[The poet] is the rock of defense for human nature; an upholder and preserver, carrying everywhere with him relationship and love. In spite of difference of soil and climate, of language and manners, of laws and customs, in spite of things silently gone out of mind, and things violently destroyed, the poet binds together by passion and knowledge the vast empire of human society, as it is spread over the whole earth and over all time" (preface, *Lyrical Ballads,* 1800).

Sirluck has shown, Milton takes issue with the Comenian philosophy of his correspondent throughout the pamphlet. The education he discusses here is clearly a liberal one, and distinct from the vocational training emphasized by the reformers, despite Milton's commonplace appeal to the "utility" of his program. One suspects, in fact, that this appeal and the period's virtually unanimous hostility to words have done much to forestall the basic disagreements uncovered only quite recently; different though Milton's "substance" and "wisdom" clearly are from the Comenian catchwords like "things" and "science." Milton's educational designs are vital for reasons chiefly national *and* cultural; and the place he gives to poetry and literature in relation to the teaching of languages is but one particularly strong testimony to his position (introduction, *CPW,* 2: 189–93). Still, at the outset Milton does single out three groups, including the ministry and the "trade of Law," as suffering particularly from the lack of proper educational policy. And when toward the conclusion of his curriculum he does mention the vocations of his scholars, he skips briefly over "parliament or council" to linger on the pulpit thus: "There would then also appear in pulpits other visages, other gestures, and stuff otherwise wrought than what we now sit under, oft-times to as great a trial of our patience as any other [i.e., stuff?] that they preach to us" (Hughes, p. 637A).

Though we could hardly call his education vocational, it is in fact the pulpit that Milton proposes to reform in his plan—and reform altogether, one is tempted to add. The emphasis is upon poetry among the organic arts because of the nature of its communication, Milton claims at the theoretical level. But it is particularly vital *for the psychic dispositions* of that third group in singular need of proper education. Poetry embodies the "delight" Milton proposes to add everywhere in the learning process. And it is useful, Milton had written two years earlier, "especially for those of soft and delicious temper" (Hughes, p. 670A)—we shall see that Milton suspected this to be a rather general condition. The third group is described in precisely this way, in language recalling *Lycidas, L'Allegro,* and surely Milton's own, rather more purely literary moratorium as well:

> Others, lastly, of a more delicious and airy spirit, retire themselves—knowing no better—to the enjoyments of ease and jollity; which indeed is the wisest and safest course of all these, unless they were with more integrity undertaken. And these are the fruits of misspending our prime youth at the schools and universities as we do, either in learning mere words or such things chiefly as were better unlearned.[7]

It is in this larger context that we may better evaluate Milton's justly famous definition of poetry, which Coleridge himself took to be at least adequate. In many respects his discussion resembles the theory of Sir Philip Sidney, whose *Defense of Poesy* also involves a scale of genres, from the epic (dealing with heroes, appealing to the intellect), to the lyric (treating, and appealing to, the passions).[8] Though a conceptual hierarchy is clearly at work in both texts, however, Milton's discussion can be said to isolate poetry *itself* on a scale primarily psychological and epistemological, relating it not to parallel disciplines like philosophy and history but, as it were vertically, to the other organic arts. Milton follows Sidney in defining poetry for the most part "pragmatically"; but he concerns himself with the affects of poetry per se, rather than falling in with Sidney's levels of response to the various genres. Despite his frequent glances at the moral good flowing from rhetoric, furthermore, he is also consistent in conceiving of poetry in somewhat the way Sidney conceived of *lyric* poetry. It is useful "especially for those of soft and delicious temper." And in the formulation to which any discussion of Milton's poetic must frequently return, it is "less subtle and fine" than the organic arts "but more simple, sensuous, and passionate."

Professor Rajan has rightly insisted that "the stock opposition of puritan to poet, of ascetic restraint to creative luxuriance—these do not exist at the centre of Milton's insight" (*Modern*

7. Hughes, p. 632B; whenever Milton actually wrote *Of Education,* this is an interesting recombination, and review, of the relations between university, "moratorium," and priesthood. See the letters, discussed above, to the "unknown friend" and to Charles Diodati.

8. G. Gregory Smith, ed., *Elizabethan Critical Essays* (Oxford: Clarendon, 1904), 1 : 172–80.

Essays, p. 13). If poetry does not here exist quite for its own sake, it is clearly seen as a mode of what we might call bodily knowledge. And the pamphlet may suggest that Milton had by 1644 satisfactorily reconciled the pursuit of Beauty with God's "other" decree for him, unknown in 1637; if he was, in his own ironic phrase, Church-outed by 1642, he could undertake the *education* of priests.[9] Milton's metaphors elsewhere convey similar attitudes toward poetry. He associates it with holiday and even, in "unfallen" forms, with play. Poetry is "recreating intermission," essential to the health of the spirit "in this body"; it is the remnant of Adam and Eve's "casual" discourse.[10] But in that same account, written two years before the letter to Hartlib, Milton seems to be proposing the institution of poetry readings, perhaps as an adjunct to the pulpit—so that the voice of Wisdom may be heard in the streets. *Whose* wisdom he still need not say, apparently. The implied situation is far indeed from Urania's status at the beginning of all things. In the invocation to book VII Milton summons her thus:

> The meaning, not the Name I call: for thou
> Nor of the Muses nine, nor on the top
> Of old *Olympus* dwell'st, but Heav'nly born,
> Before the Hills appear'd, or Fountain flow'd,
> Thou with Eternal Wisdom did'st converse,
> Wisdom thy Sister, and with her didst play
> In presence of th'Almighty Father, pleas'd
> With thy Celestial Song
>
> [VII. 5–12]

Milton's final views of poetry, which somewhat starkly oppose a true eloquence (and even vehemence, the property of satiric railing) to a visually conceived "formalism" or technical "decency," suggest a realization of the problems we have discussed briefly here. And it is difficult to resist proposing that this was an inevitable effect of maturity. Indeed, as we shall now see, Milton

9. Hughes, p. 671B. My discussion differs in emphasis from both Sirluck and Parker (1 : 253–59), to which interested readers may refer.

10. *RCG,* Hughes, p. 670A; the passage is very close to pp. 636B–37A. See above, pp. 30–32.

knew long before that the chief danger in poetry is the likelihood that wisdom can be all too easily mistaken for an "airy vision," a mere imagination. It was not just tradition that led Milton to insist ultimately that the temples of poetry resided "fast by the oracle of God" (adapted from *PL* I. 12).

A Poetry of Wisdom

Taking Milton's pamphlet of 1644 as the crucial theoretical document, then, we may say that Milton's description of poetry makes its social function central. Poetry becomes the keystone to the curriculum and thus to that collective, institutional effort to "repair the ruins of our first parents" (Hughes, p. 613A). Thus defined, it is obviously a vehicle for the perception of truth, like the system of education in which it forms a part. Even given the selective target of that education, it was no deterrent to its proponent in 1664 that a vehicle thus conceived requires a nation of prophets, audience and poetry alike. And the following November, Milton could write the following concerning the nation's general "thirst after knowledge and understanding which God hath stirred up in this city":

> What could a man require more from a nation so pliant and so prone to seek after knowledge? What wants there to such a towardly and pregnant soul but wise and faithful laborers to make a knowing people, a nation of prophets, of sages, and of worthies? We reckon more than five months yet to harvest; there need not be five weeks, had we but eyes to lift up; the fields are white already. [Hughes, p. 743B]

We might easily conclude on the basis of this millennial optimism, which we may assume is not completely rhetorical in purpose, that Milton lacked all awareness of poetry's limitations as a social instrument. But if this is missing from the *Areopagitica,* or from *Of Education,* the explanation must lie in the purposes of each text and only secondarily in the possibility that they have not yet become an *issue* in Milton's thinking—to which the formal prose writings can provide only a limited index. At any rate, it is illuminating to trace Milton's attitude toward poetry's difficulties; for he was never really ignorant of them, in the usual sense of the word. From his earliest half-serious speculation in the Prolusions (1628?–1632), Milton's remarks about poetry can be said to revolve around a set of relations which only gradually became problematic: the complex relations of poet, audience, poem, and wisdom.

The academic Prolusions are primarily rhetorical occasions. It is misleading as well as difficult to abstract from them a theoretic position—if we confine our search to *obiter dicta.* Milton said during one of them that he preferred his audience to think of his performance as "said in jest." [11] Indeed, the young Milton thought of them in much the way he came to think of poetry. They are an arena partly transcending the legalism of oratory's laws, even though they occupy the moment of imaginative release prior to the disputation with the closed fist of logic. Like holidays they institute a comic license and allow a speaker—by virtue of the "occasion and the genius of the place," even if not of his "mind and disposition"—to jest and fictionalize deliberately.[12] Throughout these exercises one anticipates the distinction in *Of Education* between poetry and the other arts (especially logic). More than once Milton implied about them what he said outright of his subject in *Whether Day Is More Excellent Than Night,* that it "seems to suit a poetical performance better than it does an oratorical competition (Prol I, Hughes, p. 596B; CE 12 : 123). Thus, although these rhetorical ceremonies are singularly unreliable as a source of straight theory, they embody an association between oratory and poetry that Milton was never entirely to abandon; and Milton spoke of them with virtually the same rather pejorative language with which he faintly praised poetry. At one point in the first Prolusion, he sharply distinguishes the literary occasion which requires "credence" from its auditors from Greek mythological poetry, in which a knowledge of the arts is clad in "the beautiful vestments of fiction." [13] The

11. Prol II, Hughes, p. 603A; CE 12 : 151. See chap. 1, n. 8.

12. Prol VI, Hughes, p. 617A; CE 12 : 227. For a self-consciously fictional formulation relevant to the concerns and techniques of *Paradise Lost,* see Prol I, Hughes, p. 599B; CE 12 : 134–37.

13. Prol I, Hughes, p. 598A–B; CE 12 : 129. The relevant passages are as follows: "the gentler Muses, nay Philosophy itself, very close to the gods,

Latin of this passage, with the intensive *ob* probably responsible for the translator's vaguely antiprelatical "vestments," emphasizes how close we are in this kind of theory to an antipoetics both traditionally Christian and current in English empiricist and educational speculation.

Moreover, several passages in the Prolusions do supply us with the germs of Milton's mature poetic theory in the aspect which concerns us here. In particular he seems to be acutely aware of the ambiguous position of the sage as simultaneously a source and recipient of wisdom. In the attack on scholastic philosophy in the third Prolusion, Milton speaks somewhat uncharacteristically as a *reader* of school philosophy and thus as a student—a comember of his own audience. He objects that the schoolmen satisfy none of the ordinary criteria for speakers, whether in poetry, rhetoric, or history—the very criteria he himself must presently consider: "This quarrelsome contest of discordant views does not seem able to develop eloquence nor to teach wisdom, nor to incite to brave deeds." He complains specifically that the philosophy of the schools is by its very nature hostile to poetry, joking that "There was never a place for them on Parnassus" except a neglected corner at the bottom of the hill, "where . . . the sound of Apollo's lyre shall never reach." The rough similarity to that secular poetry of Hell, whose authors sing "thir own Heroic deeds" is inescapable throughout the Prolusions; there is even an elaborate curse on a boorish hearer "whose back is forever turned on true and sound wisdom" (Prol III, Hughes, p. 605B; CE 12 : 163, 165). Milton locates the essence of this basic incompatibility in two related areas. The intrinsic confusion of scholastic philosophy is embodied in "verbal wrangling," a logomachy we encounter in an archetypal form in the Chaos of *Paradise Lost*. As for the matter of this pseudophilosophy, Milton's critique echoes both humanism and science; it exists "nowhere in

---

forbids us to give credence . . . to the picture of gods in the poets, especially to the Grecian. . . . they have drive into one place men who were wandering in woods and mountains after the fashion of wild beasts, and they have established states, and, inspired by the divinity, they first have taught all learning whatsoever that has been handed down to this day, clad in the beautiful vestments of fiction [*obvestitas fabellarum*]. . . . they have left a knowledge of the arts, happily begun for posterity to finish."

the nature of things; but certain airy visions [*leves quaedam imagines*] flit before minds disordered by trifling ideas and destitute of more accurate wisdom [*rectioris sapientiae*]."[14] And, again from the standpoint of the reader, Milton defines the result in a visual metaphor he will later use to discuss false poetry:

> He [the reader] is perplexed, as though at a crossroad uncertain where to stop, whither to turn, and hesitating in his decision, while so many weapons are hurled on both sides close together that they take away the light itself and produce a deep darkness in the subjects, so that, as a result, the labor of the reader now becomes such that imitating the daily labors of Ceres, he seeks Truth over the whole surface of the Earth with a burning torch and finds it nowhere, and at length is reduced to insanity, so that he wretchedly thinks he is blind, where there is nothing for him to see. [Prol III, Hughes, p. 608A; CE 12 : 167]

The passage has tantalizing similarities both with the letter to Charles Diodati discussed earlier and with *Paradise Lost,* in which a belated peasant at one point sees "or dreams he sees" the revels of some faery elves. These are connections we cannot pursue here, beyond the simple observation that Milton in 1637 associated *himself* with that questing figure in a letter which Irene Samuel takes to signal a philosophic conversion (*Plato and Milton,* pp. 9–10; see above, pp. 24–26). We must restrict ourselves to noting that in this passage it is the *reader* who is a traveler reduced to insanity by words. The entire discussion, assuming as it does the possibility of a "more accurate wisdom," militates against the scholastics on virtually the grounds used by Bacon to divorce reason from poetry: "It [poetry] was ever thought to have some participation of divineness, because it doth raise and erect the Minde, by submitting the shews of things to the desires of the mind; whereas reason doth buckle and bowe the mind unto the nature of things."[15] By making "the nature

14. Prol III, Hughes, p. 606B; CE 12 : 169. See Bacon's similar observations on the schoolmen's variety of degenerate learning, in book I of *The Advancement of Learning: Selected Writings of Francis Bacon,* ed. Hugh G. Dick (New York: Random House, 1955), pp. 183–84, hereafter cited as Dick.

15. *The Advancement of Learning,* book II, Dick, p. 244.

of things" the ground of reference here, Bacon would appear to appropriate a true mimesis for science alone, while Milton's "accurate wisdom" can accommodate a poetic vehicle. It is of course this ground of reference for "imitation" which distinguishes the two so sharply, especially when we compare Bacon's "desires of the mind" with Milton's *rectior sapientia.*

We are probably closer to Milton's characteristic view of this period in a passage such as the following, which reveals a convenient escape route from the difficulties of mimetic theory and even some measure of the skeptical affectivism (and Italianate imagery) with which Milton complemented it. He is speaking specifically of divine poetry: It rouses "to high flight the mind, buried in earthly dross, establishes quarters among the temples of the sky; and, as though inspiring with nectarean breath and besprinkling the whole with ambrosia, instils in a measure heavenly blessedness and suggests a kind of immortal joy" (Prol III, Hughes, p. 605B; CE 12 : 163). The insanity mentioned as the plight of the reader of scholastic philosophy is more often the poet's problem, the danger which threatens to leave the epic poet in book VII without an audience for half of *Paradise Lost:*

> Return me to my Native Element:
> Lest from this flying Steed unrein'd, (as once
> *Bellerophon,* though from a lower Clime)
> Dismounted, on th'*Aleian* Field I fall
> Erroneous there to wander and forlorn.
> Half yet remains unsung, . . .
>
> [VII. 16–21]

With a glance at the narrative fiction of the poet/traveler, Milton moves to the context of composition, the lowest level of procedure in his own evolving poem. In doing so, he in effect recapitulates the social reappearance of the sage described in *Of Education.*

The seventh Prolusion, in the English translations misleadingly entitled "In Defense of Knowledge," similarly treats the danger of such visions from this quite different point of view—by insisting on the necessity not merely of knowledge but, more particularly, of the approach to Wisdom (*sapientia*) through the access of art (*per artem*). Milton does not mention the Fall directly; nor does he spell out the purpose of the arts, as in the later tractate. Instead he offers a tantalizing, and quite hypothetical, myth of the soul's progress, one which in some respects resembles both *A Mask* and Raphael's lecture to Adam in book v of *Paradise Lost*. Imperishable, it would return to its destined mansion "after it sojourned spotlessly and chastely on earth for a while." Like other seventeenth-century exponents of the myth, however, Milton continues; and his version of the commonplace critique is especially evident in the diction of the Latin. What he has been describing, he says, was indeed the unique gift to man from "the great framer [*opifex*] of the Universe":

> This is the sole contemplation, according to the judgment of almost everybody, by which our mind, without the aid of the body, remote [*seducta*] and as it were wrapped up in itself [*conglobata*] copies the eternal life [*aevum*] of the immortal gods with an extraordinary delight [*voluptate*].
>
> This, however, without knowledge [*sine arte*], is altogether sterile and joyless, yea, indeed, worthless. For who can contemplate and examine seriously the ideal forms of things, human and divine, of which nothing can surely be known, unless he has a mind saturated and perfected by knowledge and training? So, in short, for one who lacks knowledge every approach to a happy life is seen to be cut off [*interclusus*]. [Prol VII, Hughes, p. 623A–B; CE 12 : 255]

Seen in its proper context, this important passage points to the quite real pleasures of "sole contemplation," with which Milton later may have identified purely literary pursuits and even the "Hammersmith period" of vocational preparation, subsequent to Prolusion VII.[16] The characteristic Renaissance judgment of that state as sterile and joyless, though, is equally clear, however dutifully it is expressed. It underlies what Milton considers the prac-

16. Long known as the "Horton" period; see Parker, 2 : 779–80. Prol VII is traditionally assigned to 1632 and is usually viewed as a final required declamation for the M.A. degree; see Parker, 2 : 774–75.

tical irrelevance of the myth as a basis for education or ideology —a judgment which he implicitly recapitulates, in a much less playful context, in his curriculum of 1644.

Certain passages in Milton's earliest work, then, suggest some awareness of poetry's difficulties; and sketchy as they are, these would appear to link such problems with linguistic and epistemological realities since the Fall. There is no place on Parnassus for the scholastics, one feels, merely because they are "verbal"; there are no things answering to their words. We must remember that Milton is not concerned with poetry primarily here. But all the same it is difficult to escape the impression that even in such off-guard moments he is interested in the paradox of a true poetry—one which will embody an accurate wisdom in a manner not merely verbal. In much of this early discussion we are not far from the more explicitly literary rejection of verbal curiosities so important in *The Reason of Church Government* (1642). The impression is confirmed when we remember that from the beginning Milton (like other Renaissance critics in England and on the Continent) associated poetry with the curriculum and thus with the end of learning, the recovery of the primal wisdom. An essential focus in any complete study of Milton's theory must be the persistent conjunction of truth and poetry, especially in those knotty passages of definition. Professor Rajan is surely right in saying that Milton's "conception of the sage corresponds quite adequately to his conception of the poet" (*Modern Essays,* p. 4).

As for our more narrow purposes, we can only recall once again that the dangers of poetry are not considered in the tractate of 1644. If they had been, we might have discovered that poetry, somewhat like the art of rhetoric in the view of Cicero and Quintilian, tends to pull apart into the private visions of a prophet and—perhaps worse—the mere technique designed only to bedazzle its audience traditionally associated with sophistry. Because poetry is both sign and vehicle of the prophet's joyful communication, evidence of that threshold where Grace descends again to Nature, we may anticipate quite hypothetically that the practical difficulty lurking in these theoretical premises will concern the relation of the vision to the art, of talent to discipline, and—most immediate to our inquiry—of poet to image and poem. Milton reserved his most blistering professional irony for the mere mechanics of writing.

Ushers or Interpreters

From the beginning, then, Milton's theoretic remarks on poetry are curiously, if traditionally, ambiguous. It seems clear that if we take the position that these remarks amount to a coherent theory we should not fall into the common error that Milton simply identifies the poetic imagination with all enemies to a Christian humanism. If it is not clear in *Of Education* whether Milton's theory there is fundamentally "expressive" or "affective," at least his *placement* of poetry in the scheme of the arts suggests that poetry is close to being the subtle knot that makes us postlapsarian man—or that it is best able to *appeal* (from some other vantage point?) to that sensuous margin where body becomes soul. I have suggested that Milton complicates the issue, to some extent, by disallowing the distinction. At his most sanguine, and in a discussion of more social emphasis, he again thinks of poetry simultaneously as something peculiarly human in the nature of its appeals and as a useful technology in the Commonwealth: an intrinsically neutral (if dangerous) ordinance of man which can potentially rival "the office of a pulpit" (*RCG*, Hughes, p. 669B). At the heart of his theory, then, there seems to lie a view of poetry which, for all its limitations, is both more expansive and more skeptical than postromantic theory. Connecting poetry alike to its origins and its public, Milton's theory (if I read it correctly) amounts to a view of aesthetic culture in its relation to political and religious life. Its central insight, however, is basically antipoetic, in the sense that if images are radically human (or "natural") historically they have had a way of becoming more than images. Psychologically, indeed, they tend to harden into idols or icons; and though we cannot equate the terms "poetry" and "images" here, Milton all but formulated William K. Wimsatt's "verbal icon."

Milton's most significant solution to this problem, I believe, was not to reject such images but more clearly to "site" his poetry, perhaps from the ode *On the Morning of Christ's Nativity* onward. But before we consider these implications of Milton's theory, it will be helpful to turn to the enemies of "true poetry," the kind feared in book VII and denounced in book IX of *Paradise Lost:* that poetry which, divorced from both its origins in the Holy Light and its effects in the "acts" of its audience, becomes the stimulant and sign of the poet's mad rapture, on the one hand, and a mere technical performance, "premeditated verse," on the other. Associated with commercial greed as well, this poetry is portrayed in visual metaphors, imaging the furniture of a "corporeal" religion. Like the frontispiece of *Eikon Basilike,* which Milton attacked on similar grounds, it presents itself primarily for the dumb gaze of the idolater.[17] *Paradise Lost* itself is full of sensuous appeals, and visual imagery is especially predominant in the first two books, significantly located in that region of "darkness visible." Milton habitually accompanies such imagery with a frontal and often harsh commentary. Hence it is helpful to notice that frequently in his prose comments on "images" Milton justifies the literary propriety of what might be called the mode of prophetic satire. If poetry was sensuous, it was more fundamentally a sensuous form of discourse, a kind of speech; and Milton came to conceive of "true poetry," in particular, in oratorical terms. Fraught with difficulties though the terms may be for modern theoreticians, "vehemence" and its presumably intrinsic affect (the "act of worship" with which we began?) seem virtually irreducible in Milton's mature thinking about poetry. The eloquence, even the "hoarseness," of *Paradise Lost* and *Lycidas* is a special measure of the poems' "truth." But if this is one crucial center of Milton's poetic, we arrive at it only through his discussion of images, those greatest enemies to what Milton called the true poem.

Perhaps we can be more specific about what Milton means by images and clarify Milton's views of the identification which modern readers too readily assume between images and poetry. Quite early Milton was in the habit of speaking about poetry as

17. The purely discursive equivalent is the "ragged notions" and false bablements discussed as the inevitable result of present educational policy in *Of Education.*

though in itself, in its secular aspect, it were "untrue"—not false, necessarily, but morally neutral or indifferent. Throughout *Paradise Lost,* but especially in the catalogue of devils, the many sources of what we could call secular poetry, sources often located "Fast by the Oracle of God" (*PL* I. 12), are also the sources of "human religion." Milton also insisted on this continuity between human art and institution much earlier. In the fifth Prolusion he declared it impossible

> to prevent the most loathsome mixture of error from entering every day all learning. Error indeed is so potent or poisonous that it can either substitute its own image for snow-white Truth, or it can join to itself by some unknown artifice a brilliant appearance of Truth; by which art, so it seems, it frequently deceives even great philosophers and claims for itself honors and veneration due to Truth alone. [Prol v, Hughes, p. 611A; CE 12 : 195]

Milton's objections to the "mere images" for which modern readers are likely to justify him are grounded in this syncretic view of art and the imagination's products, the insistence that we cannot separate poetry from other secular institutions because of the nature of aesthetic contemplation, as it were. Both by temperament and by choice Milton was the fiercest opponent to literalism of the imagination.

We can get closer to the core of Milton's objections by recognizing that his thought on the subject is not couched in literary terms. He describes the target of his attacks more generally as "the depravities of the Church." Without falsifying his context, however, we can say that his remarks on imagery focus on two areas: (1) the "carnall" apprehension of the superstitious man—the observer of Art / Truth (Art here defined primarily in a visual metaphor); (2) the gestures of the *maker* of art—the "very act of prayer," in particular, which is superior to any decency imaginable. As Milton's use of the word "decency" suggests, the useful distinction is ours rather than his and reflects the degree of specialization necessary in critical discourse of the mid-twentieth century. This central concept in the aesthetic of George Herbert (and the informing raison d'être of poems and even whole books in the seventeenth century) [18] is related in Milton's writing only to human invention, the product of an atheistic imagination, as Milton's prose account of Comus's "easy-hearted man" suggests:

> the superstitious man by his good will is an Atheist; but being scarr'd from thence by the pangs and gripes of a boyling conscience, all in a pudder shuffles up to himself such a *God* and such a *worship* as is most agreeable to remedy his fear. [This fear] renders likewise the whole faculty of his apprehension carnall, and all the inward acts of *worship* issuing from the native strength of the Soule, run out lavishly to the upper skin, and there harden into a crust of Formallitie. [*Mask,* 163; *Ref, CPW,* 1 : 522]

Simplistic as its psychology may seem, this passage is as clear and immediate as Milton ever makes his "explanation," outside of *Paradise Lost.* He discovers an irreducible fear as the basis for all corrupt worship and identifies the object of that worship with God which it projects, "shuffles up." Perhaps because this passage contains what is for Milton an archetypal genesis of idolatry, we find it repeated in the prose and poetry alike; writing like this, indeed, is one good reason to call Milton's prose half-formed poetry. This version is particularly interesting for the way Milton proceeds from the bodily image to the relationship between the Bible and superstitious men. The "upper skin" becomes a diseased "crust" and simultaneously, it would seem, a rind divorced from heart. Then all this is applied; it is an explanation of how men come to see religion as a system of signs external to themselves and to the intention of the informing Spirit:

> Hence men came to scan the *Scriptures,* by the Letter, and in the Covenant of our Redemption magnified the external signs

18. See *A Priest to the Temple,* chap. 13, "The Parson's Church": "All this he doth, not as out of necessity, or as putting a holiness in the things, but as desiring to keep the middle way between superstition, and slovenliness, and as following the Apostles two great and admirable Rules in things of this nature: The first whereof is, *let all things be done decently, and in order:* The second, *let all things be done to edification,* I. Cor. 14" (*The Works of George Herbert,* ed. F. E. Hutchinson [Oxford: Clarendon, 1941], p. 246, hereafter cited as Hutchinson).

> more than the quickning power of the *Spirit,* and yet looking on them through their own guiltinesse. . . . They knew not how to hide their Slavish approach to Gods behests by them not understood, nor worthily receiv'd, but by cloaking their Servile crouching to all *Religious* Presentments, sometimes lawfull, sometimes Idolatrous, under the name of *humility* and terming the Py-bald frippery and ostentation of Ceremony's, decency. [*CPW,* 1 : 522]

The entire passage parallels an important thematic development in book 1 of *Paradise Lost,* in which the poet moves phantasmagorically from psychic to institutional manifestations of "superstition," from the despair racking Satan to the incursions of the archetypal demons into their particular historical careers, when they were known by "the names of men." The god thus imagined by the superstitious man has a function basically magical, to remedy fear. As Milton proceeds to describe the origin of this corrupted "decency," his satiric prose is a powerful vehicle for the analytic point that there is no distinguishing the "upper skin" of the superstitious man—continuous with the now corrupted soul and "faculty of apprehension"—and the *object* of superstitious reverence, the "decent" frippery which is at once imagined and worshiped, a projection of fallen man mistaken for an image of God.[19]

It is probably a mistake to speak too quickly of Milton's Platonism here or to conclude that Milton is incapable of responding to religion (or to passages of his own writing, for that matter) in any but dissociated ways, in terms of "surface and reality." As always in confronting the minds of great poets, such reductions can only extend our methods into the phenomena we seek to describe and fail to account for the subtleties. What Milton is analyzing here is not in fact religion but the loss of self involved in *anxious* Christianity. Despite the rhetorical deflation (indeed, largely by virtue of it), he insists that the form of worship, even the visible Church, *is* the corporate soul of the individual idolater, that any dissociation of appearance from real-

19. Burton's anatomy of the soul makes it clear that the essential continuity of the soul is a commonplace. See *Anatomy,* pp. 135–48.

ity in observing things religious can only be a figure of speech. While words like frippery," and especially the theatrical imagery more common elsewhere, amount to a terminology of abuse, they are also precise. Milton is attacking a staged religion which obscures "the act of prayer," a religion to human observers denoting a cloak for guilty nakedness and to higher prospects fully expressing the soul's imprisonment in its "indifferent" extensions. Taking the analysis a step further, we could say that in this and other passages Milton is, in effect, elaborating on something like the *anima conglobata* of the fifth Prolusion—that mind involved as though before the Fall with *sola contemplatio,* consequently seduced and even "cut off": the mind "without knowledge" *(sine arte*). As we have seen, the attack on that mind also involves a rejection of "secular" poetry.

That poetry has this institutional dimension for Milton is clearest perhaps from the way in which his antiprelatical pamplets of the 1640s contrast the naked comeliness of Truth (or the Gospel) to the "imagined" decency of ceremonies and images—including those involved in official exegesis of Scripture. Milton's focus here as elsewhere is not exclusively on poetry. But given the astonishingly syncretic nature of Milton's attacks, "poetry" is not inaccurate—either in Miltonic or modern terminology—as a term to describe all human artifice. Indeed, metaphoric assaults like the following (from *Of Reformation*), so close to passages of *Paradise Lost* in idea and diction, reveal more clearly than any critical discussion the peculiar status art of all kinds inevitably has in emotional, political, and religious life:

> Sad it is to thinke how that Doctrine of the *Gospel,* planted by teachers Divinely inspir'd, and by them winnow'd, and sifted, from the chaffe of overdated Ceremonies, and refin'd to such a Spirituall height, and temper of purity, and knowledge of the Creator, that the body, with all the circumstances of time and place, were purifi'd by the affections of the regenerat Soule, and nothing left impure, but sinne; *Faith* needing not the weak and fallible office of the Senses, to be either the Ushers, or Interpreters, of heavenly Mysteries, save where our Lord himselfe in his Sacraments ordain'd; that such a

> Doctrine should through the grossenesse, and blindnesse, of her Professors, and the fraud of deceivable traditions, drag so downwards, as to backslide one way into the Jewish beggery, of old cast rudiments, and stumble forward another way into the new-vomited Paganisme of sensuall Idolatry, attributing purity, or impurity, to things indifferent, that they might bring the inward acts of the *Spirit* to the outward, and customary ey-Service of the body, as if they could make *God* earthly, and fleshly, because they could not make themselves *heavenly,* and *Spirituall:* they began to draw downe all the Divine intercours, betwixt *God* and the Soule, yea, the very shape of *God* himselfe into an exterior, and bodily forme, urgently pretending a necessity, and obligement of joyning the body in a formall reverence, and *Worship* circumscrib'd, they hallow'd it, . . . they be deck't it, not in robes of pure innocency, but of pure Linnen, with other deformed and fantastic dresses in Palls, and Miters, gold, and guegaw's fetcht from *Arons* old wardrope or the *Flamins vestry:* then was the *Priest* set to con *his motions,* and his *Postures* his *Liturgies,* and his *Lurries,* till the Soule by this meanes of over-bodying her selfe, given up justly to fleshly delights, bated her wing apace downeward: and finding the ease she had from her visible, and sensuous collegue the body in performance of *Religious* duties, her pineons now broken, and flagging, shifted off from her selfe, the labour of high soaring any more, forgot her heavenly flight, and left the dull, and droyling carcas to plod on in the old rode, and drudging Trade of outward conformity. [*Ref, CPW,* 1 : 519–22]

Milton's target here is that corporate identity which the world—and imagination—produces; and he speaks of it in something like the way he and other Renaissance apologists speak of poetry. In submitting the shows of things to the desires of the mind, what was the mimetic poet doing but attributing "purity or impurity to things indifferent, that they might bring the inward acts of the spirit to the outward, and customary eye-service of the body?" Though the language is somewhat different, this is the basis of Milton's admiration for poetry in *Of Education,* as it is for Sidney's *Defense;* even *Hamlet,* that theologically resonant play, is centrally concerned with the idea of bodily knowledge and the problems of coming to know through images both verbal and visual.[20] In short, it was an essentially poetic act, whether in or out of Scripture, "to draw down all the Divine intercourse, betwixt God and the Soul, yea the very shape of God himself into an exterior and bodily form."

But as this passage makes clear, the analytic point of Milton's attack is the practical inextricability of this "poetry"—which he so admires in Scripture—from what he elsewhere calls in more general terms "the ordinances of men." [21] Strange as it seems to postromantic readers, Milton sees all art—and hence, poetry—as inevitably and quintessentially institutional at the same time that it is elementally human. Involved as he truly is in a "modern" controversy over human nature, Milton would seem to insist that our fictions are necessarily substantial and social as well as private and literary—that the purely poetic instinct is continuous with an instinct to *lose* as well as to build and transform the self in symbolic forms.

To describe this passage as an attack on poetry or the poetic instinct in man, moreover, is to point at a central irony in Milton's satiric prose here and elsewhere. Throughout the prose works, but especially in the antiprelatical period, it is often impossible for a reader to assign blame for religious, political, and even literary conditions in England and the Church. Is it a conspiracy of the prelates or human nature? In his last prose work (*Of True Religion, Heresy, Schism, and Toleration,* published in 1673), Milton will not tolerate Catholics, one suspects, because the "enemy" is more general than he had supposed earlier—it is the idolatrous instinct in most men. In *Samson Agonistes* this

20. See Maynard Mack, "The World of Hamlet," *Yale Review* 41 (1952): 502–23.

21. *AP* (1642). See also the discussion of the knowledge of God in *CD,* book I, chap. 2: "Both in the literal and figurative descriptions of God, he is exhibited not as he really is, but in such a manner as may be within the scope of our comprehensions, yet we ought to entertain such a conception of him, as he, in condescending to accommodate himself to our capacities, has shewn that he desires we should conceive. For it is on this very account that he has lowered himself to our level, lest in our flights above the reach of human understanding, and beyond the written word of Scripture, we should be tempted to indulge in vague cogitations and subleties" (Hughes, p. 905B).

kind of distinction is partly the basis for the Nazarite's attack on "the nation." But in the most partisan early pamphlets and even in *The Reason of Church Government,* Milton would have us believe that only a few bishops stand in the way of that millennial renewal described in the *Areopagitica.*

I have called poetry the true object of attack in this passage from *Of Reformation* because quite consistently in Milton's scattered bits of poetic theory it occupies that intermediate state in the bodying forth of the soul's self; and the fact is that Milton is either indecisive or deliberately ambiguous. Because this paragraph embodies both a psychic and an institutional history, it is improper to describe either clerical / royal persons or the psyche as—exclusively at least—the vehicle or tenor of metaphor. The reason lies in the paradoxical fact that while Milton is himself describing the needlessness of poetry in matters of faith, and its actual dangers in matters of worship, polity, and politics, he does so in a manner which we and most theorists of Milton's time would recognize as in some sense poetic. Faith may not need the "weak and fallible office of the senses," but Milton apparently does. This, to seventeenth-century if not to modern readers, is the rationale for Milton's language, his figures of speech, and especially the palpable fiction of the passage. There can be no doubt that in moving from the doctrine of the Gospel, that perfectly refined book already "sifted from the chaffe of overdated Ceremonies," to the heavy labor of the "droyling carcas" Milton has himself drawn down "the Divine intercours betwixt God and the soul" into "an exterior and bodily form." Even as he denies the need of the senses, he is exploiting them to the utmost; the senses—or is it the priests?—are mere "Ushers, or Interpreters, of heavenly Mysteries." [22] Later they would be "Sewers or Seneschals" in a culinary and ritual setting also hinted at here. It is because Milton *refuses to say which* that we may call his target poetry. And we do violence neither to Renaissance theories of

22. An usher was a student appointed to help in class instruction; see Donald L. Clark, *Milton at St. Paul's School* (New York: Columbia University Press, 1948). In *Areopagitica* Milton wrote, of the writer's diminished "authority" under censorship, "I hate a pupil teacher, I endure not an instructor that comes to me under the wardship of an overseeing fist" (Hughes, p. 736A).

poetry nor to Milton's own remarks through the prose works in suggesting that for the moment Milton has knowingly, in poetry, replaced those ushers.

Poetry and the Legislation of Mankind

It is *The Reason of Church Government* (1642) in which the issues we have traced reappear in their most complete and interesting combination. Usually cited as an autobiographical "source," the preface to the second book probably reveals more about decorous or persuasive appeals in polemic warfare than it does about Milton's biography, the inner aspects of which still elude us. The preface begins with a discussion of postlapsarian knowledge in its "existential" aspect—its burdensomeness—and the abuse of men by "fleshly doctrines" in the hands of "the great merchants of this world." The effect of this burden, Milton says, is the kind of alienation which produces prophets. Upright men "are made the greatest variance and offence, a very sword and fire both in house and city over the whole earth," and Milton cites Jeremiah as the exemplar of such a response. From Jeremiah he moves to the "ancient prophets," to John, to the testimony of "the wise poet" (Sophocles, the poet of Tiresias, who "knew more than other men"), to the natural response of *"every* good and peaceable man" responding to the motions of God, and finally to the *ethos* of the pamphlet itself, the relevance of such a summons "for me." In a passage which appears to be closely related to the letter of 1633 (accompanying Milton's sonnet on Time) he emphasizes his own talent, the biblical one also treated in sonnet XIX, and expresses fear of a Divine reproach concerning the gift of language—used for vain subjects but absent in the "cause of God and his Church." [23]

We might notice at this point that both the imagined reproaches imply that the single voice of Milton could make the crucial difference as to the outcome of the present political and religious struggle: an assumption of considerable interest to the student of Milton's poetics. For the optimism, which we have

23. See Macon Cheek, "Of Two Sonnets of Milton," *Renaissance Papers* (Columbia, S.C.: University of South Carolina Press, 1956), pp. 82–91; rpt. *Modern Essays*, pp. 125–35.

become too inclined to dismiss as rhetorical stance, becomes evident just as Milton moves into his self-presentation as a writer of prose. In this section of ethos, he dwells at length on poetics—the role with which he defines himself professionally, in which he can "without apology speak more of himself than I mean to do" and from which he dissociates himself so self-consciously in this pamphlet. That is, Milton apparently considers poetry as *excluding* the material of the present pamphlet—a segregation of literary functions he may have reconsidered later, at least by implication, in the invectives of his epic poetry. In fact, the analysis of poetry itself in the preface includes a discussion of vehemence as a mode of poetry, even while distinguishing sharply between the present occasion (calling for that "cooler element" of prose) and the projected plan of Milton's life. It would seem that the "interrupted pattern," the forcing of rude fingers, is a very nearly archetypal image in Milton's works and life alike. Even as he distinguishes one identity from another, private poet from prose warrior for truth, he hints at an aesthetic which will as it were include the one within the other.

There is another point we may easily lose in examining the way Milton zeroes in on his own life plan. The relation of the quasiautobiography/poetics to the framing context—the opening remarks on knowledge and the sequence of prophets—may seem ponderous and pretentious. But it is a truly organic continuity. It has been pointed out that in Milton's poetry a "picture" contained by a frame of commentary may burgeon and seem to transcend that matrix altogether. But Milton ends the preface to book II of *The Reason of Church Government* speaking of the "under-service to God," and of its relation to his "destiny" from childhood. It is perfectly clear from his claim to have been "Church-outed by the prelates" that he has not forgotten his own place in the line of prophets. The entire passage is a tantalizing document on the relations between prophecy, poetry, and politics.[24]

With this much of the passage's context in mind, we can turn to the more purely literary discussion. Milton begins the passage with an apology for speaking "unusual things of myself" in

24. For an illuminating study, see Fixler, *Kingdoms of God.*

prose, where a writer expects many readers "of no empyreal conceit." Because of the breach in decorum some account of the occasion is necessary. And taking pains to amplify its importance, Milton points to the discovery (by whom we are not told, unfortunately) that the style of his writing "was likely to live" (*RCG,* Hughes, p. 667B). Milton seems to suggest here that style in itself is not associated intrinsically with either poetry or prose —or necessarily with the vernacular. "In English or other tongue, prosing or versing, but chiefly this latter." Even without what follows, however, it seems clear that he already associates his style (in 1642) with English verse.

We cannot take all that Milton says here as material of great value for biography, of course, at least for the biography of the period Milton is describing. Such remarks as these have the kind of clarity that comes only in retrospect, like the continuity in Milton's prose career as seen from the vantage point of the *Second Defence* (1654) (*CPW,* 2 : 1–2). Concerning Milton in 1642, however, we can perhaps be more certain. Even for readers conditioned by Milton's own retrospective comments on his life plan, it would be difficult to miss the strongly affirmative manner of this entire preface, spoken as it seems to be by someone who has discovered, perhaps recently, what his portion in this life is to be and who is trying to make sense out of a radical intrusion on his early career. More particularly, Milton dates his own assent to this gradually revealed identity not from the writing of the *Nativity* (Christmas 1629, where one authority has placed Milton's most basic literary and religious crisis) but from the Italian journey or shortly thereafter: broadly speaking, sometime in 1639. One cannot deny, of course, that 1639 is a convenient date for Milton's purposes in 1642. The year of the first bishop's war nearly coincided with Milton's entry into the pamphlet controversy. Perhaps there is even good reason to doubt the existence in 1642 of an integral identity to be "historified," in Erik Erikson's phrase (Erikson, pp. 53–54). Milton's conception of the poet is curiously all-embracing, and he sought to institute in the figure of the poet a volatile mixture of social parts, as the discrepancies we have traced have made evident. Yet, if only because we do have later poems from Milton's highly professionalized hand, we cannot easily dismiss these references in favor of biography whose only materials are the poems. We must turn with some sympathy to the thoughts which, in Milton's words, "possessed me." These, he tells us, were of two kinds. He was persuaded by the acquaintances of the Italian journey and "friends . . . at home" as well as by an "inward prompting which now grew daily upon me" to undertake the labor and study necessary for the literary legacy—in Milton's oft-quoted words, "something so written to after-times, as they should not willingly let it die."[25] It is this effort, Milton writes in 1642, speaking (we must admit) in very general fashion—this "labor and intense study [that] I take to be my portion in this life" (Hughes, p. 668A).

Throughout the preface, Milton is concerned to establish how much he is giving up for the purpose of embarking on what he later calls "a troubled sea of noises and hoarse disputes." His largest polemic purpose is to emphasize the discontinuities between poetry and pamphleteering. Here, however, he turns immediately from the product of such studies to the often discussed life plan—and to the practical matter of how he would *spend his time* should he live to "write as men buy leases, for three lives and downward." We do not lose touch with the concern for style and the focus on the poetic products; Milton returns to them shortly in interesting detail. But he now turns to social and didactic poetry as a kind of religious duty. "There ought no regard be sooner had than to God's glory, by the honor and instruction of my country." He specifically prefers this end to the merely literary distinctions of arriving at the second rank among the Latins, or making "verbal curiosities the end (that were a toilsome vanity)." Thus he sees his posture in social terms and (once again) in the light of the humanist and scientist rubrics of *verba et res:* "to be an interpreter and relater of the best and sagest things among mine own citizens throughout this island in the mother dialect" (Hughes, pp. 671A, 668A).

We should not read such words in the light of distinctions

25. Hughes, p. 668A; the phrasing anticipates the accounts of the writer's motives and morale in *Areopagitica,* Hughes, p. 735A–B. There an author writes "to the world."

Milton failed to make until later in his career. He is attempting to justify himself as a poet/citizen of a religious *and* political nation; and consequently, it is impossible to distinguish personal from national pride. The disingenuousness of Milton's modesty in confining himself to "these British islands as my world" is not purely rhetorical. There is complexity in Milton's attitude, some sense of impulses difficult to reconcile, as the syntax suggests: "not caring to be once named abroad, though perhaps I could attain to that, but content . . ." What emerges most clearly here, however, is the vagueness, the lack of felt difficulties, in Milton's didactic literary theory: the needlessness, the unwillingness, or perhaps the real inability to distinguish the artistic problems of person, argument, and poem. The implication is clear that "God's glory" has a peculiarly local connection with England—a traditional connection obscured only, Milton contends, by "the unskillful handling of monks and mechanics"—and all He needs is a poet.

The prime emphasis in this paragraph is on Christianity, England, the vernacular, and the "mechanical" obstacles to a poetry of wisdom. In the next paragraph Milton seems closer to his organizing distinction between the activities of "the mind at home"—a more spacious but less real place than the insular locale of Britain or the home of "Truth herself"—and the polemic wars. The discussion of formal and topical alternatives for the poet is in its entirety a list of "what the mind at home, in the spacious circuits of her musing, hath liberty to propose to herself." Milton pretends to return to this distinction when he mentions "with what small willingness I endure to interrupt the pursuit of no less hopes than these," when he tells us he must forbear "beholding the bright countenance of truth in the quiet and still air of delightful studies, to come into the dim reflection of hollow antiquities sold by the seeming bulk."

But it is important that we take this in part as a debating point. For when we turn to the theory itself, we find not merely "literary hopes." The material preliminary to the central theoretic discussion is curiously double in its emphasis at once upon the possibility of an eternal and primarily literary fame and the patriotic desire "to be an interpreter and relater of the best and sagest things among mine own citizens." Indeed the relative neutrality of these words for the poet's activity suggests the sense of an almost magical efficacy of those "sagest things," not to mention the openness of English ears to them. Milton seems to hold that the one is to be achieved through the other, that true fame can come only through the choice to be local, temporary (or at least temporal)—even to be in some measure *unprofessionally* literary; thus Milton's insistence that this island—or "these British islands"—will suffice to be his world.

Whether or not this is *felt* as paradox, Milton's way of framing this section of his preface to book II—as a description of the hopes of his literary career—obscures an interesting and recurring additional rhythm in the preface. It is a movement from words to things, and the distinction underlies Milton's rejection of "verbal curiosities." More than once, Milton moves from considering "the mind at home," at liberty in "the spacious circuits of her musing," from this literary, private, and potentially solipsistic activity to the redefinition of this luxury as "abilities . . . bestowed . . . to some . . . in every nation." Recalling his earlier distinction between the *anima conglobata* and the social uses of knowledge (*ars*), Milton redefines his own liberty as a private poet—his pastoral days through the Hammersmith period?—as the luxurious use of a certain ability which is an "inspired gift of God," a talent, and not merely a technology. Milton's own syntax reveals the nice complexity of his analysis, as well as the dialectic quality of the entire preface: "These abilities, wheresoever they be found, are the inspired gift of God, rarely bestowed, but yet to some (though most abuse) in every nation." Then, as though elated with discovery, Milton immediately moves to his catalogue of the various forms of power flowing from this talent—power, in Milton's words, "besides the office of a pulpit." The discussion of this poet's power, obviously related to the claim of Milton's having been "Church-outed by the prelates," is the focal point of Milton's theoretic discussion and the final phase of the rhythm I have mentioned.

Milton prefaces his account of the mind at home by suggesting that the bridge between pure poetry and good citizenship—that is, the *subject,* Britain's noble achievements—is actually extant, like the "great argument" of *Paradise Lost.* The archetype is there; all that is needed is the truthful signature. This, of course, is why Milton makes so much of being "content with these British islands as my world." Despite the many guesses offered, it is difficult to say, thus far, just what the archetype *is* in this passage: possibly a version of the conflict with Norman incursions against native "English" liberty, though this is usually considered a later interest for Milton. The important point here for our purposes, in any case, is Milton's deliberate choice of a world in which the true native *gesta* have been obscured by "monks and mechanics"—employing, we are tempted to add, considering the context, the "skill of Artifice or Office mean" (*PL* IX. 39).

In turning to the discussion of formal and topical alternatives open to the private poet, Milton invites us once again to consider the sacrifices of the poet entering the busyness of pamphlet warfare. Despite the way Milton presses the debating point here—the distinction between public and private man, poetry and prose—what is impressive is the way in which Milton's definition and his actual discussion serve to enhance a continuity rather than a dichotomy between the two. Once again, we might say that the key for Milton is the audience of Christian heroic poetry; if poetry's province is the mind at home, human fallibility requires a return to nature *per artem.* And Milton's decision to confine his muse to his native islands clearly puts tremendous burden on the relationship between the poet and his audience. Milton at this point denounces monkish artifice in obscuring the true history of Britain partly because he sees the truth of Christian history as requiring only the services of a scribe. Still, the busy pamphleteer pretends to be pressed for time, which (he says) "serves not now." And he seems to dissociate the occasion of *The Reason of Church Government* from the literary hopes he must leave: "I might seem too profuse to give any certain account of what the mind at home, in the spacious circuits of her musing, hath liberty to propose to herself." (Hughes, p. 668B). We have encountered this language before, together with "realistic" qualifications which occurred to Milton even as a university student. Yet this is the general rubric, the strategic apology mentioned earlier in the preface and governing the entire consideration of formal and topical alternatives. We are encouraged to view the survey of genre and subject as this particular *kind* of example. And to an extent Milton does stick to an almost purely literary level. We are given models of diffuse and brief epic, alternative modes of structure ("whether the rules of Aristotle herein are strictly to be kept, or nature to be followed"—a choice which Milton appears to approve).[26] We descend, as in Sidney's survey of the genres, from epic to dramatic tragedy and finally to lyric.

It is hardly necessary to point out, however, that this is not the luxury of *any* mind at home, even in such a literary golden age as the seventeenth century. It has been clear for some time that the passage is closely related to the Trinity manuscript, on which Milton was working at about this time (see Parker, 1 : 190; 2 : 843). Clearly, in addition, these are the remarks of a professional poet, as the references to the "critical art of composition" and the allusions to "them that know art" testify. The passage would seem to be both a kind of literary prospectus and the obiter dicta of a practicing poet. How free *is* that poet's mind at home? In fact, Milton's considerations of what it might propose are so far from being purely literary that they amount to a discussion of literature's relation to the Church, then a treatment of the individual poet's (that is, Milton's) power in the Church and State. Milton's terms for the subject of the ideal epic are restrictive: he wonders "what king or knight, before the conquest, might be chosen in whom to lay the pattern of a Christian hero." With the advantage of being a Christian, he is inclined to think that the choice Tasso gave his Italian prince can be duplicated in "our ancient stories." Only "the fate of this age" and possible adversities in "our climate" might prevent this achievement. As for his own patron, Milton does not indicate to whom "the like offer" might be extended (Hughes, pp. 668–70, esp. p. 669A; cf. *PL* IX. 21).

In truth, only one subject really occurs to the mind at home—

26. The exact wording is as follows: "whether the rules of Aristotle herein are strictly to be kept, or nature to be followed, which in them that know art and use judgment, is no transgression but an enriching of art" (Hughes, p. 668B).

the pattern of the Christian hero; the nature of the epic's archetypal pattern is clear if its action is not. More significant, however, is the social province of the literature Milton has in mind. What determines the formal choice between epic and dramatic "constitutions" is not a scale of genres per se but the pragmatic question of which is "more doctrinal or exemplary to a nation." Indeed, the central concern which emerges from a careful reading of *The Reason of Church Government* directly anticipates the theory in *Of Education:* it is the sense that a poet (again, Milton?) is needed to supplement if not to take over the nation's religious instruction. Implied in the preface to Milton's second book is the virtual institutionalization of literature and perhaps of a national / religious poet in precisely that area of national life vacated by a prelatical Church.

For Milton turns, at this point in his discussion of literary hopes, to a consideration of the ideal poet's abilities and powers. He does so rather abruptly, as if to imply that the poet's hopes are indistinguishable from his religious and social matrix and even, perhaps, from a rather specific cultural program. By shifting from a discussion of genres to the matter of abilities, Milton in effect reminds us that the preface is an extended ethical argument, as well as a partial poetics. Stylistically, the sentence which opens the section resembles the description of poetry's place in *Of Education:* "These abilities, wheresoever they be found, are the inspired gift of God, rarely bestowed, but yet to some (though most abuse) in every nation" (Hughes, p. 669B). Are these abilities actually rare, or is it simply a matter of abusing a received technology? A sentence like this makes its point partly by rhythm alone and in the way it negates and qualifies its own process. Unlike Milton's section on the forms and subjects, a section governed stylistically by formal balance, Milton follows this passage with a list of the powers of someone with these abilities. He includes as much as one would in a Ciceronian period but emerges from the sentence with a point of view cumulatively double and only temporarily single. He is clearly celebrating the abilities, both for their own sake and for what they can accomplish in the nation. Within the quoted passage, the emphasis comes down hard on "every nation." To this extent, England is like *any* nation, the Italy of Tasso, say. But the gifts are *rarely* bestowed, even if to some in every nation. Milton does *not* say that most *people* abuse a gift universally endowed. The "some" in his sentence refers to those rare recipients of God's gift (be they pagan or Christian—*wheresoever* found); most of that *some* abuse the ability. The effect, again, is twofold. Milton suggests that most *nations* will suffer the same fate as the talent, and perhaps even that England has suffered thus through the unskillful handling of monks and mechanics. But the possibilities for a nation which does contain one of such abilities are almost unlimited.

As if to emphasize the departure stylistically, Milton follows this opened period with his list of powers held by someone with these abilities. After circling and circumscribing his own career with an extraordinary precociousness of conscience,[27] Milton turns to the benefits flowing from the presence of such a figure:

> . . . but yet to some . . . in every nation; and are of power, beside the office of a pulpit, to imbreed and cherish in a great people the seeds of virtue and public civility; to allay the perturbations of the mind, and set the affections in right tune; to celebrate in glorious and lofty hymns the throne and equipage of God's almightiness, and what he works, and what he suffers to be wrought with high providence in his church, to sing the victorious agonies of martyrs and saints, the deeds and triumphs of just and pious nations, doing valiantly through faith against the enemies of Christ; to deplore the general relapses of kingdoms and states from justice and God's true worship. Lastly, whatsoever in religion is holy and sublime, in virtue amiable or grave, whatsoever hath passion or admiration in all the changes of that which is called fortune from without, or the wily subtleties and refluxes of man's thoughts from within; all these things with a solid and treatable smoothness to paint out and describe. [Hughes, pp. 669B–70A]

Formally, this catalogue of the powers corresponds roughly to the descending scale of genres in the earlier survey. Milton describes the social affects of epic (noting without special attention

27. See above, the concluding pages of chap. 1, and n. 7 in this chapter.

the ideal circumstance of a "great people") tragedy ("to allay the perturbations of the mind, and set the affections in right tune") and lyric. But the catalogue is not precisely correspondent; for toward the end, Milton seems to focus on what *subjects* the poet can in general sing. And there is an addition to the earlier survey which is perhaps significant, especially in view of the optimistic assumption, noted earlier, about the relation of poet to audience. What is new in the discussion is the propriety of satire in the province of poetry; to single out the relevant comments, poetry is "of power, beside the office of a pulpit . . . to deplore the general relapses of kingdoms and states from justice and God's true worship."

It is well to be clear on Milton's precise view of this deploring; for we know that vehemence comes to be a central question in his mature discussions of aesthetic propriety. Vehemence, indeed, seems to have become an issue as Milton's conception of the poet found him more and more at odds with the society of which he is here the spokesman. It is tempting to suppose that *Lycidas* is such a poem in its entirety, and especially in the dire warning of the two-handed engine. It is often read, to be sure, in the bitter tones of that warning, and the headnote to the 1645 reprinting has too frequently been taken as a part of the poem (see below, chap. 4). Certainly the elaborate framing of the poem's "eager thought" and its ending suggest that *Lycidas* does not deplore the relapse of a kingdom; nor does the poem foretell the ruin of the corrupted clergy, as Michael Fixler has recently reminded us (*Kingdoms of God,* p. 61). It does not embody, in other words, any simple view, at least on *Milton's* part, of the connection between poetry and prophecy, which Bacon in any case had called "divine history" and brought into the legitimate realm of divine poetry (Dick, p. 230). The kingdoms to be deplored in *The Reason of Church Government* are mentioned with a comfortable distance. Whatever changes occurred in Milton's view of poetry and its relation to political prophecy between 1638 and 1645, it is relatively clear from *The Reason of Church Government* that English poet and kingdom in 1642 are basically at one, presumably in practice as in theory, and also that Milton regards satire as part of poetry's song. As we have seen, poetry itself cannot be dissociated from politics and religion throughout the preface. Critical issues considered separately and so skeptically in the twentieth century are mingled with an abandon which embarrasses our preconceptions. But the way in which Milton turns immediately from the option of what we might call satire to a passage of pure mimetic theory in general puts the issue beyond doubt:

> . . . all these things with a solid and treatable smoothness to paint out and describe. Teaching over the whole book of sanctity and virtue, through all the instances of example, with such delight to those especially of soft and delicious temper, who will not so much as look upon Truth herself, unless they see her elegantly dressed; that whereas the paths of honesty and good life appear now rugged and difficult, though they be indeed easy and pleasant, they will then appear to all men both easy and pleasant, though they were rugged and difficult indeed. [Hughes, p. 670A]

This is a classic passage of mimetic theory, in the tradition of Sir Philip Sidney and of Bacon. And merged as it is with a facile didacticism, it dramatizes nicely the problems of a poet writing in this tradition. Milton clearly sees poetry as a form of human discourse, inferior to "Truth herself." But while there are important qualifications in his attitude toward the audience of poetry, there is hardly the note of condescension we find in seventeenth-century justifications of ancient fables as mysteries to be veiled from vulgar display. Indeed the net effect of a passage like this is at once more complicated and optimistic than Hobbes's view of fablers, for example, particularly regarding the Miltonic poet's solidarity with his audience. Poetry is helpful "to those especially of soft and delicious temper"—an emphasis slightly different from the letter to Hartlib, in which poetry itself is "sensuous" and "passionate." If poetry happens to be good for those of soft and delicious temper, Milton goes on to suggest, we are all more or less in that predicament—those of us, at least, in what Milton conceived as "my world." The perception of Truth herself is the ultimate end of all Art, and Milton seems to say that Art—or poetry—can do more truthfully (perhaps because more self-consciously) what the prelatical Church in its encouragement of idolatry was doing only "imaginatively." In fact, Milton appears to identify the vision possible in poetry with the immediate, face-to-face perception described by Paul in 1 Cor. 13. Regardless of how the paths of honesty are "in deed," Milton argues, they seem in poetry—with all due insistence on the seeming—what they will be in the aspect of eternity, "both easy and pleasant."

It is only within the context of this mimetic and pragmatic theory of poetry, then, that Milton defines the function of the satirist. Satire, if we may call it so, is conceived as within the province of poetry, a literary mode and not an all-encompassing social position. Despite the fact that Milton in 1642 and earlier conceives of the poet as potential prophet, the nation too is one of prophets. Poetry itself, moreover, is treated in connnection with the contemplation of Truth herself. Milton frequently reminds us of his general distinction in the preface by saying that in embarking on "a troubled sea of noises and hoarse disputes" he has left off contemplating "the bright countenance of Truth in the quiet and still air of delightful studies." Indeed he stresses that he has been "put from" such studies, to "come into the dim reflection" of pamphlet warfare (Hughes, p. 671A). Such images and distinctions, later to be incorporated within the metaphoric and discursive economy of *Paradise Lost,* add to the resonance of such a recurrent phrase as "true poem," particularly when Milton uses it in the context of discussing the poet in society.

If the paradox in "true poem" is incipient, it is nonetheless real. Milton clearly thinks of the ideal poet as one who contemplates Truth; and he seems to have viewed his own leisurely study as such a contemplation. He was the quintessential poet only through the Hammersmith period, such assumptions would appear to suggest. But as we have seen, poetry also includes something like satire within its province. The poet is inevitably a citizen, an interpreter and relater more than a sage. Like Yeats—and Milton was concerned with many of the same postromantic alternatives—the poet for Milton cannot escape the discursive nature of his posture, despite the fact that he is no mere fabricator of verbal curiosities.[28] A true poem rejects elements in-

28. See Kermode, *Romantic Image,* pt. 1.

herent in the conflict between poetry and the world; as I have suggested above, it mediates between Truth herself and "our youth and gentry" (not to mention those "libidinous and ignorant poetasters") in the manner supposed to be the business of the Church. Milton's ideal poem here is not far from having the ontological status of Herbert's *The Temple*. But a true poem is also a more vulgar thing, in the sense that Herbert's "Church-Porch" is vulgar, precedent to the "mystical repast" of "The Church" proper. Somehow, it must combat the appeals of those poetasters whom Milton attacks more than once in the remainder of his preface—perhaps by including and modifying them.

Milton does not say just *how* this benefit from poetry can be effected, though he offers one specific suggestion. What concerns him primarily is that the ignorant and libidinous poetasters, with no sense of decorum, have made "the *taste* of virtuous documents harsh and sour." [29] With the purpose of captivating an audience for his true poetry, Milton appears to call for an instituted, doctrinal poetry as a vehicle for wisdom alternative to the pulpit, a vehicle which will bring the *whole* soul of man into activity. And it is poetry which is both regular and somehow bodily, corporeal, answering a need almost physiological, "because the spirit of man cannot demean itself lively in this body without some recreating intermission of labor and serious things." If poetry is a game, however, it is a game well managed. In calling for his program, Milton specifically contrasts it indeed with Charles I's *Book of Sports* (1633):

> It were happy for the commonwealth, if our magistrates, . . . as in those famous governments of old, would take into their care, not only the deciding of our contentious lawcases and brawls, but the managing of our public sports and festival pastimes; that they might be, not such as were authorized a while since, the provocations of drunkenness and lust, but such as may inure and harden our bodies by martial exercises to all warlike skill and performance; and may civilize, adorn,

29. To a remarkable extent throughout his writing—in *Of Education* even more than *Paradise Lost*—Milton's root metaphor in matters of knowledge is digestive. His scholars, in particular, will know "how to manage a crudity" —in Burton the special liability of gluttons, epicures, and idle persons (*Anatomy,* p. 136) and a disorder opposed to "maturation."

> and make discreet our minds by the learned and affable and artful recitations, sweetened with eloquent and graceful enticements to the love and practice of justice, temperance, and fortitude, instructing and bettering the nation at all opportunities, that the call of wisdom and virtue may be heard everywhere, as Solomon saith: "She crieth without, she uttereth her voice in the streets, in the top of high places, in the chief concourse, and in the openings of the gates." Whether this may both be, not only in pulpits, paneguries, in theatres, porches, or what other place or way may win most upon the people to receive at once both recreation and instruction, let them in authority consult. [Hughes, p. 670A–B]

Milton dissociates himself at this point from "them in authority," and unfortunately it is not entirely clear what he has in mind: poetry readings, perhaps, among other things. The rest of the discussion is personal and has the effect of making the theoretic passage more immediate and more evidently biographical. But the transition is abrupt, almost as though Milton sensed the presumption of acknowledging the poet as the legislator of mankind; and Milton returns to the organizing apology and appeal to the interrupted career.

The entire argument of the preface implies certain harmonies which modern readers—and even Milton himself, somewhat later—find naïve and even perhaps embarrassing; in particular, the facile (though moving) association of purely literary hopes and intentions with the sense of 'myself [as] anything worth to my country." But if any aspect of *The Reason of Church Government* reveals a predominant attitude, it is the way Milton returns to the antithesis between poetry and pamphlet, finally to accept this discontinuity in his career. To make this decision, he says quite distinctly, is to turn away from "beholding the bright countenance of truth . . . to come into the dim reflection of hollow antiquities sold by the seeming bulk." He is to some extent a victim of circumstances. "Urgent reason" has plucked him from the accomplishment of his intentions by "an abortive and foredated discovery"; he has been "put from" beholding truth; he is "Church-outed" by the prelates. But such passages do not strike us as complaints. "Church-outed," in particular, is a sarcastic coinage for what the prelates wrongly imagine they *can* do. If there is anxiety in these closing lines of the preface, there is also confidence and strength. In a passage which anticipates sonnet XIX, Milton suggests that the great and true poem is already *there*. It needs only the writing down, and mere time is all but irrelevant—at least for the definitive poem Milton has in mind. This, I think, is the rationale for Milton's covenant with "the knowing reader," for "going on trust with him toward the payment of what I am now indebted." [30] What matters in the meantime is "the yoke of prelacy, under whose inquisitorious and tyrannical duncery, no free and splendid wit can flourish" (Hughes, p. 671A). The attack on prelacy is linked with the abuse of poetry itself, as it was in Milton's description of those who obscured the true British achievements, the "monks and mechanics." Here Milton dissociates himself—and that true poem —from conventional and youthful artifice. This definitive poem is a work

> not to be raised from the heart of youth, or the vapors of wine, like that which flows as waste from the pen of some vulgar amorist, or the trencher fury of a rhyming parasite; not to be obtained by the invocation of dame memory and her siren daughters, but by devout prayer to that eternal Spirit, who can enrich with all utterance and knowledge, and sends out his Seraphim, with the hallowed fire of his altar, to touch and purify the lips of whom he pleases. [Hughes, p. 671A]

Here Milton is preoccupied with time—with its relation to his talent and the poem. His attack on "the trencher fury of a rhyming parasite," virtually repeated in book IX of *Paradise Lost,* is presented as a justification for the covenant, as well as a plea for the necessity of political calm; the payment of his debt is not an everyday, bodily matter. It is as though Milton were deliberately turning to the world, back into time, in order to establish those ideal conditions for "free and splendid wit," a social theater for

30. Hughes, p. 670A; I do not mean to suggest that the work in question is *Paradise Lost.*

poetic action. Three years later, of course, he seemed to think of it as all but accomplished.

I have emphasized that Milton's overriding purpose is to justify his presence in the pamphlet controversy by lingering on what it is he turns away *from*. The choice as it is defined here is clearly imaged as a descent into a realm portrayed satirically as animal and bodily. In its materiality it resembles Hell or Chaos in *Paradise Lost*. But we have seen that Milton's organizing distinction obscures a poetics which can, practically speaking, include such distinctions, and the discussion as a whole worries the relation between a poem, particularly a true poem, and a world in which poets write in a "trencher fury" and prose is sold by the "seeming bulk." More important, perhaps, is the deliberateness of Milton's choice, pretended if not real. He appeals to "any gentle apprehension" for sympathy in his dilemma. But his conclusion, again anticipating the language of sonnet XIX, specifies that the Church, to which Milton was "destined of a child," particularly commands *his* energy. The concluding passage is worth quoting in full:

> But it were the meanest under-service, if God by his secretary conscience enjoin it, it were sad for me if I should draw back; for me especially, now when all men offer their aid to help, ease, and lighten the difficult labors of the church, to whose service, by the intentions of my parents and friends, I was destined of a child, and in mine own resolutions: till coming to some maturity of years, and perceiving what tyranny had invaded the church, that he who would take orders must subscribe slave, and take an oath withal, which, unless he took with a conscience that would retch, he must either straight perjure, or split his faith; I thought it better to prefer a blameless silence before the sacred office of speaking, bought and begun with servitude and forswearing. Howsoever, thus church-outed by the prelates, hence may appear the right I have to meddle in these matters, as before the necessity and constraint appeared. [Hughes, p. 671B]

It is evident to any honest reader of Milton's prose that the difficulty of discovering a theory of poetry is exceeded only by that of formulating its use. It seems clear from our survey, partial as it may be, that it is probably a mistake to assume that there is a theory; despite Rajan's admirable essay, we may not be convinced that Milton said "something systematic" about his art, least of all in the area Milton called "the critical art of composition" (*Modern Essays,* p. 3). On the whole it seems safer to examine the details of specific texts and then proceed, somewhat skeptically, to whatever position they suggest—for a given circumscribed period. In particular, it is important to take into account the rhetorical purposes of such passages of "theory." Perhaps the most serious temptation, to which I shall partly yield, is the theory-and-practice approach. For it is essential to remember that in Milton's prose we do not *have* literary theory as such. The most revealing bit of Milton's theory occurs in a passage he himself likens to poetry, one in which he will speak more of himself than decorum allows. Milton's most interesting theory, indeed, occurs in a passage of self-defense, in the context of rhetorical ethos. The theory which emerges revolves around the central fact of Milton's life that he was by vocation, *professionally,* a poet. Whatever difficulties the admission may involve us in methodologically, no candid account of Milton's poetics can escape the likelihood that we are closest to the center of Milton's aesthetic in such "antipoetic" remarks as that the poet "ought himself to be a true poem" (*AP,* Hughes, p. 694A).

What can we make of such remarks? It is undoubtedly true that at some level they can translate to mean something like, "To be a true poet, a man must live the good life" (Samuel, *Plato and Milton,* p. 67). Must we conclude, however, that Milton's theory leaves us this much up in the air? Only, perhaps, if we too narrowly pursue the theory-and-practice approach (that is, read Milton's prose as though it were Wordsworth's *Preface* or the *Biographia Literaria*)—and if we are particularly rigorous about our modern theoretic allegiances. Modern literary criticism, or at least many of the heirs to the New Criticism, seems particularly ill equipped to confront this kind of writing. One solution may be to recognize that such remarks as Milton's patently take us *behind* the literary work—or the work of art in general—into the realm of its "occasions" and, perhaps more threatening, the area of *auctoritas.* The more carefully we look at Milton's prose, I believe, the more difficult biography and biographical criticism become, at least in the modern applied meanings of those words. For what we should recognize is not that we should read *Paradise Lost* as biography but more nearly the opposite: that the person we discover in the so-called autobiographical passages of Milton's prose is a quite fictional creature, with quite extraordinary similarities to the "person" who presents *Paradise Lost.* For whatever reasons, Milton seems to have recognized this dilemma and deliberately built into structures avowedly poetic that same *auctoritas* and those occasions. Far from being a useless Christian humanist fiction, the ideal poet, with all his magical powers, reappears in the figure of the poet within *Paradise Lost,* equipped with a virtually magical control at times over the poem's "events." So, for that matter, does the uncouth swain, whose ironic fallibility introduces the "prospect high" of book III. What we need in reading Milton's oeuvre is a critical vocabulary which is flexible enough to allow us to see poetry and prose alike, not as occasions more or less confessional but as "scenes" which involve a largely fictional character we can call the poet—a fictional character more familiar to us perhaps in more recent literature and related in ways probably unknowable to the *real* John Milton.

But, because of Milton's view of poetry, *poet* is an ambiguous term. The point becomes clear if we reconsider our discussion of satire. What we call satire is something Milton describes, as he generally describes true poetry, in oratorical terms. Though it is a proper part of poetry, he describes it as *speaking* vehemently. It is in fact part of that "true eloquence" which Milton opposed to mere poetry—which in its secular aspect he discussed in visual terms, as though it were an icon or "corporeal resemblance." Indeed, Milton speaks of language itself as somehow corporeal, a function of body. If poetry is visual in the form of its appeal it is also a corporeal form of discourse, conversant (like any polity) "about the visible and external part of man." Poetry is especially dangerous because the visible and external man are one; man "in this body" is all skin, so to speak.

But although Milton's true poetry is conceived oratorically, this does not deny the recognition that poetry itself is "natural"; on the contrary, as even the criteria of "simple, sensuous, and passionate" suggest, it is only that the nature is seen as a lapsed nature. Poetry is natural in the sense that man's images, properly viewed, cannot be separated from his self; it is with real awe and alarm that Milton speaks of the "lavishness" with which the inward acts of worship "run out to the upper skin." What often appears to be a doctrinaire praise of poetry is actually grounded in a lifelong view, at bottom ambiguous, that poetry is elementally human. The gift of language, since the Fall (and especially with the advent of science), has become the reality which Bacon called "circuit of speech." But if the mind or fancy was apt to rove, as it was even before the Fall, it was also prone to fix its gaze on the verbal level, that sensuous rind of discourse with which Milton consistently accused his enemies of being obsessed. This basic and ambiguous view underlies both the celebration of poetry in *Of Education* and Milton's latest refusal in *Of True Religion* to tolerate Catholicism ("the common enemy") on the grounds of the people's natural proneness to idolatry. It seems also to inform Milton's suggestion to institute what may be public readings of true poetry in the ideal commonwealth mentioned in *The Reason of Church Government*.

Milton's root perception in this matter is psychological and perhaps fundamental to Protestantism, although his metaphors are predominantly social, political, and commercial. The formulation in *Of Education* is not very helpful in this context, although it is interesting that Milton relocates poetry on those grounds into a position "precedent" to logic—he seems to speak of its pedagogical utility. Similarly, it does not help us much to read again and again that poetry is a form of error unless we recover that primal meaning of the word as imaged in the morally neutral wandering enjoyed by Adam and Eve before the fall.[31] Poetry then can become an imaginative tool which—in a limited fashion—can make the best of our "crookedness." One early passage is helpful in balancing the absolute claims of

31. See, for example, the usage in Chapman's translation of the *Odyssey* (*Chapman's Homer,* ed. Allardyce Nicoll [New York: Pantheon, 1956], 2 : 14 n.).

Truth and the "veneration due to Truth alone" against the powers of artifice to deceive the wariest of men:

> [Error] indeed is so potent or poisonous that it can either substitute its own image for snow-white Truth, or it can join to itself by some unknown artifice a brilliant appearance of Truth; by which art, as it seems, it frequently deceives even great philosophers and claims for itself honors and veneration due to Truth alone. [Prol v, Hughes, p. 611A; CE 12 : 195]

This is abstract, to be sure, though its balance anticipates Milton's mature poetic. Granted that poetry is the projection of a superstitious man, an immediate representation of his carnal vision and at the same time the object of that vision; and granted that an "unknown artifice" can deceive even great philosophers, what difference can this possibly make in reading Milton's poetry? From such passages as this we can only guess that making an artifice known might be one way to make a poem true and distinguish that kind of artifice from Truth herself. Fortunately, we can be more specific both about connections between Milton's early poetry and prose and even about Milton's ultimate strategies for confronting this dilemma.

The Prolusions may strike us as being intolerably self-conscious, even jejune, about the distinctions we have discussed in this chapter, so much so that a connection between the Prolusions and Milton's early poetry is inconceivable. Looking at Milton's work as an oeuvre, however, we can surely agree that if Eliot was describing anything in calling Milton's verse "dissociated" it was just this apparent self-consciousness. One of the Prolusions, in theme, imagery, and tactics, has much in common with Milton's first religious poem in English; and the ode *On the Morning of Christ's Nativity* has the curious feature that it is a "staged" as well as an aesthetic success. Milton's fun in the second Prolusion (*De Sphaerarum Concentu*) is quite similarly concerned with the paradoxical association of inexpressible subject and discursive occasion.

> A few words . . . suggest themselves to be pronounced, as they say with open hand and with rhetorical embellishment, about

> that famous heavenly harmony concerning which very shortly there is to be a disputation with the closed fist: consideration of the time being observed which now presses me on and restrains me, I would prefer, however, that you, my hearers, should regard these things as said in jest. [Prol II, Hughes, pp. 602B–3A; CE 12 : 149–51]

Like the *Nativity*—in both the "humble ode" and the insistently "occasional" proem—the second Prolusion is full of rhetorical hesitation and self-depreciation: the refusal to allow a formulation avowedly poetic to go unqualified. The speaker, appropriately enough, presents himself as "one somewhat sluggish and for the most part possessed of a dull wit"—not unlike the author of the humble ode itself or the uncouth swain of *Lycidas*.[32] The conclusion in particular is close to the strategies of the *Nativity*. In both works, the self-consciousness has the effect of dramatizing (as well as protecting) the poet. It keeps him from having to *enact* the music of the spheres. In both instances, however, the "poet" nearly—and I think recognizably—does so anyway, in the Prolusion following a flight exactly analogous to stanzas XII–XV of the hymn. Appropriately again, the lame conclusion is forced upon the orator by Time.

In considering such details, we dare not insist that this rhetorical hesitancy was a personal or psychic function for Milton—though what we do know of his personality, his training, and especially his all-encompassing concept of vocation may suggest the special attraction such devices held for the young poet. Rather, what I am getting at here is an early concern with a poem's "situation" and particularly the way in which, even in his earliest serious English verse, Milton mingles what we may tentatively call poetic and rhetorical devices within poems, even to the point of framing "poetic" passages. Such relatively *separable* passages, early and late in Milton's work, imply the presence of the poet, and more specifically that fictional poet described in the Prolusions. The pretense of artlessness in Milton's early work may in fact be no pretense; but later it is frequently associated with the presentation of *contemplatio sine arte* and ought to be viewed as

32. In *Lycidas,* however, it is "our thought" that is "frail."

a strategy in *Paradise Lost,* if not earlier. In a passage which is often read biographically, the poet cites the paradox that his apparent blindness is precisely what qualifies him for claiming to possess a true poetry—though it exposes him likewise to particular dangers:

> from the cheerful ways of men
> Cut off, and for the Book of knowledge fair
> Presented with an Universal blanc
> Of Nature's works to me expung'd and ras'd,
> And wisdom at one entrance quite shut out.
> [*PL* III. 46–50]

When the poet descends later in *Paradise Lost,* to sing "more safe," his remark about wandering mad "on th'*Aleian* field" makes explicit a danger of book III's subject and location which the Milton of the seventh Prolusion, at least, would immediately have recognized and associated with the seduction of contemplation and poetry themselves:

> I acknowledge indeed that one who is commonly reclusive and withdrawn in studies is much more ready to address the gods than men; either because he is almost uninterruptedly at home among the higher powers, with little knowledge of, and quite inexperienced in, human affairs; or because, by the continuous contemplation of divine things, the mind, made as it were larger, tossing itself about with difficulty within the narrow confines of the body, becomes less adapted to the more exquisite gesticulations of greetings. [Prol VII, Hughes, pp. 624B–25A; CE 12 : 263]

To a great extent, then, the narrator's action in *Paradise Lost* realizes (however "imaginatively") the potential of someone who has completed the cycle of learning, a kind of priest and prophet whose art has the power—and the fragility—of Prospero's. In Milton's words, he is—or "will seem to be"—an Orphean figure, "whose power and authority the stars will obey, the land and the sea will follow implicitly." He will experience "a certain divine extension of magnitude," Milton wrote in that speech of the 1620s, and will "wrest away from fate a certain preliminary immortality." One aspect of this knowledge will be virtually prophetic and sounds strikingly like the education of Adam later dramatized in books XI and XII of *Paradise Lost:* "At length many accidents and consequences of things will become clear so suddenly that nothing in life can happen quite unexpectedly, nothing by chance to one who has gained possession of this stronghold of wisdom" (Prol VII, Hughes, p. 625B; CE 12 : 267).

It is not far from such a position to the vatic theory written two centuries later by Percy Shelley. And partial though it has been, our survey illustrates the limitations of viewing Milton as a "classic" (or for that matter as a Puritan) and no romantic. As the most helpful of Milton's theoretic expositors has observed, such antitheses are particularly misleading in the area of Milton's poetics. Whatever the discontinuities between romantic and modern poetics, Coleridge retrieved Milton's word "sensuous" for Eliot and others, accepted as adequate his definition of poetry, and decided to illuminate chapter 13 of the *Biographia Literaria* with Raphael's fascinating lecture on the Oneness of the Almighty. Furthermore, we may recall Coleridge's claim, however disputed now, to have gained the essentials of his idealism *prior* to reading the German philosophers, in the writings of the English Platonists.[33]

The epigraph to chapter 13 is of particular interest to us because, however misunderstood, it seems to have become a touchstone for the early nineteenth century's habit of defining poetry organically (*PL* v. 469–88). Milton's image epitomizes the Oneness of the Almighty. Beginning as a logical analogy, it evolves into a microcosm of the *scala naturae,* which is shown literally to include human psychology as part of the divine continuum—"if not depraved from good." Unlike Coleridge, however, Milton went on in the passage to suggest a slight difference between the "several spheres" of angel and unfallen man. Perception differs in degree, "of kind the same." But "discourse / Is oftest yours, the latter [intuitive reason] most is ours" (v. 488–90). By ending the passage where he did, and by retaining only the innocuous "if not

33. For my discussion of romanticism I am much indebted to M. H. Abrams, *The Mirror and the Lamp: Romantic Theory and the Critical Tradition* (1953; rpt. New York: Norton, 1958), hereafter cited as Abrams.

depraved from good," Coleridge in effect identified the vision of Milton's unfallen archetypal Man—or rather of the angels—with that of the true poet.

There is a passage in Shelley's *Defence of Poetry* which may also be based on Milton's organic symbol. Its thought is clearly not Milton's. But it adds a consideration distinctly Miltonic in the submerged complaint about the poet's condition. "Poetry," Shelley wrote in 1821,

> is at once the center and circumference of knowledge; it is that which comprehends all science, and that to which all science must be referred. It is at the same time the root and blossom of all other systems of thought; it is that from which all spring, and that which adorns all; and that which, if blighted, denies the fruit and the seed, and withholds from the barren world the nourishment and the succession of the scions of the tree of life. It is the perfect and consummate surface and bloom of all things.[34]

In speaking of poetry as a form of knowledge, Shelley identifies the products with the processes of imagination and even with the poet's materials. It is decidedly not his most felicitous theoretic writing, to be sure; the imagery is rather unusually abstract and even allegorically appliquéd. Poetry here becomes a kind of internal correlative to his own *Mont Blanc*. By implication the poet is given even more than Adam or the angels: the insight—though by no means the power—of Milton's Almighty himself.

The great difference between Shelley and Coleridge here, of course, is Shelley's interest in the *conditions* for poetry's development, the removal of the blight—leaving aside the question of what exactly *constitutes* poetry for Shelley. In its most fully articulate form, as Raymond Williams has shown, the social and political failure to acknowledge the true legislators of mankind is not so much a fact as a complaint carrying with it "the felt helplessness of a generation." [35] And the difference in emphasis

34. *Shelley's Critical Prose,* ed. Bruce R. McElderry (Lincoln: University of Nebraska Press, 1967), p. 30.

35. Raymond Williams, *Culture and Society* (1959; rpt. Garden City: Doubleday, 1960), p. 52.

from Coleridge brings Shelley closer to the center of Milton's later theory, when the figure of the prophet began to overshadow that of the poetic priest.

What distinguishes Milton from the romantics who made such complaints, I believe, is not a nineteenth-century monopoly on the isolation of the artist but Milton's original decision to exploit available traditions and techniques—we shall single out the conventional devices of epic—so as to embody the perception within the strategies and the structural economy of actual poems. By this I mean the mediating presence—*spectacle* might be a better word for it—of the poet within a given poem: the dramatized mental action, at times expressing our collective dissociation, often officiously corrective, sometimes even apparently absent *as mind* from an act of pure and collective contemplation. For all the recent discussions of the poem's rhetoric and its presumed affects or targets, surely one primary experience in reading *Paradise Lost* is the action of the poet's mind. We shall see that there are also moments of what would appear objective rendering in which the world of the poem's narrative (we are often reminded of its imaginary status) in some wondrous way answers to the voice of that poet.

Thus, as we have seen, even Milton's most explicit poetic theory is readily assimilable. And at times it seems more attuned to other ages than his own. Dennis seems to have known the formula now considered central in Milton's theory; and like the romantic critics who followed him, he applied the formula to distinguish poetry from prose. Whereas Milton focused at least partly upon the relative utility of poetry in a school curriculum with particular if ideal aims, Dennis went on to attribute the poem's "passion" to the artist's involvement with his poem, a relation in the nineteenth century variously called interested, subjective, or personal (see Abrams, chap. 9). Apart from the fact that we *have* Milton's poetry, what makes such appropriation legitimate—romantic or otherwise—is in part Milton's phrasing in this as in other passages of his theoretic prose. More than once when he discusses poetry, there is at least the pretense of uncertainty or revision; poetry should be subsequent "or indeed rather precedent" to logic and rhetoric. From his wording, indeed, it is not entirely clear whether his theoretic focus is on the art, the artist, or the audience; so pervasive is the organizing analogy between curriculum and psychology in his letter that he seems to be well on his way to the mature statement—somewhat clearer and less *generic*, perhaps, in singling out the recipients of poetry's benefit—that the poet engenders delight "to those, especially, of soft and delicious temper," those (presumably) who retain a youthful sensibility upon which poetry can work. The ultimate emphasis in Milton's letter to Hartlib, then, would appear to be "affective" and in keeping with Renaissance versions of Horace. Postromantic readers may not altogether approve; and we should be wary of attempts to put Milton in the vanguard of the latest New Poetry. But if Milton never entirely escaped the pragmatist's approach to poetry as a kind of technology, at least he retained the correlative view that, as an art, poetry can best exploit the vestigial sympathy between the souls of poet and audience.

But Milton's conception of "affect" needs further explanation; for it is primarily with the *truth* of poetry that Milton's theory, like much modern theory, is concerned. Coming to the poem from a reading of Milton's explicit and incidental remarks about poetry, we would not wish to locate the truth of *Paradise Lost* in the poem's "referential value" since, as Isabel MacCaffrey has observed, the poem presents itself to some extent as the ground of all reference.[36] It presents, among other things, "Hesperian Fables true, / If true, here only" (IV, 250–51). Nor is the truth of *Paradise Lost* a "formal" or primarily aesthetic truth; though again, Milton clearly thought extensively about aesthetic experience and deliberately presents "images" in *Paradise Lost*. In his epic and elsewhere, Milton exploits a discourse which virtually transcends the realm of poetry and aesthetics, at least in passages where it succeeds in its intended flights. Such successes are at times actually staged. But the *affect* of such discourse, we might say, is "sincere action"—if by this we mean a psychic and moral gesture which is unpremeditated and, as it were *un*staged, a virtual copy of unfallen action in the Garden. The term *affect*

36. Isabel MacCaffrey, *"Paradise Lost" as "Myth"* (Cambridge: Harvard University Press, 1959) chap. 1.

in modern critical usage normally applies to something subsequent to the action of a poem. And for this reason it may be helpful to recall the passage with which this chapter began, in which Milton clarifies the distinctions—a carefully worded defense of extemporaneous prayer: "The worship of God singly in it selfe, the very act of prayer and thanksgiving with those free and unimpos'd expressions which from a sincere heart unbidden come into the outward gesture, is the greatest decency that can be imagin'd" (*AP, CPW,* 1 : 941–42). The passage comes from the *Apology* of 1642, when Milton's aesthetic—his antipoetics, modern critics would call it—seems relatively mature and consistent. Characteristically, Milton defends just those qualities of extemporaneous prayer which are under attack by his adversaries in the pamphlet controversy, the "very act" of prayer which informs the unpremeditated "outward gesture." With a fine irony he identifies this act (not its verbal aspects, we should notice, but the *inward* gesture "singly in it selfe") with a commonplace aesthetic ideal of the seventeenth century, an ideal (he may be suggesting) which is also indefinable: "the greatest decency that can be imagin'd."

In urging that the very act of prayer is more decent than a formally perfect "ordinance of man," Milton was generating an aesthetic, partly private, which in its implications is at once fundamentally Protestant and potentially secular. Milton habitually thought of poetry in relation to Truth herself. And characteristically he conceived of it as being, like ritual, potentially "formalist." As such, poetry is always an "ordinance of man." A major impulse in Milton's English verse, from *Lycidas* and even the *Nativity* onward, is consequently to transcend mere poetry, to use it as the more or less self-proclaimed vehicle to an archetypal Truth. To the extent that *Paradise Lost* represents the meandering discourse of its author and even its own making, we might say that even Milton's first epic, for all its maintenance of decorum, is an "indecent" and ipso facto a true poem—at least if its language involves the reader in the act of prayer by internalizing and reforming liturgy. Ever mindful of poetry's dangers, especially the potential opacity of fallen language for either poet or audience, Milton cannot be said to have forgotten one early literary aim, couched in what was for him, even in 1642, something like a paradox: to write a public poem, "doctrinal and exemplary to a nation" (*RCG,* Hughes, p. 669A).

Milton's high-sounding remarks about the poet, then, can be taken as having some implications for the strategies of poems; specifically, I believe, they account for what we might call the sense of poetic process within Milton's English verse—for what in *Lycidas* may be called the context of the oat's "procedure." [37] It appears that the origins of a poem themselves become part of a poem's "world." In the English verse from the *Nativity* on, at any rate, there is little of what we might call pure poetry displayed without a context, more or less immediate, that does not appear to qualify or "originate" it in some way, even to the point of "denying" it. Exactly in what way poetry is qualified or situated we need not pause to examine here. Stanley Fish argues persuasively that Milton locates the action of *Paradise Lost* within the mind of its reader (see above, p. 6). I shall focus on its double origins in the darkness of the poet's mind, itself in effect represented, and in the Holy Light, of which the poem in part claims to be an expression.

In this chapter, however, we have examined some aspects of Milton's theoretic concerns and even speculated on the biography which underlies *The Reason of Church Government* and Milton's initial appearances as a pamphleteer. Hence we may turn at this point to a more detailed consideration of two of Milton's earlier literary texts. In both *A Mask Presented at Ludlow Castle* (1634) and *Lycidas* (1637), I believe, we find that the theoretic suspicions which pervade Milton's entire prose career could also figure as significant parts of masque and poem. In *A Mask,* Comus is associated with what the Lady calls "dear Wit and gay Rhetoric," while rhetoric itself is metaphorically linked with the staging of the masque's realm of "visible forms." It is in Milton's "nearly anonymous" appearance as a poet in *Lycidas* that narrative and drama diverge in a manner unmistakably strategic. The poet in the elegy is projected as a character somewhat like the contemplative man of the Prolusion—but at the same time like

37. In recent years, "process" has been taken to refer primarily to composition; see above, chap. 1, n. 11.

the hard-pressed *litterateur* of *The Reason of Church Government.* Readers have long recognized that *Lycidas* centers to a great extent on the fate of poetry (and pastor-alism), once its archetypal Orpheus dies. The irony of particular interest to us—this time on the level of what Milton called "the critical art of composition"—is created by an objective portrayal of the penetration achieved by the uncouth swain's wisdom—all this precisely as we gain ironic distance on the poet himself in the narrated *ottava rima* conclusion.

PART TWO

3

Vehemence and Rhetoric in *A Mask*

A Mask Presented at Ludlow Castle (1634) may serve to illustrate one way in which Milton's early views on discourse actually inform the details of a highly wrought literary and social occasion. All the patterns in the poem are in some way antithetic; for our purposes, a certain kind of utterance emerges in opposition to a rhetoric which actually includes the masque's visual scene, the sensible extension, in Rosemond Tuve's phrase, of "images verbally commenced."

What the common (and sometimes vague) complaints about the "rhetorical texture" of *A Mask* often fail to reveal is that there are several styles in the masque (we must of course include its music and its staging) [1] and that its modes of discourse call attention to themselves as separate elements in the thematic and metaphoric design. To focus only on the verbal ones: Comus vows to exploit "well-plac't words of glozing courtesy," and the Elder Brother refers to an extravagant claim early in the poem as a piece of rhetoric: "Keep it still, / . . . not a period / Shall be unsaid for me" (584–86). Comus himself sets off his festival against "Puritan" attitudes partly on stylistic grounds: "Strict Age and Sour Severity / With their grave Saws in slumber lie" (109–10). So distinct is this consciousness of what Milton would have called formalistic rhetoric in the poem that it verges on self-parody.

It is the Lady's response to Comus's climactic temptation which most clearly reveals the radical continuity between verbal and visual rhetoric as well as the distinctions Milton encourages among

1. On the poem's staging, as distinct from its "scene," see John G. Demaray, *Milton and the Masque Tradition* (Cambridge: Harvard University Press, 1968).

the masque's various types of discourse. Speaking more for herself (or to the familiar audience) than in response to Comus, she begins thus:

> I had not thought to have unlockt my lips
> In this unhallow'd air, but that this Juggler
> Would think to charm my judgment as mine eyes,
> Obtruding false rules prankt in reasons garb.
>
> [756–59]

The Lady may not be gracious, at least in any trivial sense, but she is *right* on almost every count here. In the context of courtly ceremony—that is, viewed as part of the Lord President's retinue—Comus *is* a courtly entertainer of sorts, and what he offers, however gorgeous, is the heavily institutional wisdom of "false rules." At one point, anticipating Satan's similarly facile association of food and wisdom in *Paradise Lost* and *Paradise Regained,* he says, "Be wise, and taste." More important here for our purposes, however, is the juxtaposition involved in the phrases, "my judgment as mine eyes" and "false rules prankt in reasons garb." [2] The connection would appear to suggest a distinction between clothes and reason, between eyes and judgment. And it may suggest that rhetoric itself, in our general sense, is manipulated almost materially in the piece, much like the masque's lighting, staging, and costume. To put it another way, the physical scene of the masque is an extension of rhetoric into precisely that area of appeal which Milton later appropriated "theoretically" for poetry itself.

The link between rhetoric and concrete setting is more explicit in the published version than in the manuscripts. Continuing the speech quoted above, for instance, Milton develops the notion of an alternative style to Comus's "profane tongue":

> To him that dares
> Arm his profane tongue with contemptuous words
> Against the Sun-clad power of Chastity
> Fain would I something say, yet to what end?
> Thou hast nor Ear nor Soul to apprehend

2. In *PL,* Belial's ignoble stoicism is expressed with "words cloth'd in reason's garb" (II. 226).

> The sublime notion and high mystery
> That must be utter'd to unfold the sage
> And serious doctrine of Virginity,
> And thou art worthy that thou should'st not know
> More happiness than this thy present lot.
> Enjoy your dear Wit and gay Rhetoric
> That hath so well been taught her dazzling fence,
> Thou art not fit to hear thyself convinc't;
> Yet should I try, the uncontrolled worth
> Of this pure cause would kindle my rapt spirits
> To such a flame of sacred vehemence
> That dumb things would be mov'd to sympathize,
> And the brute Earth would lend her nerves, and shake
> Till all thy magic structures rear'd so high
> Were shatter'd into heaps o'er thy false head.
>
> [780–99]

Parts of this passage are sometimes quoted to establish succinctly what the poem as a whole is about, even by readers who go on to join Comus in rejecting rhetoric. Read carefully, however, these lines establish a rationale for the entire balanced structure of Milton's masque. In explaining why the Lady will *not* indulge in "sacred vehemence" (and dwelling instead upon what would follow if she did), Milton's lines reveal a focal concern with "apprehending" and its relation to language. The lady insists (as we can imagine the young Milton insisting) that doctrine is inseparable from sublime notions and high mysteries and that (for most of us) it must be quite literally involved in utterance of some kind.[3] And she does so in language which describes the threatened "sacred vehemence" as a combination of Orphean harmony and the apocalyptic voice of the judging Redeemer. It is precisely true that Comus and his magic structures outglitter the Lady's speech; indeed the splendor of the facade, part of which *is* his language, is essential. But his language must be *patently* a structure, and both the Lady and the audience have the pleasure of knowing him for what (or who) he is. The Lady implies that

3. All of this is close to what both Raphael and Milton say about "likening" and about epic poetry, respectively, in the invocations and especially in book v. See below, chap. 8.

what Comus has done with rhetoric is analogically like what he has done with his art in general, and hence with the whole creation. In another significant zeugma, she observes that Comus has neither "Ear nor Soul" to apprehend sublime notions and mysteries. Without an ear for the supremely musical (and wondrously destructive!) "sacred vehemence," Comus is left only with "dear Wit and gay Rhetoric"—a taught discourse in which rules precede spirit. Here, such discourse is deliberately coupled with epithets referring to setting—its costliness, its visual affects. Seen from this point of view, Comus's palace bears a resemblance to Babel that is more than coincidental, as the sense and sounds of his next speech emphasize. "She fables not," he admits, and invites her company in his rejection of "moral babble." [4]

Comus's appeal is of course philosophically "libertine." We distort its implications, however, if we read into its arguments the social implications of nineteenth- or twentieth-century radicalism. For it is clear throughout that the arguments add up to an invitation to fall in harmoniously with the "canon laws of our foundation." So consistently does Milton's language become virtually palpable that such phrases acquire an almost inevitable gestural dimension. They function somewhat like the Elder Brother's remark I have already quoted, a remark which in its entirety reads, "Lean on it safely, not a period / Shall be unsaid for me" (585–86). Though working at different psychological levels, Milton hints, staging and gesture are linked in the masque's grandest design with the poetry's *musical* utterance and hence with the mysteries and forms to which all discourse ultimately refers. If Comus himself is more the officious stage manager than the more powerful Attendant Spirit (played by the Egertons' musical tutor Henry Lawes), it is because, as Milton would later complain about most poets, his use of language throughout is "artificial." He is portrayed as a kind of rhetorical technician.[5]

It can be argued that, while the extent of "struggle" in *A Mask* is largely intellectual in its definition, it is best indicated in the

4. On Milton's grounds for reforming priestly education, including the specific objections to "ragged notions and babblements" (Hughes, p. 632A), see the second section of chapter 2, above.

5. See Willa M. Evans, *Henry Lawes, Musician and Friend of Poets* (New York: MLA, 1941).

fable by noticing the degree to which Comus can cause confusion in the Lady's mind between two distinct species of rural inhabitants—swains (the "sheep" of this earthly "pinfold") and the transformed monsters that make up Comus's own train. The chief means to this end is Comus's and the masque's attempt to cause confusion in what it really is that *we* see—to pretend, in other words, that the entire scene before us, so to speak, is a "faery vision." Milton's delicacy in complimenting the Egertons is exquisite. By making the environs of Ludlow into a pastoral landscape, Milton actually heightens the sense in which that world is shimmeringly close to both Heaven and Hell. Thus, when Comus, hoping to gain a "queen," tells the Lady that he took her brothers for "a faery vision," it is important to remember the ceremonial occasion from which the fable never really parts. But the remark is also part of Comus's strategem and indicates his taste in visions. Similarly with the claim that the progress of the masque is a journey "like the path to Heaven"; the ceremonial compliment is obvious, but the likeness is also part of Comus's corrupted doctrine of imitation: "We that are of purer fire / Imitate the starry Choir" (111–12).

The fact that the form of the masque calls attention to itself as metaphor suggests that one of Milton's primary distinctions in the entertainment is between forms of "workmanship" or, if we like, between art and life. Comus's confusions would make human beings into parts of masques, into costumes, artifacts. He would have us mistake the vermeil tincture for the lip. More particularly, he would eliminate the masque's "crucial" distinctions, between swains and fairies, between day and night vision, the "sober certainty of waking bliss" he himself acknowledges to be expressed in the Lady's song, on the one hand, and those "wise" effects of his own potion, namely, the "delight beyond the bliss of dreams" (813). Psychologically, what Comus wishes to institute in Milton's masque is the "clear illusion" of Fancy, whose "wild work" is in this case precisely the herd of "ugly-headed monsters" now surrounding the son of Circe.[6] It is not so much grave saws which lie in slumber for the duration of the masque

6. See *PL* v. 95 ff., and *Anatomy*, pp. 139–40.

as Reason herself, retired "Into her private Cell when Nature rests" (*PL* v. 109).

Again, likeable or not, the Lady is our best guide to the kinds of perception involved. The brothers pray that the stars and moon will "unmuffle" (331); and of course, after she hears Comus's speech, the Lady refers to the "Sun-clad power of Chastity" (782). But when Comus throws his magic dust, there is a crisis of sorts, rendered in the published version as follows:

> A thousand fantasies
> Begin to throng into my memory,
> Of calling shapes and beckoning shadows dire,
> And airy tongues that syllable men's names
> On Sands and Shores and desert Wildernesses.
>
> [205–9]

The masque as a whole insists on the relationships between shapes, shadows, and tongues—and the landscape in which they appear. Like the faery vision of the "belated peasant" at the end of book I in *Paradise Lost,* the uncreated forms in this passage (the "fantasies" which throng into the Lady's memory) are related to the imperfectly created shapes that traditionally peopled the antimasques and, more immediately, to Comus's crew of ugly-headed monsters.[7] Clearly they stand at the opposite pole in vision from the visible form of Chastity, or "Reason's mintage moulded in the face."

That visible form of Chastity, seen and apprehended by the audience as well as by Alice,[8] reminds us that vision is not to be rejected in the masque but merely "placed." Lady Alice herself tells us that her ear is "my best guide now" (171). She correctly hears the monstrous imitation of the starry choir as "noise" but supposes it (temporarily) to be

> The sound
> Of Riot and ill-manged Merriment,
> Such as the jocund Flute or gamesome Pipe

7. See Enid Welsford, *The Court Masque* (Cambridge: Cambridge University Press, 1927), chap. 7.

8. Rosemond Tuve, *Images and Themes in Five Poems by Milton* (Cambridge: Harvard University Press, 1957), p. 148.

> Stirs up among the loose unletter'd Hinds,
> When for their teeming flocks and granges full
> In wanton dance they praise the bounteous Pan,
> And thank the gods amiss.
>
> [171–77]

What the Lady has mistaken the noise to be, it seems, is a pastoral festival of gratitude (for natural abundance)—a "natural" version of that presumably more doctrinal dance and song toward which the whole of Milton's entertainment moves.

We need not dwell on the function of music in the masque. Rosemond Tuve has ably demonstrated its importance in her attempt to provide a more balanced response to Milton's art (*Images and Themes,* pp. 113–15). I would only add the further observation that the function of song is defined at several points in the masque as being opposed to that of rhetoric. We can summarize by saying that, if rhetoric in the poem serves as analogy to the staging of masques, then song is analogically the true art which correctly expresses gratitude for the creation. The Lady requests Echo not to "imitate the starry Choir" but rather to "give resounding grace to all Heav'n's Harmonies" (243). At points like this Milton seems close to Herbert, part of whose purpose in *The Temple* was to answer God's love in music; for both poets, it is music that "shall finde thee" (Hutchinson, p. 36). We should perhaps add the qualification, however, that although the Lady Alice does sing the marvelous song, "Sweet Echo," her most important dramatic act is to *threaten* Comus with what she calls sacred vehemence, an Orphean music which is both primitive and apocalyptic. It is the Spirit, played by Lawes, who does most of the singing in the performance.[9] It is even possible, in fact, that the epilogue, which Lawes seems to have sung, is in effect the sacred vehemence which the Lady had threatened, stripped (but for a few lines) of its overtly suasive purpose. The Spirit refers to his accomplishment partly in musi-

9. The Spirit sings to Sabrina and "Back, Shepherds"; most important, however, the stage direction of the Bridgewater MS suggests that in the original performance Lawes may actually have sung the lovely poetry of the epilogue: "The dances ended, the Spirit sings or sayes." There is music extant for the final ten lines.

cal terms; and in a complimentary gesture much like the actual staging of "visible forms," he injects the parenthetical "List mortals if your ears be true" (997). Milton's great poetic flight of the masque seems to be deliberately framed, as the musical focus of both entertainment and art. This much the deletion and relocation of sensuous description from the manuscript version seem to suggest.[10] By taking us to a "true earth" drenched in this description and thence ultimately to the Christian and Neoplatonic realm of the "inexpressive nuptial song," the Spirit's song both defines and embodies the crucial role of song in the masque.

Such distinctions between different modes of discursive appeal are potentially (and even crucially) Miltonic, but they are neither original with Milton nor limited to the arts. Both sight and hearing in Renaissance psychologies are faculties of the sensible soul; the eye "sees the whole body at once," while it is hearing, "by which we learn and get knowledge," to quote from Burton's survey of the commonplaces (*Anatomy,* p. 138). Milton's use of the distinction, in fact, can serve as a useful caveat for those readers who seek biographical controversy in every Jonsonian allusion to the "soul of the masque." The allusion seems more technical in nature, involving references to music and thus to aural dimensions of discourse. Nor does the juxtaposition of "Ear" and "Soul" necessarily deny the pleasures of the eye or detract from the elaborate stagings traditional in the Jonsonian masque. Indeed, visual appeals were traditionally associated with the province of poetry, as the etymology of fiction (*fingere,* to mould, shape) suggests. The combined appeals of the masque itself made it an ideal form to project the workings of the imagination, whose social agents (Burton found, in a passage Milton undoubtedly read) were poets and painters; in them "imagination forcibly works, as appears by their several fictions, anticks, images. . . . In men," Burton went on, "it is subject and governed by *reason,* or at least should be; but in brutes it hath no superior, and is the reason of brutes, all the reason they have (*Anatomy,* p. 140). The point which needs stress here is the explicitness with

10. See Harris Fletcher, *John Milton's Complete Poetical Works, Reproduced in Photographic Facsimile* (Urbana: University of Illinois Press, 1943), 1 : 298, 303–4, 339, 398–99; hereafter cited as Fletcher.

which Milton *places* those appeals in *A Mask,* working the responses (much as he works the very staging) into the substance of his poetry. It is almost as if the complete apparatus for perception (of the masque itself, as for all workmanship, human and divine) were provided with the entertainment, like special glasses.

4

Lucky Words: Process of Speech in *Lycidas*

> He spake: and to confirm his words, out-flew
> Millions of flaming swords, drawn from the thighs
> Of mighty Cherubim; the sudden blaze
> Far round illumin'd Hell
>
> *Paradise Lost* 1. 663–66

Some of the significant information about *Lycidas* is so obvious (in the Miltonic sense, "in our way") that we may easily miss it. The pastoral elegy is the first poem Milton agreed to have published; [1] with the "nearly anonymous" initials "J. M.," it is unobtrusively but finely located at the end of a memorial volume of elegies entitled *Justa Edovardo King* . . . For the historian, it is thus Milton's first poetic gesture, indeed the first semipublic presentation of himself *as a poet,* regardless of when the private recognition confronted him. The mere *fact* of its publication (in however modest a volume) is one measure of the poem's completeness, of its autonomy; it argues on Milton's part a willingness to submit a piece of English verse to public scrutiny and to call it, as he would in fact subtitle both his epics, a poem; it was somewhat later, in a volume designed to display the maturing genius of "Mr. John Milton," that he would designate it, more particularly, a monody.[2]

1. "Shakespeare," which appeared in the second folio (1632), was anonymous; the only other English publication prior to *Justa Edovardo King* . . . was *A Mask,* "not openly acknowledged by the Author" but dedicated to Lord Viscount Brackley in 1637 by Henry Lawes. See Parker, 2 : 1205 ff., app. 1.

2. See Louis L. Martz, "The Rising Poet, 1645," in *The Lyric and Dramatic Milton; Selected Papers from the English Institute,* ed. Joseph H. Sum-

All this is the more interesting when we observe that the poem itself, in its untraditional aspects, is articulated in much the same manner as earlier Miltonic performances—performances which were only *in part* poetic; and more than one of these dealt in effect with the "cool element of prose" and the vocational alternatives available to his left hand. To take the clearest example, we are dealing here with a published and partly signed poem which *by itself* fulfills the purpose of both the letter to the unknown friend of 1633 and the "Petrarchian stanza" for which the surrounding prose is an ironic apology. Like Milton's earlier works, of course, *Lycidas* is occasional; in particular it resembles the *Nativity,* whose occasion—Christmas morning, 1629—is by virtue of the framing proem involved with the hymn itself in a partly functional way. But for the reading public, the *Nativity* dates from 1645, not 1629, as we have seen. And it is perhaps necessary to stress that Milton's dates in the 1645 volume are in part apologetic and autobiographical in nature; however ironically intended, they too are meant to be taken as part of the poem's occasions for the reader of 1645.

What matters here for our purposes, then, is that *Lycidas* is the first "professionally decorous" poem Milton submitted to public scrutiny without "external" apology (except the rubric for the entire volume)—but that *within the poetic structure* (however we describe it) there is a *staged* occasion. The poem is indeed partly about poetry, as Brooks and Hardy have observed; but more immediately it is about its own making. To put it another way, the extrinsic causes of this particular poem—the historical and autobiographical contexts of *poesis*—have been incorporated within the design of the poem. Would it be too much to say that, in the pastoral elegy which may well have sealed the professional commitment of its author, part of the actual poem is the person of its poet? And that by a daring, though not unique, extension of this formal decision the poet becomes virtually identified with the sun or Son, the Word toward which all poetry (if "lucky") tends?

---

mers (New York: Columbia University Press, 1965), pp. 3–33, hereafter cited as *The Lyric and Dramatic Milton.*

Despite the fact that readers of *Lycidas* continue to discuss the poem as though discourse were a central concern, few have been inclined to give full due to its own bivalent manner of presentation—that curious mixture of narrative and drama—as an element actually in the poem's construction. With the exception of a few essays, notably those of Rosemond Tuve and Isabel MacCaffrey, criticism of the poem in this aspect has not much advanced beyond the brilliant (if somewhat uneven) study of John Crowe Ransom, published in 1938.[3] Indeed, the basic question of the poem's mode is still a matter of debate. It is a question bearing on Milton's poetics as well as on the practical matter of reading *Lycidas* and Milton's poetry in general from *A Mask* onward. Quite clearly, to judge from recent studies, the poem itself invites the kind of inquiry which is routine in the reading of most poems; its choreography is so unmediated that William G. Madsen is quite right in asking, for example, "How can the person who plaintively and ineffectually calls on the dolphins suddenly speak with the unambiguous accents of authority?"[4] Though the shift (at line 165) is not unique in the poem, readers have long recognized the passage in question as crucial; for D. C. Allen it comes at the point "where philosophy bows to theology, where grace takes over from nature, where the lyric peripety occurs."[5] What happens in the following lines of consolation (165–81) is for M. H. Abrams a new phase in the evolving thought of the uncouth swain; the poem represents the speech

3. Tuve, "Theme, Pattern, and Imagery in *Lycidas*," in *Images and Themes*, pp. 73–111, reprinted in *Milton's "Lycidas": The Tradition and the Poem*, ed. C. A. Patrides (New York: Holt, Rinehart & Winston, 1961), pp. 167–200; Isabel MacCaffrey, *"Lycidas:* The Poet in a Landscape," *The Lyric and Dramatic Milton*, pp. 65–92. Ransom's essay, also reprinted in Patrides's anthology, was first published in *American Review* 1 (1933): 179–203, 444–67, and reprinted in *The World's Body* (New York: Scribner's, 1938), pp. 1–28. For convenience, subsequent references to the criticism, where possible, will be to the collection of Patrides.

4. William G. Madsen, "The Voice of Michael in *Lycidas*," *Studies in English Literature* 3 (1963): 4. The point at which the swain's voice perhaps returns, at "Now Lycidas, the shepherds weep no more" (p. 6), can also be regarded as authoritative, and unnaturally knowing, about what is in effect the poem's internal *audience*.

5. D. C. Allen, *The Harmonious Vision* (Baltimore: Johns Hopkins University Press, 1954), pp. 68–69. See M. H. Abrams's similar point in Patrides, *Milton's "Lycidas,"* p. 229.

and discursive insights of the natural man throughout, with the important exception of the narrative conclusion. For Madsen on the other hand, the lyric peripety occurs "because the angel [Michael] does indeed melt with ruth and reveal to the uncouth swain that there are 'other groves, and other streams' than those of the pastoral tradition." [6]

Given such disparate answers, it is best to look closely at the irreducible circumstances surrounding two of the poem's critical shifts, from the petition to the consolation, and from the "vision" and farewell to the narrative section dismissing the uncouth swain to "fresh woods and pastures new." With these passages as focuses, we may further clarify the matter of the poem's mode and the sense in which we can say that the poem "incorporates its occasion"—and time—as part of a poetic structure. Though grounded in metaphor, *Lycidas* is "figurative *speech,* from beginning to end," as Miss Tuve reminds us. More particularly, I believe that the poem's mere discourse becomes a uniquely Miltonic vehicle in the paradoxical economy of Christian pastoral; more than simply staging the unripe thoughts of the uncouth swain, the poem represents "immediate" acts of God through the time-bound but ultimately lucky medium which Raphael, in book VII of *Paradise Lost,* calls "process of speech."

We are still told that the "Angel" of that famous line is Michael, though the reading ignores both the implications of Milton's punctuation and the suspension of the period leading into the line.[7] The Trinity Manuscript includes *no* punctuation, indicating only, perhaps, that the line is to be read, and run into the next line, without a pause. And the first published version reads

6. Madsen, "The Voice of Michael in *Lycidas,*" p. 5. Aside from relying upon the identity of "Angel" with Michael (see below), Madsen would here ascribe an unmediated speech (i.e., unaccompanied by some such narrative commentary as "Last came and last did go") to a supernatural voice, whereas all other speeches are clearly assigned to the swain. Even "the Pilot of the Galilean Lake" is thus accompanied.

7. Thus Douglas Bush in his excellent *The Complete Poetical Works of John Milton* (Boston: Houghton Mifflin, 1965). Hughes and Patrides place a comma after "now," and (respectively) a comma/colon at the end of the line. John T. Shawcross (*The Complete English Poetry of John Milton* [New York: New York University Press, 1963]) properly omits all punctuation.

> Look homeward Angel now, and melt with ruth,
> And, O ye dolphins, waft the haplesse youth.[8]

The additional commas we usually encounter following "home-ward" and "Angel," with their tacit assumption that the Angel is Michael, seem to have become part of the text of *Lycidas* much later. It was Thomas Warton who claimed to be the first to point the line properly, explaining the emended punctuation as follows:

> The great Vision and the Angel are the same thing; and the verb *look* in both the two last verses has the same reference. Moreover, if in the words *Look homeward, Angel, now,* the address is to Lycidas, a violent, and too sudden, an apostrophe takes place; for in the very next line Lycidas is distantly called the hapless youth.[9]

We may be surprised at Warton for failing to notice that the apostrophe to which he refers actually begins in line 154, and consequently that the weight of the whole sentence, with its impressive balance, suggests the identity of the "thou" with the "Angel now" of line 163. But Warton is surely correct in saying of the line following the crux that Lycidas is there called hapless youth "distantly." One suspects, indeed, that this sound observation is the basis of his pointing and explanation. He has in effect seen the discontinuity in sense with which more than one eighteenth-century reader was uncomfortable.

As the variorum debate took shape, the crux was always defined in quite the same way; either the Angel was Michael, equivalent to the "great Vision," or it was Lycidas himself. Thus, when Robert Thyer, the editor of Butler's *Remains* (1759) and contributor to Newton's variorum edition, proposed an alternative reading to Warton's, he too was met with legitimate objections. For Thyer, "Look homeward Angel now and melt with ruth" was translatable to "You, O Lycidas, now an angel, look down from heaven," and the line then completed sensibly the sentence begun at line 154 (Todd, 6 : 9). But how can looking

8. For both early versions, see Fletcher, 1 : 52–56, 185–89, 346–52, 434–43.

9. Henry J. Todd, *The Poetical Works of John Milton . . .* (London: J. Johnson, 1809), 6 : 9, hereafter cited as Todd.

downward from Heaven be said to be looking *homeward?* and why is the shipwrecked person to melt with ruth? In answer to questions like these, and worried in general about the poem's logical consistency, Warton noted at line 177:

> Even after Lycidas is received into heaven, Milton does not make him an *Angel*. He makes him, indeed, a being of a higher order, the *Genius of the Shore,* as at v. 183. If the poet in finally disclosing this great change of circumstances, and in this prolix and solemn description of his friend's new situation in the realms of bliss after so disastrous a death, had exalted him into an Angel, he would not have forestalled that idea, according to Thyer's interpretation, at v. 163. [Todd, 6 : 51]

We may conclude this survey with Charles Jerram's review of "the contrary interpretation" and the accepted gloss in Scott Elledge's recent anthology:

> It has been objected that if a full stop be placed at "surmise," the present line is required to complete the sentence beginning at "whilst thee, etc.," which would otherwise be unfinished, and of which Lycidas is the subject throughout; and that, even with the semicolon there (l. 152), St. Michael's apparition is merely introduced parenthetically, as part of a local description, and never directly apostrophized. This is perhaps strictly true; but a poet is not always bound by the strict laws of grammatical construction, and the sudden turn of address from Lycidas to the archangel (who is now a prominent figure in the description) strikes powerfully upon the reader's imagination. Another argument (which at first sight appears plausible) is founded upon the coincidence of the present passage and of ll. 183 ff. in structure, language, and sentiment, with certain lines in the First Eclogue of Sannazaro (ca. 1520), in which a drowned man is thus addressed by his mourning friends: "At tu, *sive* altum felix colis aethera, *seu* jam / Elysios inter Manes, etc. . . . / *Aspice nos* mitisque veni, *tu numen aquarum / Semper eris laetum piscantibus omen.*" But even admitting, as we surely may (cf. especially l. 184), that Milton had the above passage generally in view, we need not assume that he copied

> his original with such exactness as to make the subject of his "look homeward" correspond with that of "aspice" in Sannazaro.[10]

The argument appeals to criteria like poetic license and the poem's "striking" effects in dissolving what was problematic in the eighteenth-century readings. The account of poetry as a mode antithetic to the "strict laws of grammatical construction," indeed, anticipates postromantic studies which similarly divorced image (or symbol) from discourse in any form. But Jerram does provide the kind of evidence which is all-important in such matters, a *precedent* for Thyer's reading. Even if Sannazaro becomes in Jerram's account an "original" to be kept "generally in view" by real poets and exactly "copied" only by poetaster-grammarians, the possibility that "Angel" could "be" Lycidas is now considerable on grounds entirely extracritical, thus at least putting the rug back under the critic's feet.

The suggestion is more plausible when we consider two details in the pastoral eclogue composed perhaps in late 1639, mourning the death of Milton's friend Charles Diodati (August 1638). The *Epitaphium Damonis* provides no precedent for any feature of *Lycidas.* But clearly and simply it does employ two devices also at work in *Lycidas,* one of them to my knowledge unrecognized: the overt request to the departed to pity those who remain at home, and (more important) the potentially Christian musing about the name or identity of the departed "now." If Sannazaro provides a precedent for "Look homeward . . . and melt with ruth,"[11] *Epitaphium Damonis* shows us that by 1639 Milton could play with the identity or name of his dead friend and even, perhaps, with the idea that it is involved in multiple apotheoses[12]—"Now, since you have been granted the rights of heaven, stand by my side and gently favor me, by whatever name you are called." The central passage, which I believe helps us to unpack the crux in *Lycidas,* is as follows:

10. Scott Elledge, ed., *Milton's "Lycidas" Edited to Serve as an Introduction to Criticism* (New York: Harper & Row, 1966), pp. 308–9.

11. Sannazzaro's eclogue is reprinted in *The Pastoral Elegy: An Anthology,* ed. T. P. Harrison, Jr. (Austin: University of Texas Press, 1939), and briefly discussed by J. H. Hanford in Patrides, *Milton's "Lycidas,"* pp. 46–47.

12. I am developing a point made by Northrop Frye in his "Literature as Context: Milton's *Lycidas*" (Patrides, *Milton's "Lycidas,"* p. 204).

> Heroumque animas inter, divosque perennes,
> Aethereos haurit latices et gaudia potat
> Ore Sacro. Quin tu, coeli post jura recepta,
> Dexter ades, placidusque fave, quicunque vocaris,
> Seu tu noster eris Damon, sive aequior audis
> Diodotus, quo te divino nomine cuncti
> Coelicolae norint, sylvisque vocabere Damon.
>
> [205–11]

[Among the souls of heroes and the immortal gods, he drains ethereal draughts and drinks joy with holy lips. And now, since you have been granted the rights of heaven, stand by my side and gently favor me, by whatever name you are called. Whether you are to be my Damon, or prefer to be Diodati (by that divine name, "God-given," you will be known to all the heavenly host), in the woods you will still be Damon.] [13]

We need not limit ourselves to insights which these two poems provide in the way of precedent or quasianalogue; *Lycidas* is a far greater poem than both. But with such possibilities for line 163, "Look homeward Angel now and melt with ruth"—possibilities which recall Hamlet's efforts to get the right name for the ghost—let us consider this portion of Milton's English pastoral elegy.

The best case for justifying the Thyer reading (with some modifications) must finally be established from within the poem and its poetry—if we call *Lycidas* as it was finally displayed at the end of *Justa Edouardo King* . . . (1638), where it first appeared, the poem, as distinguished from the poetry—the various fragments of the manuscript version.

This section of the poem, we may recall, evolves from a previous pretense of discursive collapse after the fiction of the floral procession [14]—the passage which explains or justifies that fiction as the kind of false surmise one needs on such occasions and in such a world as this, to "make the going easier" (as Virgil's Lycidas puts it in the tenth eclogue), "to interpose a little

13. The translation used here is that of Douglas Bush (*Complete Poetical Works,* p. 166). Milton is playing obviously on Damon/Daemon.

14. Here and elsewhere I depart from the reading of Rosemond Tuve, whose "Theme, Pattern, and Imagery in *Lycidas*" remains to my mind the best single essay on the poem.

ease." [15] In what follows, the movement is from a passionate address to an all-inclusive "thee" toward finer discrimination between the several elements in the section's addressee; beginning with speculations about the location or name of "Lycid," it ends with a particular assertion of an identity (the ultimate form of location) which subsumes all other identities (previous or subsequent)—such as the "Genius of the shore" which bothered Warton. The idea that the identity or name of the dead somehow includes that of the poet himself is of course perfectly traditional in the pastoral elegy; this is why the poet hopes for lucky words to favor *his* destined urn, and as we shall see the convention may be involved again in the narrative coda to the poem. The point I wish to make here, however, is simply that "Angel" is the final identity or location for Lycidas—the single word which signals the poet's (and poem's) ultimate *apprehension* of Lycidas. "Wherever you are (wherever your body, and, in the context of the poetic procedure, in whatever nominal realm, creatural, mythological, etc.)" [16]—the poem seems to be saying, in effect, distinguishing almost immediately between "thee" and "thy bones"—"Whether your bones are north or south, look homeward as an Angel now, and pity us." The poem's deliberate technique and the temporal dimension of discourse itself obscure two separate points important to a full understanding of this passage. First, the long sentence beginning at line 154 ("Whilst thee the shores and sounding Seas . . . ") is *as a whole* governed by "Whilst," a word which works against the length of the period in its insistence on the simultaneity of the looking homeward and, say, the visit to the "bottom of the monstrous world." [17] Secondly, as I have suggested in my paraphrase, the poem's mode of progression

15. *Quo te, Moeri, pedes?* A convenient text, with translations, is that of E. V. Rieu, *Virgil: The Pastoral Poems* (Baltimore: Penguin, 1954).

16. Distinguished as "levels" in Frye's essay; see Patrides, *Milton's "Lycidas,"* pp. 203–4.

17. In his essay on the "Affective Structure" of *Lycidas,* Wayne Shumaker quotes lines 154–58, for many critics "the most powerful part of the elegy" (Patrides, *Milton's "Lycidas,"* pp. 133–34). Shumaker suggests the affective strength of the whelming water as the source of this power. My point is that while we may want to stop, so to speak (as many readers have thought *Milton* does in the curse on "the fatall bark"), Milton keeps on us the steady pressure of syntax, forgotten by too many critics because considered a radical

keeps this immediate act of God in the background, confronting us instead with the uncouth swain's process of speech. There are thus virtually three separate orders of experience compressed into the "now" of line 163: "now" in the context of the poem's occasion, as Thyer explained—now that you're dead, namely, in 1637; "now" in the perspective of the Taskmaster's eye, *sub specie aeternitatis,* a point of view from which all "nows" are "as ever" and in which all acts are "immediate"—this is the "now" adumbrated in words like "Whilst" (or, in Marvell, "Mean while"); but also "now," at this point (and perhaps subsequently) in the *poem's* argument.

In moving toward this name for Lycid, the poem also generates other movements, similarly anticipated. In a sense, "Ay me" is a most immediate reality in the poem; as I have said, it is the closest thing here, apart from vowels in general (or tears on the manuscript) to the kind of inarticulate grief already controlled when it is called, for instance, a "melodious tear" or "moist vow." All such phrases adumbrate a radical paradox in the poem's strategy, the sublimity of humility, the magic of pastoral uncouthness; and one element in this strategy is the poet's careful control of fiction. Traditionally, as Milton remarks in his own *Logic,* "every likeness hobbles" (CE 11 : 195), and we might say that one way to make poetry "true" is to point frankly to the limp; in this passage, as I have indicated, Milton is careful with the exact meaning of every "thee." At the same time, he begins to use pejorative or qualifying diction—diction indicating make-believe—*together with* the naturalistic view of Lycidas's end. That is, the "Ay me," the most *unmusical* view of ultimate reality, begins to be redefined as fiction. We move in the poem, and not merely from north to south; we move also discovering that we cannot entirely escape the "false surmise" from which this segment was initially supposed to release us. It is as though the speaker recognizes the

---

threat to the truth of "poetry," and here, deliberately, all but drained from the poem—until "Look homeward Angel now." The point, then, is that syntax, the reminder that the poem is indeed a "process of speech," forces the reader beyond this attitudinal stasis, however attractive; and forces, too, the poem's miraculous discovery of Lycidas's ultimate identity, an "Angel now." See Jon S. Lawry, " 'Eager Thought': Dialectic in *Lycidas,*" *PMLA* 77 (1962): 27–32, reprinted in *Modern Essays,* pp. 112–24.

antimony between true and false surmise as itself false, and he begins to freight his naturalistic language with fictive signposts; he patently *imagines* fates worse than death, implying that they have as little to do with the real Lycidas as fables with truth.

> . . . where'er thy bones are hurl'd,
> Whether beyond the stormy *Hebrides,*
> Where thou perhaps under the whelming tide
> Visit'st the bottom of the monstrous world;
> Or whether thou to our moist vows denied,
> Sleep'st by the fable of *Bellerus* old,
> Where the great vision of the guarded Mount
> Looks toward *Namancos* and *Bayona's* hold.
>
> [155–62]

The point of these lines, it turns out, is that it little *matters* where. The geographical realm itself turns out to be a fable in the poem's economy of self-revision, and the poem as a whole (if we may speak of such a processive work thus) rejects all fable. At worst, the poem can amount only to "moist vows"; it rejects all attempts at verbal magic. But there is a disarming quality in its self-consciousness, its awareness of poetry's nature and limits, as of "frail thought" in general.[18] To return to my interpretation of line 163: because we are frequently reminded in this fashion of the poem's *process,* a narrowing circumlocution of the ultimate formula or name for Lycidas; because the syntactic parallel in lines 154–62, the most important "fixed" frame of reference, insists that the addressee of line 163 (as of the entire section) must be at least *somehow* related to the generalized "thee" beginning the passage which will finally locate Lycidas; and finally because the poetic effort to discover Lycidas is a central concern of passage and poem, we may conclude that it is Lycidas who is now (both eternally and from this point in the poem) asked to look homeward and to pity. In view of our analysis thus far, then, we

18. In the MS this originally reads "sad thought"; the revision, which brings into sharp focus the epistemological dimension I am attempting to describe, is the basis of my disagreement with Rosemond Tuve on the reading of "false surmise." See n. 14 above.

may say that the syntax of the two lines we have been examining points to a central impulse in the poem's final movement: the distinction between realms "fabulous" and real, and the continuing coexistence of both orders.

> Look homeward Angel now, and melt with ruth
> And O ye dolphins, waft the hapless youth.

Lycidas *is no more*—not even "distantly"—the hapless youth he was, for example, in line 154, where *all* aspects of his identity, now distinct, were fused in "thee."

In getting at the larger implications of such a reading, it may be helpful to recall John Crowe Ransom's brilliant essay of 1930, and a critical observation which has been insufficiently explored in later criticism (Patrides, *Milton's "Lycidas,"* p. 79). For all its mistakes, "A Poem Nearly Anonymous" points squarely at an irreducible and untraditional "insubordinacy" in Milton's procedure:

> Pastoral elegies are dramatic monologues, giving the words of a single shepherd upon a single occasion; or they are dialogues giving, like so much printed drama, the speeches of several shepherds in a single scene. They may have prologues, perhaps so denominated in the text, and printed in italics, or in a body separate from the elegy proper; and likewise epilogues; the prologues and epilogues being the author's envelope of narrative within which is inserted the elegy. The composition is straightforward and explicitly logical.
>
> Milton's elegy is otherwise. It begins without preamble as a monologue, and continues so through the former and bitterer half of the passage on Fame. . . . At this point comes an incredible interpolation: ". . . But not the praise, / Phoebus repli'd, and touch'd my trembling ears . . ." And Phoebus concludes the stanza; after which the shepherd apologizes to his pastoral Muses for the interruption and proceeds with his monologue. But dramatic monologue has turned for the moment into narrative. The narrative breaks the monologue several times more, presenting action sometimes in the present

> tense, sometimes in the past. And the final stanza gives a pure narrative conclusion in the past, without the typographical separateness of an epilogue; it is the one which contains Milton's apology for the "Dorick" quality of his performance, and promises that the author will yet appear in a serious and mature manner as he has scarcely done on this occasion.

Ransom's essay is admirable partly because for the most part he is willing to read the poem, rather than document Milton's biography. He is in fact concerned with what was for Milton a central matter in poetry and poetics, as well as ethics—the "person" of the *poem,* which Ransom unfortunately confuses at times with the person of the poet. Ransom must conclude that the final *ottava rima* stanza is something distinct from "the poem," because it "contains *Milton's* apology for the 'Dorick' quality of *his* performance" (my italics).[19]

Ransom's conclusion from these untraditional details is that "Milton's bold play with the forms of discourse constitutes simply one more item in his general insubordinacy. He does not propose to be buried beneath his own elegy" (Patrides, *Milton's "Lycidas,"* p. 80). But we might say rather that by including a narrative dimension in his poem—both within and after it, so to speak, in the ottava rima conclusion—Milton both emphasizes his poem's temporalness and perhaps implies a gradually emerging "independent" reality more or less correspondent to the uncouth swain's discursive process. If we look steadily at the poem's uncouthness, I suggest—keeping in mind the conventional burden of Christian pastoralism and the *sermo humilis*—we find that the uncouth swain dallies not only with false surmise but also "by occasion"—precisely by virtue of "lucky words"—with Truth. Although I have shifted contexts for Milton's phrase, the "by occasion" is important here as similar ironic parentheses are in all of Milton's early work. Readers have long felt that a good deal of the occasion of *Lycidas*—the poem's outside, as it were—is built *into* the poem.[20]

19. Patrides, *Milton's "Lycidas,"* p. 79; like Brooks and Hardy (ibid., pp. 151–52), Ransom takes Doric to mean "rough," "homespun"; "It was written smooth, and rewritten rough" (ibid., p. 71).

20. This matter, related to the question of "when the real poem begins/

We can thus no longer ignore, or dismiss as being poetically irrelevant, what Eliot might have called the dissociated texture of Miltonic poetry written even much earlier than *Paradise Lost*. Whether or not Milton is even in *Lycidas* writing English "as though it were a dead language" (Eliot, p. 141), it is clearly necessary to determine the literary function of such formulas as eager thought, lucky words, and the like—phrases we have ignored till now perhaps because they appear to be the furniture of a Baconian (or worse) antipoetics. Such roughnesses, abound in this poem and, like the distancing in the narrative conclusion, enhance the impression of the poet's uncouthness. But as with much earlier products of the Christian *sermo humilis,* they amount to *strategic* apologies and are properly viewed as elements essential to the poem's oddly internal action (Patrides, *Milton's "Lycidas,"* p. 203). What I believe these ironic hesitancies in *Lycidas* sug-

---

ends," is a commonplace in the criticism. For these readers, the poem "begins with a statement of the occasion which prompted it" (David Daiches, in Patrides, *Milton's "Lycidas,"* p. 103), and "the actual elegy" does not begin until the second verse-paragraph; the poem ends before the *ottava rima* stanza (p. 105); the impression is that of Milton "doing his duty." Even Brooks and Hardy must invoke "Milton, the self-conscious young poet": "Evidently this is not the first time he has come forward with an immature performance" (ibid., p. 137). The most elaborate recent statement about the poem's "occasion," that of Isabel MacCaffrey, is particularly helpful: "The opening of Lycidas . . . is brutally direct. Declining to observe the decorum of a public event, the poet in his Argument noncommittally recites the private occasion. His claim to the role of prophet is modestly confined to immediate history; he will foretell 'the ruine of our corrupted Clergy'" (*The Lyric and Dramatic Milton,* p. 66). It seems to me misleading to mistake, as Mrs. MacCaffrey does here, the poem of 1645 for the poem of 1638. As Fixler has implied (*Kingdoms of God,* p. 61), Milton's view of poetry in its relation to prophecy may have changed between 1638 and 1645. Milton in the 1638 *Lycidas*—in the poem—foretells nothing, and one may doubt that a gloating Milton of 1645 would ever seriously have identified the fall of the clergy with the definitive stroke of the two-handed engine. But there is the further point that to some extent one occasion of the poem *is* an intrinsic aspect of Milton's performance, whether in the 1638 or 1645 versions. To some extent this is true of all exhibits of the Christian *sermo humilis* or, for that matter, of Christian pastoral (see Erich Auerbach, *Literary Language and Its Public in Late Latin Antiquity and in the Middle Ages,* trans. Ralph Manheim [New York: Pantheon, 1965], pp. 27–66). Hence it is a mistake to distinguish too severely between the "decorum" of the poem per se and the "brutally direct" recital of "the private occasion" of *Lycidas*. The question here is the extent to which this poem's occasion is *part of* the poem—or, as we now say, the poem itself.

gest is that the poem calls attention to itself as a verbal process, not so much "told as earthly notion can receive" (*PL* VII. 179) as involving its readers in a sequence of fiction, fact, and vision which in part undercuts its own "validity."

The fact that *Lycidas* is so familiar as to have become an incantation obscures its deliberate attempt to escape that status and the kind of opacity which Milton would have associated with religious formalism or (in 1641) "senceless Ceremonie" (in *Ref, CPW,* 1 : 526). Modern readers, particularly those of holist bias, have ignored the poem's famous roughness (pretended and real) and in particular the way in which, even in its finished form, it dramatizes its own composition:

> That strain I heard was of a higher mood:
> But now my Oat proceeds,
> And listens to the Herald of the Sea
>
> [87–89]

The poem insists, or comes to insist, that we remember at all times where we are; and it does so largely by maneuvering in and out of narrative and dramatic modes. It is necessary to remind ourselves, for example, how imperceptibly the poem seems to begin, almost as though it were specifically designed for the last position in the book in which it first appeared. The anonymous speaker asks the Muses to begin only in line 14, and the first suggestion that anything unusual is forthcoming by way of answer—that anything is happening, as it were—comes in line 76, the first major break in the poem's continuity, when Phoebus actually *answers* the poet.

That break is emphatic, for Warton marking the irruption of a "sublime strain" (Todd, 6 : 31); it is the first full stop within a line. More disturbing than the mere pause, however significant that may be for a poet of Milton's metrical precision, is the irony involved merely in the introduction of a response and in the sudden establishment of a narrative aspect to the poem—however traditional that may be per se. At the very point the poet is farthest, as it were, from fondly dreaming, when his speech verges on a proverbial style and on desperately "unpoetic" obiter dicta, the utterance is distanced by becoming part of a narrative "history." The poem's most immediate context—the bitter reaction of the poet "now"—is framed in a new perspective, one presumably more definitive than the previous words because judging them and—potentially, at least—moving beyond them into an "other" realm altogether.

At least one interesting detail in the Trinity Manuscript provides evidence that the preoccupation with history, or with what happens in the poem, does not involve us in a uniquely modern approach to the poem. With one portion of his stylistic inheritance (and legacy), the poem's abundant expletives, the manuscript shows some signs of tampering. Again, we encounter the objection of considering textual matters so curiously; and again the neoclassic theorists and poets who see this as a merely technical problem and expletives a "feeble aid" may well give us pause.[21] But I would venture to say the line, which in 1638 reads "Whom universal nature did lament," originated, like other portions of the poem, as a fragment somewhat unrelated to the poem's finally perceived modes of coherence. In the manuscript it reads "whom universal nature *might* lament" (my italics) and forms part of a rather decorated passage on Orpheus and Calliope. Milton recognized both his own self-consciousness about "the golden hayrd Calliope" and the way in which the poem's "final" manner allowed—indeed, encouraged—him to enact more immediately, as it were, the "might." The final poem—as distinguished from the earlier poetry—makes distinctions throughout between what is true "now," what *might* be (in dreams or fables), and what *did* happen, in either the historical or imagined past, whether in or out of the poem. As I have suggested above, it can be argued that in *Lycidas* Milton conflates these last two pasts. As poem, the elegy verges at all times on fond dreams (the sort to which Milton's belated peasant is prone in the first book of *Paradise Lost*) and on the solipsism involved in all fictive thought. But this poem is also *res gesta;* Milton makes it at once something the poet does and something that is happening. In short, he makes a poem which appears to have entered history.

The minor textual detail, then, reflects (in the poem's emergence from poetry, it may have anticipated) the shift we have

21. See, e.g., *An Essay on Criticism,* line 346.

already examined in the poem, the shift from a frontal declaration which is distinctly atemporal to a narrative segment which has the effect of framing and "historifying" that declaration. To put the connection too bluntly, obiter dicta ("is") are suddenly reviewed, as it were, and become fiction ("might") or fable ("did")—though we may not perceive this structure until rather late in the poem.

The very fact that there *is* a procession of figures modifies their pronouncements to a degree by locating them in a temporal context. It is not even made clear to what extent the procession is separable from the procedures of the swain's oat—to what extent we should view them as *merely topoi,* the projections or excuses of a poet all too human. Are we to think of the swain as located *in* the pastoral landscape when his oat overhears the various strains of the speakers? Does the landscape itself exist throughout the poem, as Isabel MacCaffrey seems to suppose, in arguing that the argument alone unfolds in time? [22] Or does the entire poem (as Northrop Frye suggests) take place within his fancy, as the conclusion (particularly the reference to the swain's touching "various Quills") seems to imply? That Milton intended such ambiguities—anticipated and sought to provoke such questions—is evident, for example, in the way he modulates between the response of Hippotades and the poet *in propria persona:*

> It was that fatall and perfidious Bark
> Built in th'eclipse and rigg'd with curses dark,
> That sunk so low that sacred head of thine.
>
> [100–02]

The narrative or historical dimension here, virtually forgotten by the time we reach the final word "thine," is unequivocally reestablished with the elaborate and conventional description of Camus.

An even clearer instance of such control is Saint Peter's speech (108–31), the narrative dimension of which is important only because it is insisted upon. "Last came and last did go / The Pilot of the Galilean Lake" (108–9). He came and he "did go." Perhaps we are likely to forget; this voice, we are told in advance, did not have the last word—its speech is over before we can re-

22. *The Lyric and Dramatic Milton,* p. 69.

spond to it. But this factual information aside, the clarification which follows the speech is equally explicit in telling us of the *effects* of the "dread voice." It "shrunk [the] streams" of Alpheus —an apocalyptic motif to which we shall return. It is a mistake to view such details as merely connective *topoi,* akin to the ancient *topos* of conclusion exploited in the concluding stanza, the sunset: a line to be translated into an extrapoetic context.[23] For by now it is clear (and even clearer subsequently in the poem) that in *Lycidas* there is implied an emerging, evolving landscape, in part answerable to the voices of its inhabitants—as in the end they turn out to be. The landscape partly "answers to" Saint Peter's voice (as it does more completely to the one which follows, despite its skepticism) in the very way universal nature "did," not "might," to Orpheus.

But this is to get ahead of ourselves. At the point when Phoebus interrupts the poet, at least at the syntactic level, there is no such attempt to distinguish the realms I have discussed; there is indeed no effort to isolate narrative from monologue. Coming as it does, articulated with the previous complaint, the reply of Phoebus serves only to make the monologue dramatic and perhaps to deny the presumption that the opening of the poem, however crude, is *merely* fond dreaming. One suspects, indeed, that such well-defined categories for earlier portions in the poem are available only to a speaker with clearer eyesight, one who hovers between pessimistic naturalism and Christian consolation —or perhaps to a reader coming to the poem's beginning all too freshly from the poem's *ending.* In any case, Phoebus, we should notice, merely speaks of "all-judging Jove" and of the final pronouncement of Heaven (in the manner of Raphael, or the Attendant Spirit of the *Mask*), without attempting even to accommodate that realm—as "Milton himself" later will attempt to do in the vision of Lycidas's reception in the sweet societies of Heaven. All that we can say of Phoebus's unobtrusive presence at this point is that it implies a different "now" in the poem from the one first established and that this new coordinate places both deeds and words in a temporal continuum or sequence—including the words and narrated acts of this poem. Within the poem,

23. See E. R. Curtius, *European Literature and the Latin Middle Ages,* trans. Willard Trask (New York: Pantheon, 1953), pp. 90–91.

as in the history which ends in Phoebus's Heaven, there is represented a progress toward pure eyesight and definitive judgment—a progress which I think includes a final pronouncement on the deed that is *Lycidas*.

It may be helpful at this point to recapitulate. It seems that a case can be made for reading line 163: "Look homeward *as* an Angel now, Lycidas—that is, now that we've found you by naming you." Taken in this way, the line involves us in no abrupt shift in addressee (from the "thou" of line 157 to Michael); and better yet, we return more gracefully to the world's pitiable condition, emphasized at similar points in Sannazaro and in the *Epitaphium Damonis*. At line 163 Lycidas is an angel partly because throughout the poem he has been (and subsequently will be) so much else. As in Donne's poetic and meditative arguments—or in *Paradise Lost*—the "now" here marks, not a vaguely temporal reference to the dimmer world after the shepherd's death, but (secondarily, perhaps) a point in the *poem's* progression of imagined identities for King, identities redefined as more or less fictional. "Angel" is the culminating identity for Lycidas, though it is not the final one; it immediately precedes the natural analogy connecting Lycidas with the day-star (that finely elemental hyphenation), the paradox that he is "sunk low, but mounted high," the extended description of the heavenly reception. Finally, Milton accomplishes his coda with the reference to a pastoral genius and the conclusion, in which for the first time narrative and the ottava rima stanza (rather than the traditional conclusion in the *canzone*, the *commiato*) emerge as norms for the poem as a whole.[24]

24. Given Milton's knowledge of Italian forms and style, so admirably illustrated by F. T. Prince in *The Italian Element in Milton's Verse* (Oxford: Clarendon, 1954), I am not convinced that the last verse-paragraph "undoubtedly corresponds in its own way to a *commiato*" (Patrides, *Milton's "Lycidas,"* p. 154). If a concluding *ottava rima* stanza seems peculiar here, we need not say that it merely "rhymes *like* an *ottava rima*" (ibid.; my italics). The core of the poem is the paradox that Lycidas is not dead. Untraditional though it may be, the use of a "normal" stanza form here, instead of the recognizable apparatus of conclusion, is as appropriate as the avoidance of apocalyptic responses to the poem's final lines. Indeed, the stanza serves, with the final action and outlook of the swain, to work against such resonances, though without entirely eliminating them.

It is deliberately, then, that the poet calls attention to the rudeness of his effort in phrases like "melodious tear," the only kind of meed of which the speaker first seems capable. The poem's informality is most evident when a given section collapses into patent fiction, when the melody is recognized as merely a tear, without any value as meed, and perhaps without an audience—as in "Ay me, I fondly dream." The most extended section of this sort is in fact the point where a naturalistic reading of *Lycidas* is likely to end the "real" poem (see above, n. 20). It follows the imagined procession of flowers, in which prayer does verge on dream (or mere "poetry"). The laureate hearse where Lycidas lies is recognized as a fiction—but only after it has virtually achieved another status. And the poet, with a matter-of-fact "For" returns to the pretense of logical progression, as though not yet seeing (with the reader) that the new movement is also a form of eager thought, in itself a fictional or even false surmise:

> For so to interpose a little ease
> Let our frail thoughts dally with false surmise;
> Ay me!
>
> [152–54]

But it hardly seems necessary to suggest, after so many studies of *Lycidas,* that the poem as a whole does not propose this function for poetry.

Indeed, as I hope to show in the remaining pages of this essay, it is essential to relate the insights of the uncouth swain to this eager thought and not to assign new speakers, for example, to the consolation. For from this point to the end of the poem (and of *Justa Edouardo King* . . .), three sections present not different speakers, I believe, but the spectacle of *the poet* (or his person) mediating in the manner of a priest between the shepherds (at once the poem's symbolic society and its audience) and Lycidas, now defined as an angel. On the verge of distinguishing now between realms heretofore not clearly perceived as separable, the poet-priest turns first to the woeful shepherds (lines 165–81) speaking from above (to some extent from "God's prospect high"), then to Lycidas speaking from below (where those wandering in the "perilous flood"—anyone "here"—need a good genius). Finally we are distanced on *all* this eager thought in the stanza. In a sense, these final sections explicate the potential of that deliberately "mystic" line 163 with which we began.

To be more specific: within the lines of consolation following the arresting double apostrophe of lines 163–64, there is a movement toward the passionate, irrational (or "eager") apprehension of the poem's central paradox. What we notice on the stylistic level is the gradual disappearance of intellection and the commonsense awareness of incongruous opposites:

> Weep no more, woeful shepherds, weep no more,
> For *Lycidas* your sorrow is not dead,
> Sunk though he be beneath the watery floor;
> So sinks the day-star in the Ocean bed,
> And yet anon repairs his drooping head,
> And tricks his beams, and with new-spangled Ore
> Flames in the forehead of the morning sky:
> So *Lycidas,* sunk low, but mounted high,
> Through the dear might of him that walk'd the waves,
> Where other groves and other streams along,
> With *Nectar* pure his oozy Locks he laves,
> And hears the unexpressive nuptial Song,
> In the blest Kingdoms meek of joy and love.
> There entertain him all the saints above,
> In solemn troops and sweet societies
> That sing, and singing in their glory move,
> And wipe the tears for ever from his eyes.
>
> [165–81]

The lines are not often explicated, perhaps because they embarrass readers who mistake them for a statement of belief, an ultimate truth with which Milton outfaces his audience. Actually the passage is better called a vision.[25] It is a highly daring dramatization of a difficulty inherent in the paradoxical mode: by calling attention to paradox in a passage of persuasive rhetoric (or indeed in any verbal formula), a poet is likely to rationalize it: "sunk low, but mounted high." Milton gets around this difficulty

25. As it is, for example, by Isabel MacCaffrey in *The Lyric and Dramatic Milton,* p. 89.

in two basic ways, I think. First, the connective tissue of discourse, the apparatus of intellection here describes (and hence, controls) a paradox, while a more *inherently* paradoxical diction, by extending or redefining the sense of an earlier line in the poem, enacts the same paradox in a purer form: "Sunk though he be beneath the watery floor." [26] Secondly, the rationalizing apparatus itself—most obviously the quasilogical analogy but including the "other" which is only implied in purer images like "Nectar pure" and "blest Kingdoms"—disappears as we move upward (glancing back last perhaps in "sweet societies") into the ineffable "blest Kingdoms meek of joy and love."

In lines 182–85, I have suggested, Lycidas is addressed from beneath, apparently from the shepherds' point of view. He is now capable of *dispensing* "fair recompense" and can be good to all . . . shepherds? The recipient of Lycidas's good is not made entirely clear. Surely the shepherds do not ordinarily "wander in that perilous flood"—as do pilots, for example, in *Paradise Lost*. But it is clear that the "all who wander" is meant to include anyone "here"—as in line 163, where even as the poet names Lycidas as an angel he still thinks of himself (presumably with us) as being at home, so to speak. The question of the poem's ending, therefore, would seem to be the distinctness of the speaker's location with respect to Lycidas and the shepherds. The shepherds are apparently dissociated from all those who wander in the perilous flood; and unless the voice is at this point collective, speaking for all those shepherds (and thus for the poem and even book), we may say that the speaker himself, as priest, no longer locates himself "here," at home. For the speaker, as for Lycidas, the danger is now "there"—even though the flood seems to have enlarged so as to include more than the reference of the poem's headnote. The speaker, one might even venture, has already arrived at that shore, which is now not the shore of England but the harbor of the "blest Kingdom."

Or so the poet imagines. The greatness of the poem's conclusion lies partly in the way Milton reminds us, in the manner of

26. The shift in the metaphor for "world" is operative but subtle; "monstrous world" is both *mundus* in the abstract and the realm of creatures like responsive dolphins.

the *Nativity* ode, that "this must not yet be so" or is so only within the confines of a poem.[27] After all, like *Paradise Lost,* the poem seems to end more than once. We have seen how, earlier in *Lycidas,* the poet interrupts a section—the procession of flowers or the assumption of a persona like the dread voice which shrinks the streams of Alpheus—with a reminder in effect of the poem's unluckiness or even of its origins. This skeptical voice is as much an intrusion on the poem's "poetry" as the sad occasion dear is on "the mellowing year." When it is close to the occasion it calls attention to the poem's uncouthness by calling it a melodious tear; at its most skeptical (or indeed, honest) it stresses the poem's *origins*—the matrices in literary, imaginative, and social reality from which poetry (and this poem) in varying degrees emerges. The first words of the poem are superficial instances of such origins, like the initials J. M. at the close. Another instance is the satiric voice of Saint Peter; the poet must subsequently pray for the return of the pastoral world. Most important to our present discussion is a solipsistic origin for the poem in the mind of the poet: "Let our frail thoughts dally with false surmise." As we have seen the line is peculiarly appropriate to a particular section of the poem, the floral procession; but to an extent it describes the entire performance of *Lycidas.* The long prelude strikes us as *preliminary* material to the poem proper—a rationale, it would seem, for its very composition. And to our surprise the purest vision—that of the "blest Kingdom"—seems to be immediately qualified in a similar way, as though to suggest that the poem is not yet all there:

> Thus sang the uncouth Swain to th'Oaks and rills,
> While the still morn went out with Sandals gray;
> He touch't the tender stops of various Quills,
> With eager thought warbling his *Doric* lay:
> And now the Sun had stretch't out all the hills,
> And now was dropt into the Western bay;
> At last he rose, and twitch't his Mantle blue:
> Tomorrow to fresh Woods, and Pastures new.
>
> [186–93]

27. My discussion of the poem's conclusion is indebted to Isabel MacCaffrey's essay. See especially *The Lyric and Dramatic Milton,* pp. 87–92.

Perhaps the prime irony here is formal, in the sense that this section, describing and distancing us on both poet and poem, is both a narrative and ottava rima, not the traditional *commiato* of the *canzone*. The abrupt shift to a narrative mode locates the entire action of the poem in the past and implies that the speaker of this section is impersonal, or at any rate decidedly *not* the uncouth swain whose eager thought was most of *Lycidas*—indeed, the new voice has magical access to the swain's thoughts, as revealed in the last line. The passage, in fact, anticipates similar shifts in *Paradise Lost,* where a dialectical or dramatic portion is "answered" on what might be thought of as a definitive narrative level. In *Paradise Lost,* this strategy allows the poet to realize the effects of the Word at some level in the poem's cosmos "beneath" its origin. Here we may describe the shift as moving in the opposite direction—from the sphere of mere words more or less lucky, more or less articulated with the poem's occasion, to the less personal sphere of the Word: a world in which pastoral phenomena, now presented as it were objectively (*without* the poet's mind), "independently" answer to the swain's eager thought (including the passage of Christian consolation) and *make* the words lucky.

It is a brilliant, and daring, solution to a problem which for Milton was not entirely artistic—not, at least, until *Lycidas.* The coda appears at first to be part of the apology which informs the poem from the beginning, part of what I have called the poem's (not the poet's) skepticism. The coda thus describes quite exactly *almost* the whole poem. But if the "various Quills" can be said to include the narrative which mentions them, surely the ottava rima conclusion at least is something more than eager thought, as even the ironic exactness of "Doric lay" suggests. The nature of that something more, I think, is partly adumbrated in the insistent end-stopping—the fragmentation of line units and of syntactic and, implicitly, cosmic relationships—within the ottava rima stanza. Just as the narrative stanza is divorced formally from the rest of the poem's eager thought, the lines within the stanza are disjoined in such a way as to image the apparent unrelatedness of singer, song, and cosmos. Lines 189–90, in particular, stress a "naturalistic" divorce between mind and matter; the uncouth swain's eager thought had nothing to do with the time of the day, and the way the stanza *reads,* the relation between the various quills and Doric lay seems almost accidental.

In truth, however, Milton is at pains to stress such a disjointed world partly because this "objective" reality contains powers of consolation missing from the poem's merely dialectical portions. The audience for the uncouth swain is the "Oaks and rills"; the Orphean correspondences are irretrievably lost with the death of Lycidas. All that happens in response to the song is the passing of time; if the morn is personified, she wears gray and is "still." But in another sense time has vanished from this last portion; the "now" of the last eight lines covers the entire day, or at least from late in the morning to sundown.

The last four lines deal (in the second of two sentences in the stanza) with what appear to be more temporal references. But now, instead of the compressed formula "day-star" adduced (with apparent success) as a natural and naturally paradoxical analogy to console the shepherds, we have the mere sun, within a natural and supernatural, not a logical, order, first presented with recognizably apocalyptic activity (it "had stretch't out all the hills"), then providing a terribly final end to one day: "And now was dropt into the Western bay." What is curious about these lines is that they are recognized (by readers alert to Milton's modulations in and out of *als ob*) as pastoral or diurnal references only *secondarily.* The phenomena of lines 190–91 seem sufficient for faithful action at least on the part of the uncouth swain, whose final thoughts are definitively reported in the poem's last line, "Tomorrow to fresh Woods and Pastures new." If the reader discovers only an apocalyptic or naturalistic outlook in lines 190–91, though, it is very likely because he has failed to read the poem carefully enough to perceive its "real" pastoral basis, gradually emerging in what Isabel MacCaffrey has called the poem's landscape.[28] For that basis has involved us in a partly logical discovery of Logos, in the Son/sun—the "dear might of him that walked the waves." And it implies a rejection of all fable, all poetry (including apocalyptic correspondences) as eager thought.

The coda, then, seems deliberately to return us to the "shape-

28. See *The Lyric and Dramatic Milton,* pp. 69, 71, 73.

less process of life," the realm from which some critics would redeem all poetry; at least it attempts to *include* that realm within its magic circle. It seeks also to distinguish between that world and the realm of poetry proper—the province of eager thought. In confronting us with what might be called one more of the poem's matrices, Milton can be said to make his poem more true. But it is important to add that the descent to time and to a recognizable space is necessarily a pretense; nor can we ask more. In removing us from the swain's vision, Milton pretends to deliver us, as so often in his poetry, from a fable (or type) to truth. But truth, here, unlike the "forms" of things in real life, is recognizable in the furniture of the poem's pastoral landscape, notably in the prime rhythm of the sun's daily cycle. It is now fully revealed outside the context of eager thought, almost beyond the sphere of poetry itself. While every human inhabitant of the poem is a swain—even the Pilot—characterized primarily by a voice to which something out there answers (and Lycidas himself is of course the archetypal figure of this kind), the poem's ending, ostensibly part of the poem's "outside" with which it has so long been confused, absorbs all endings, all "outsides" into an ultimate context of Logos, the Word which makes the poem's words lucky. Milton relies on the very presence of the ottava rima, as on the definitive basis of pastoral imagery, to contain the centrifugal, indeed atomistic tendencies of its disjunctive lines. Thus, though we recognize the literal, "eager" value of the poem's final terrors, we also instinctively *translate* them:

> And now the Sun had stretch't out all the hills,
> And now was dropt into the Western bay.

PART THREE

5

Ramus, Metaphor, and the *Art of Logic*

On 10 September 1802 Coleridge declared in a well-known letter to Sotheby that "Nature has her proper interest." Furthermore,

> He will know what it is who believes and feels that everything has a life of its own and that we are all *One Life*. A poet's heart and intellect should be combined, intimately combined and unified with the great appearances of nature, and not merely held in solution and loose mixture with them, in the shape of formal similes.[1]

In making a poem's figures the measure of the poet's vision, Coleridge was not speaking of *Paradise Lost*. By the time he wrote *Biographia Literaria*, indeed, he had found an illuminating description of unfallen perception, and hence the antithesis of the "formal simile," in Raphael's famous lecture on the "bright consummate flow'r," much of which appeared as the epigraph for chapter 13, on the imagination. Still, the earlier passage illuminates Milton's poem, even in opposing the oneness of all life (or the poet's perception of it) to that unmistakable stylistic index of Milton's supposedly dissociated sensibility, the formal simile. For while we may gather from Coleridge's chapter 13 that Raphael's metaphysics are inseparable from the psychological and discursive tenor which only gradually emerges from his speech,[2] in the poem that metaphysics is less often experienced or enacted than described. Finally, we must admit that—to the extent that *Paradise Lost* images the perceptual experience of the poet, rather than the more discursive justification it claims to present

1. See Abrams, pp. 294, 386, n. 101.
2. See *PL* v. 469–88. Aside from ending the quotation where he did, Coleridge departed somewhat from Milton's text, notably in substituting "nature" for "matter" in "one first matter all."

—the work itself in its most characteristic passages reveals less the true Coleridgean poet than the maker of similitudes.[3]

If we turn to Milton's own Ramistic discussion of the logical argument of similitude, we discover a cautious skepticism regarding the relation of metaphysics and comparative figures—whether the metaphysical ground is conceived organically or, say, numerologically. The twenty-first chapter of this early and largely derivative *Art of Logic* is certainly less interesting to students of the poetry than, say, Raphael's tantalizing remarks about his own presentation of the War in Heaven—the poem's most extended and highly explicated simile. But the handbook does reveal both the extent of Milton's familiarity with current and fashionable theory regarding the similitude and some signs of his own independence from Ramist method and even Ramist assumptions. Ultimately, Milton pulls back from linking similars with a proportion inherent in nature, only to direct attention to the maker of formal simile, whatever the context or medium of his argument. And since a total theory of knowledge is involved, the similars of the poet are as pertinent as those of the dialectician.

Milton's only formal theory of similitude appeared, then, in the handbook of logic entitled *Artis Logicae Plenior Institutio*.[4] It was published in May of 1672, between the first and second editions of *Paradise Lost* and one year after the publication of *Paradise Regained* and *Samson Agonistes*. We should not assume that the *Art of Logic* embodies Milton's considered or current opinions as a literary artist, since for the most part it is a thoroughly traditional rehandling of the Ramist textbooks: notably, the *Dialectica* of Petrus Ramus himself and the *Commentarii* of the influential prelector in logic at Cambridge, George Downame —in all likelihood Milton's two prime sources. Even if Milton wholeheartedly embraced the system he expounds and amplifies in the *Art of Logic*—a system necessarily far more indebted to

3. This was virtually the complaint of the anti-Miltonists; there is a brief review of the argument, with a short bibliography, in my article, "Some Uses of Sensuous Immediacy in *Paradise Lost*," *Huntington Library Quarterly* 31 (1968) : 211–12.

4. Full title: *JOANNIS MILTONI*, / Angli, / Artis Logicae / Plenior Institutio, / AD / *PETRI RAMI* / Methodum concinnata, / *LONDINI*, / Impensis Spencer Hickman, So / cietatis Regalis Typographi, ad / insigne *Rosae* in *Caemeterio*, / *D. Pauli*. 1672. See CE 11 : vii.

classical authors and even Aristotle than it pretends—the evidence suggests that the *Art of Logic* was largely composed long before its publication, perhaps between Milton's two degrees at Cambridge (i.e., between 1629 and 1632), a period of some controversy between the Ramists and Aristotelians of that university.[5] Appearing as it did in 1672, Milton's *Art of Logic* may best be viewed as the early production of an author currently famous for epic and tragic literary works, rather than as the poetics of a practicing artist. In its manner it is patently a university product, clarifying a traditional text and seeking to make "copiously clear" a system which had been too often expounded obscurely.[6]

The likelihood that this handbook does not really represent Milton's own theory is much less important, however, than the fact it makes unmistakably clear: that, whether or not a Ramist, he is thoroughly familiar with the schematic view of arguing by "similars"—a view, with obvious literary implications, that must have been virtually a mental habit. The three main points in the Ramist treatment of the subject may be summarized as follows.

1. Formal elements in the argument by similitude. We can dis-

5. The date of composition is unknown; see Parker, 2 : 938, n. 67. Some of the difficulties can be set aside. We need not accept Franklin Irwin's argument for a late date on the basis of the anti-Trinitarian remark, "solus pater est verus deus," and on the assumption that Milton lost faith in the Trinity after 1641, since the remark might have been interpolated (see W. S. Howell, *Logic and Rhetoric in England, 1500–1700* [Princeton: Princeton University Press, 1956], p. 215). Perhaps more serious is the claim, advanced by G. C. Moore Smith, that by 1644 Milton had lost his passion for logic ("A Note on Milton's *Art of Logic*," *Review of English Studies* 13 [1937] : 335–40). In *Of Education,* which was published with his poems in 1673, Milton does say that in logic students should have only "so much as is useful" (*CPW,* 2 : 402). But Milton is discussing the crucial last phase in his educational scheme, the "organic arts," including logic, rhetoric, and—"subsequent, or indeed rather precedent" to these—poetry. These taken together are the arts of discourse (one meaning of the Greek *logos*) "which enable men to discourse and write perspicuously, elegantly, and according to the fitted style of lofty, mean, or lowly" (p. 403). Milton merely indicates here, as in the *Art of Logic* itself, that he requires only as much logic as is useful in the highest "organic arts." His attack on logic is the conventional Ramist (and Protestant) attack on syllogistic, scholastic logic, which he elsewhere associated with both a jingling verbalism and "airy visions" (*quaedam leves imagines*) and which he had distinguished, somewhat vaguely, from a "more accurate wisdom" (*rectior sapientia*). See Prol III, CE 12 : 164–65, 168–69.

6. For the claim that Renaissance poets thought Ramus to be "nothing if not lucid . . . fit only for simpletons," see George Watson, "Ramus, Miss Tuve, and the New Petromachia," *Modern Philology* 55 (1958) : 259–62.

tinguish similars from other kinds of argument first by their signs (*notae*) and more fully by their structural elements or parts. Short signs of similitude comprised in one word are either the properties of similar things or the denial of dissimilars; the proper signs of similars can be nouns (*like, effigy, image,* etc.). In examples and in text, Milton follows his sources, making clear what Addison would still claim in 1712, that metaphor is essentially a similar, a "similitude contracted to one word without signs, which, however, are understood," [7] a formulation unacceptable to later critics.

2. Sometimes similars are fully developed and are thus recognizable from structural elements or parts as well as from the framing signs. Structurally, similars are seen to be of two basic forms, disjunct and continued; disjunct when two terms or distinct things in the context are compared with two terms or distinct things in the similar argument, continued when "as the first term is to the second, so the second is to the third" (CE 11 : 197–201). At this point Milton reveals a characteristic and important attitude in the Ramist tradition he is following: "Proportion not merely mathematical but also logical is common to all things." What follows from this premise is that, given a likeness in the "proposition" and "reddition," there is also inverse and alternative likeness among the terms themselves. Milton illustrates both the terminology and the practice with a favorite example of the Ramist writers, one which clarifies the emblematic value of Milton's later maritime similes: "As the best governors of ships oftentimes may not overcome the strength and rage of the tempest, so the most wise man may not always vanquish the invasion and violence of fortune."

> If [the terms] are similar they are also similar inversely and alternately. Inversely in two manners, obviously by inversion of the proposition and reddition, which is common to other comparatives, or of the terms, which seems proper to similars. For example, *As the pilot is to the tempest, so is the wise man to fortune;* inversely, therefore, it will be *As the wise man is to fortune, so is the pilot to the tempest.* This is inversion of the proposition and reddition. Again, *As is the tempest to the*

7. CE 11 : 195, 197; see *Spectator,* no. 303, 16 February 1712.

pilot, so is fortune to the wise man; this is inversion of the terms. Alternation is when the antecedent of the proposition is compared with the antecedent of the reddition, and the consequent to its consequent. The rule here, therefore, is that if things are similar they are alternately similar. *As is the pilot to the tempest, so is the wise man to fortune;* therefore, alternately, *As is the pilot to the wise man, so is the tempest to fortune.* [CE 11 : 199, 201–3]

3. Milton concludes his chapter by extending even further the scope of argument by similitude: *"the fictitious similitude* [the apologues of Aesop and the so-called Socratic parables serve as precedents] *has equal force in argument"* with the similars previously mentioned.[8]

To the traditional Ramist discussion of similars, Milton makes but one significant contribution. If we compare Milton's chapter with the *Dialectica* of Ramus and George Downame's *Commentarii* (1601), we discover a passage which appears in neither source. Marked in Milton's *Art of Logic* with an asterisk, the passage occurs toward the end of his definition of similars:

> * Monendum autem est similia sive contractae formae sive explicatae urgenda non esse ultra eam qualitatem quam in utrisque; eandem esse propositum assimilanti erat ostendere: sic magistratus assimilatur cani, sola nimirum fidelitate custodiae: unde illa in scholis, *nullum simile est idem, simile non currit quatuor pedibus, omne simile claudicat.*[9]

Significantly enough, Milton's caveat, apparently so skeptical on the important Ramist assumption that "proportion not merely mathematical but also logical is common to all things," replaces

8. The italics are those of the text; CE 11 : 203. In *Apology against a Pamphlet,* Milton discusses scriptural parable as "similitude": "Doth not Christ himselfe teach the highest things by the similitude *of old bottles and patcht cloaths?* Doth he not illustrate best things by things most evill? his own *comming* to be as a thiefe in the night?" (*CPW,* 1 : 898).

9. Allan Gilbert's translation: "Warning, however, should be given that likes whether of short or full form are not to be urged beyond that quality which the man making the comparison intended to show as the same in both. Thus a magistrate is likened to a dog, yet merely in the fidelity of his guardianship, whence came the saying of the schools: 'Nothing similar is identical; likeness does not run on four feet; every likeness hobbles' " (CE 11 : 194–95).

an extensive section in the sources. In fact, the passage in Downame and the traditional Ramist writers expands rather boldly the province of similitude. Illustrating the process with mathematical examples, it concludes: "Solent quidem hae voces a quibusdam ad quantitatum collationes adstringi, verum generalis sunt significationis. Num et similitudo omnis proportio est, et qualitas omnis ratio est." [10] Clearly the asterisk marks the most important "original" departure from Milton's Ramist sources in the chapter. He puts the burden of emphasis on "the man making the comparison" (*assimilanti*)—on the poet's declared intention, one might venture, in the form of a designated point of comparison. By introducing the figure of the logical inventor, or poet, Milton shifts somewhat abruptly from the intrinsic rationality presumed to inhere in all Ramist "arguments." Moreover, in citing the school formula *omne simile claudicat*—"every likeness hobbles"—Milton even more clearly diverts the general thrust of Ramist theory, which in this context begins with the proposition that "proportion not merely mathematical but also logical is common to all things" and moves (inevitably enough, perhaps, given the premise) toward the critical practice of inverting and alternating terms and elements.

What are we to make of this brief, tedious, "theoretic" text, which appears to be neither original nor current in Milton's mature thinking and writing? The only explicit discussion of simile we have places the argument of similitude in the context of logical invention, among the "artificial" arguments—those built upon intrinsic rationality, rather than upon *auctoritas*. None of the comparative arguments is precisely equivalent to the simile with which we are familiar in the epic tradition; nor does the comparative group as a whole come close to describing the complexities of Milton's own similes. Milton's chapter on similars might seem to verge on a complete treatment of simile, partly because it cites examples of this mode of argument. But as

10. "These examples are ordinarily drawn together for the comparison of quantities, but they are of general significance. For every likeness is proportion, and every quality is an argument" (George Downame, *Commentarii in P. Rami* [London, 1601], pp. 338–39, my translation; this copy, of a book usually studied in a 1669 reprint, is in the Folger Shakespeare Library).

Rosemond Tuve has said, such citation was commonplace long before Ramus; and in the case of the Ramist logics, it reinforced the oft-repeated point that logic was a general art. Literature was especially handy, it would seem, to prove that logic had a kind of existence apart from specific argumentative purposes or media.[11] Moreover, of the illustrations themselves, only two are from epic (both from the *Aeneid*), and only one of these would be recognizable as a true simile.[12] Milton adds no new examples to those accumulated in the handbooks for over one hundred years. He follows the tradition in mixing his examples from oratory, epistles, fables, and epic.

We can make better sense of Milton's slight innovation in emphasis, I would suggest, by recalling the most general purpose of the *Art of Logic* and particularly the relationship between logic and poetry. What exactly is it, first of all, that Milton wishes to clarify in handing down the art of logic? As in his letter to Hartlib, Milton wishes to avoid the "anxious" and "subtle" employment of art which can actually trammel "those whose native abilities are active and strong" (see CE 11 : 3, 7). But complementing Milton's (and the Ramists') concern for the talented individual is a Ramistic stress on the limitation of the art itself, as well as of ordinary men's epistemological resources. It is true that logic is one of God's motions in men, as Milton points out in an arresting passage about "invention" in general:

> I suppose no one doubts that the primal mover of every art is God, the author of all wisdom. . . . The assisting causes were the men divinely taught and eminent for ability who in the past discovered the individual arts. The method of discovering these was much like the method of painting; for as there are in a picture two things—the subject or archetype and the art of painting—so in the discovery of an art, nature or practise and the example of skillful men corresponds to the

11. See A. J. Smith, "An Examination of Some Claims Made for Ramism," *Review of English Studies* 7 (1956) : 348–59, esp. 351. For a useful and balanced account of the controversial matter, see K. G. Hamilton, *The Two Harmonies: Poetry and Prose in the Seventeenth Century* (Oxford: Clarendon, 1963), pp. 108–19, esp. 116.

12. *Os umerosque deo similis* ("In face and shoulders like a god"), *Aeneid* 1.589, CE 11 : 195.

> archetype, and logic to the art of the painter—natural logic, at least, which is the very faculty of reason in the mind of man, according to that common saying: Art imitates nature. [CE 11 : 11]

The final qualification here suggests the more normal emphasis in the handbook. Elsewhere Milton defines logic as "the art of reasoning well," adding the word "well," as he says, "in order to distinguish the perfection of the art from the imperfection of the natural faculty" (CE 11 : 19). The art of logic works at one remove from the practice or "experience" of perception; and speaking as a pedagogue, Milton must measure the utility of the art itself against the imperfections of human knowledge, treating logic as a way of clarifying the fallen vision. This attitude toward the refinement of verbal and rhetorical technology extends even to the raison d'être for Milton's own publication, which belongs somewhere between the traditional realms of logic and rhetoric, and seeks to make "copiously clear" the work of an author commonly considered obscure.

As we have seen, Milton came to think of poetry not only as a kind of key to the improvement of the "organic arts" but specifically as a form of descriptive clarification of moral experience. As in the *Art of Logic,* painting was to be the analogy for the way poetry teaches "over the whole book of sanctity and virtue" (in the passage above painting is the analogy for *all* the arts). Useful especially for those whose "soft and delicious" tempers have been prematurely introduced to logic, it dresses Truth elegantly; "all these things with a solid and treatable smoothness to paint out and describe" (*RCG,* Hughes, p. 670A). To some degree the position may be traced in the *Art of Logic,* and even in the passage on similars. Milton is particularly concerned that "the Theologian awake" on the rubric of *form,* for example. Yet what chiefly emerges from this discussion is a strong sense of the difficulty involved in knowing form *at all.* Form is the "cause through which a thing is what it is." Again, "the rational soul is the form of man generically; the soul of Socrates is the proper form of Socrates. . . . From form alone comes an essential distinction" (CE 11 : 59–61). Milton allows all this. Yet in the next paragraph he defines the difficulty basic to any knowing; it is precisely the confusion between internal form and sensible experience, or "figure." It is a distinction helpful in adjusting our vision to the "darkness visible" of Milton's Hell:

> [The fact that] cause is the fount of all knowledge, is understood especially to apply to form. For the cause which especially constitutes the essence, if it is noted, above all brings knowledge. But to know the internal form of anything, because it is usually very remote from the senses, is especially difficult. In artificial things, however, the form, as being external and exposed to the senses, is more easily observed. . . . But there is not true distribution of form. For the distribution of internal or external which some hold will not apply to all things but merely to the corporeal; and the external is not less essential to each artificial thing than the internal to each natural thing.[13]

Though the passage is not strictly Milton's, it would be difficult to surpass in dramatizing the problems in acquiring true knowledge. In its potential, moreover, it is thoroughly congenial to the temper of Milton's mind: notably in its openness to ordinary sense experience and in its preoccupation with the whereabouts of the "idea" relative to "the shapes and forms of things," whether real or artificial. The same interests pervade Milton's (and the Ramists') discussion of definition and description, a more characteristically Miltonic topic. Since *genus* and *form* together make up the essence of a thing (CE 11 : 239), definition is a symbol or virtual equivalent of the thing defined. A perfect definition depends exclusively upon "the causes constituting the essence of the thing defined" (CE 11 : 263) and is thus what the Ramists called a "universal symbol" of those causes. But because definition requires the knowledge of such elusive entities as form, what normally takes its place is an imperfect definition or "description," of which Milton writes the following:

> Because of the obscurity of causes and especially of forms, perfect definitions are difficult to come upon. *Description* has been

13. CE 11 : 61–63; for a reminder of this kind of difficulty, see p. 253. The observation is in Downame but not in Ramus.

> devised to supply their scarcity. *Description is* an imperfect *definition, defining a thing through other arguments,* that is, explaining the thing in some way from whatever is available.
>
> So where form cannot be had (for the genera are commonly better known) a property must be accepted in place of form or distinguishing difference, as when it is said *An angel is an incorporeal substance; or A horse is an animal that whinnies,* etc.[14]

Milton's later radical acceptance of poetry as an inescapably descriptive function of the mind is not so far beyond such passages as we might suppose. And the general assumptions informing the entire *Art of Logic*—not to mention the Fall of Man—make clearer the possible uses of similitude, to which the descriptive function of "making plain" (as distinct from proving) was traditionally assigned.[15]

We may best understand Milton's own cautionary contributions to the art of "likening" in logical and poetic argument if we bear in mind these central assumptions. And we should notice that while such discussions are epistemologically skeptical they are also traditionally "Ramist." Whatever the relevance of the *Art of Logic* to his rhetorical and poetic theory during the time Milton wrote *Paradise Lost,* the treatment of "human names" in the poem, the "alter'd style" of Adam and Eve after the Fall (itself presented in large measure as an epistemological crisis), Michael's attempt to provide Adam with a new vision—all remind us that the poet's early preoccupation with language was more than pedagogical. Although we must pick our way carefully, the *Art of Logic* is one guidepost for Milton's poems.

The handbook itself, we may recall, is what earlier generations had called a rhetoric. On the evidence that Milton employed examples from classical literary texts, A. J. Smith has maintained

14. CE 11 : 267; again, in Downame but not in Ramus.

15. "Before comparison is begun that which the comparatives argue by their nature should be better known and clearer to him with whom we discuss a comparative than is the thing argued, for something equally obscure would make nothing plain. Hence the extraordinary usefulness of comparatives stands out, for by this it comes about that an unequal knowledge of things by force of comparison is made equal. Thus the consentanies are fittest for proving, the comparatives for making plain" (CE 11 : 153).

that Milton cannot be said to have continued the Ramist tendency to merge logic and poetry. Perhaps not; but what of a Miltonic, "new" poetry? Throughout the *Art of Logic,* Milton stresses that logic, as "the first and most general" of the arts, is the art of reasoning well. More particularly, Milton wishes to dissociate logic from both words and things, to discuss (for example) a "fitness for argument" which is technically called *ratio:*

> Although it is possible to reason without words, yet from the very necessity for speaking, logic seems with perfect right to demand that whenever it is necessary words should be employed that are distinct and certainly not ambiguous and not inappropriate. Logic leaves things themselves to their appropriate arts; it considers merely what affect or ratio for arguing they have among themselves.[16]

Words themselves, moreover, have become detached from things, or at least from "arguments," as Milton suggests most clearly in his treatment of "notation" or etymology. The difficulty of discovering the nominal "symbol of some primitive argument" is simply one manifestation of the general discursive predicament: "Both that first [language] which Adam spoke in Eden, and those varied ones also possibly derived from the first, which the builders of the tower of Babel suddenly received, are without doubt divinely given; hence it is not strange if the reason [*ratio*] of primitive words is unknown" (CE 11 : 219–21). To this predicament, the development of Milton's distinction between definition and description, or of the province of the comparative argument, was to provide a partial solution. Arising in the course of a dense argument from the obscurity of "causes" (that crucial word in the opening invocation of *Paradise Lost*) to the virtual necessity of description as a mode of argument in logic and poetry, the distinction may be taken as one sign that a logic conceived in the Ramist way, as a general art distinct from both words and things, is at least serviceable for a poetry of wisdom.[17]

16. CE 11 : 25–27; throughout this passage *vox* is translated as "word."
17. See Smith, "Examination of Claims for Ramism," p. 351, and Hamilton, *Two Harmonies,* p. 116.

It is dangerous, though tempting, to speak of the relation between Ramism, Milton's handbook, and the poems in terms more specific than these. All Ramists (and most logicians) insist that "likes" are more fit for making plain than for proving, and everyone agrees on the value of similars in logical strategy. The presumed existence of a logical and mathematical proportion not quite extramental but "common to all things" was of course not the private property of the Ramists because they may have reflected it in neat, detailed correspondences between formal image and narrative context. Milton's own construction of images reveals a familiarity with this tradition, as James Whaler's treatment of Miltonic "homologation" amply demonstrates.[18] On the other hand, although Milton's omission of Downame's illustrative material and his caveat taken together obviously betoken reservations about certain Ramist views, the practical implications of this individualism are less clear. Certainly the claim that "every likeness hobbles" was not new when Milton wrote it; indeed, in using this school tag where he does, Milton confirms the impression, available elsewhere, that there are perhaps several discriminable Ramisms and that each—including Milton's—can accommodate elements both traditional and heterodox. We are obliged to admit, finally, that Milton is of little help to readers of his own similes in directing the reader to the intention of the poet or arguer—even if by "intention" he means anything so precise as an initial term of comparison. As most readers notice, the occasions of "likening" in the similes of *Paradise Lost* account for only a minor part of the total effect, schematically tight though most of them are. In replacing Downame's emphasis on the proportion "common to all things" with a passage invoking what the "assimilating" poet or arguer "proposes" to show, Milton has implicitly refused to encourage the examination of the argumentative poem itself, apart from that perplexing cause of its being, the "person" of its poet.

Even if the evidence for Milton's "departure" from Ramism bulked much more largely than it does in the *Art of Logic,* it

18. See James Whaler, "Compounding and Distribution of Similes in *Paradise Lost,*" *Modern Philology* 28 (1931) : 313–27; "Grammatical *Nexus* of the Miltonic Simile"; "The Miltonic Simile," *PMLA* 46 (1931) : 1034–74.

would be difficult to assess fairly the question or degree of Milton's Ramism; and I wish to imply no such innovation.[19] For readers of literature, I believe, the question itself has been asked misleadingly, too *ideologically,* at least if the answers are an indication. Ramism is variously held to be a cause, more or less immediate, of literary phenomena as diverse as the metaphysical style, the plain style, and *Paradise Lost.* One conclusion seems inevitable: either we are dealing with several Ramisms or we have done little more than replace Eliot's "dissociation of sensibility" with another single-cause explanation. At any rate, since Ong's *Ramus, Method, and the Decay of Dialogue* (1958), it should be much more difficult to insist that one kind of literary strategy or style necessarily resulted from what Rosemond Tuve called "the basic realism of the Ramists, their willingness to identify things with ratio, idea with thing-as-it-is." [20] We still need to know how scrupulous Milton's Ramism was. The preoccupation with whether or not Milton "was" a Ramist, moreover, has preceded a properly detailed examination of the *Art of Logic* itself.

About the poem's (as distinct from the poet's) epistemology we can be somewhat more specific. In writing the words about the poet's "heart and intellect" with which we began, Coleridge had in mind a specific kind of poetry, as M. H. Abrams makes clear: the conventional natural description presented as the transparent vehicle for human analogues or morals, exemplified particularly in the sonnets of William Bowles (Abrams, p. 294). But characteristically, in raising to the level of theory what is in part a particular stylistic objection, Coleridge obliquely helps sharpen our focus on the perceptual crisis in the narrative of *Paradise Lost:* Adam's loss of the "Presence Divine" in the universe of things and the survival only of a "track Divine"—*signs* of the Presence. This aspect of *Paradise Lost* was clearly central for Coleridge and contemporary readers in Europe, and it has remained so ever since. As presented to the reader, however, the poem's metaphysics is for the most part veiled behind what Raphael calls

19. For the most interesting and radical acceptance of Milton's Ramism, see Cope, pp. 27–49; his review of the controversy over Ramistic influence is helpful, along with that of K. G. Hamilton, noted above, n. 11.

20. *Elizabethan and Metaphysical Imagery* (Chicago: University of Chicago Press, 1947), p. 350, n. 21.

"process of speech" (VII. 7). Within *Paradise Lost,* the oneness of the Almighty may be accessible to the angels and (at the moment of Raphael's lecture) to Adam. We may recall a distinction conveniently ignored by Coleridge: even before Adam and Eve sin, they do not quite possess the intuition of the angels. As Raphael says, "Discourse / Is *oftest* yours." It does seem at times that Milton's poet becomes rapt, even to the point of reaching the unexpressive mysteries of the divine wisdom. But the reader seemingly implied by *Paradise Lost* is most clearly placed by the arguments of its similitudes, both formal and dissolved; more than the readers of other epics, he needs—he is, at any rate, offered—the relative clarity provided by the easier, but secondary, art of description. To Coleridge and his contemporaries, such a reader might well have seemed all too amenable to discourse.

It may be emphasized once again that we are concerned here with the admittedly shadowy area of Miltonic intention. In adapting Raphael's distinction for critical purposes, we do not use "process" to mean something like "existential" or merely "shapeless," as in some current critical terminology. And it may be helpful at this point to clarify the differences by noticing that the most theoretic of the poem's recent "metaphoric" readings describes the poem's "primary organization" using distinctions remarkably similar to those of Coleridge (see Cope, pp. 1–26). Speaking generally, and not of "Miltonic" metaphor, Jackson Cope takes the position that "process" should be considered as simply opposed to "superimposed" or "spatial" relationships and, consequently, that "depth metaphor" is the antithesis of a "grammatically telescoped and, hence, reversible simile." [21]

Cope cites the formulations of Sigurd Burckhardt to argue that metaphor, as "the epitome of the poetic process itself," must "ef-

21. Cope, p. 6. I am inclined to be skeptical about the convergence of Miltonic, Ramistic, and modern views of metaphor, more because of the Miltonic assumptions revealed in chap. 2 than the existence of a "Ramistic" reversibility in similes, discussed above. Cope is quite right in saying that critics long confused the method of the metaphysical poets with "the shape of the poem or the structure of its rationale" (p. 9). Do we not, however, encounter a fictional, projected poet in this poem, one whose discursive difficulties are strategic pretense and thus part of the poem's paradoxical economy? See below, chap. 8.

fect a destructive action prior to its creative function" (Cope, p. 25). Words are signs for things, but the truly poetic medium, in itself "debased by its removal from primary reference," strives to return, in Burckhardt's words, to "the corporeality which a true medium needs."[22] Thus, although ordinarily a system of "signs," language becomes poetry primarily through metaphor, in which words "not only break the distortions of discursive syntax" by restoring the "existential immediacy" intrinsic to musical and plastic media "but outrage and belie the insidious simplicity of perception which infects our ordinary use of language as a system of 'signs'" (Cope, p. 25). The poem, in Cope's account, is an "object" precisely because its language is (again in Burckhardt's term) "corporealized" and only to the extent that its texture thickens and its mere words become (through metaphor, rhyme, or pun) "things" (p. 25).

As a critic, Cope is avowedly concerned with the function rather than the nature of metaphor, and he wishes to isolate "those moments when tenor and vehicle draw so closely together that language becomes an immediate structural clarification, rather than a signatory betrayal, of experience (pp. 4–5), the term which Cope associates with "process." Given such an approach, we may conclude that the ideal poem altogether escapes such betrayal and thus obviates the necessity to distinguish those moments from what Cope calls the primary organization of *Paradise Lost.* Readers who wish to accommodate this account more particularly with the aspect of Miltonic intention that we have examined may well ask two complementary questions at this point: whose organization (or image) *is* this; and, secondly, can we speak critically of a poem which incorporates process or exploits its own discursive limitations? To judge from Milton's discussion of poetry and aesthetics, relatively consistent through the pertinent writing of the 1640s, the ownership or provenience of imagery was clearly crucial. To speak of the narrator in his chameleon aspect, merging easily with Satan and the reader, now and then rising solitarily above even the angel chorus, is not nec-

22. Sigurd Burckhardt, "The Poet as Fool and Priest," *Journal of English Literary History* 23 (1956) : 280; quoted in Cope, p. 25.

essarily illegitimate; it is simply to refer to the built-in "causes" of the poem and to the strategic articulation of its prime mysteries.

More specifically, within Milton's poetic world, it seems misleading to think of process and corporeality as antithetic terms. For if we consider the poem to involve "levels" of discourse and vision (as Raphael's "consummate flow'r" in particular suggests we might), both process and corporeality are *together* opposed to the Holy Light itself, the Logos, and thus to the very unexpressive Image which postromantic theory inclines to identify with the poem. It is helpful to think analogically in considering the wholeness of *Paradise Lost.* But unless we are willing to deny the insistently temporal experience of reading a particular long poem, we are likely to conclude, in this case, that the poem's epitome is not metaphor but something more like Raphael's narration—itself a process of speech, one "so told as earthly notion may receive." Half of Raphael's narration is in fact a simile *involving* the poem's primary metaphor, though patently it *is* not that metaphor. In a sense the most indecorous formal detail in *Paradise Lost,* it likens "spiritual to corporal forms, / As may express them best," a strategy patently "fallen" in its evident pragmatism. According to Milton's metaphoric pattern, things "corporal" are primarily (again in Raphael's phrase) "things conspicuous," roughly the sense in which I shall use "visual" in the pages that follow; and the sociable angel goes so far as to use the variant, "things . . . on Earth conspicuous" (at VI. 299). As we shall see the energy of such "simile" is considerably less for our earth than for Adam's Paradise, and the doubleness of its "reference" would appear to be deliberate. In the pages which follow I shall suggest that (1) simile provides a somewhat fuller epitome at least for the "poetic process" in *Paradise Lost* than does metaphor, partly because Milton would not have distinguished the two; and that (2) it dramatizes the process of *Paradise Lost* in three ways: (*a*) by dramatizing the poet in his various guises; (*b*) largely by referring to "things conspicuous" as the pretext for "unpremeditated" discovery; and (*c*) by itself functioning, in part metaphorically, as the "lowest" and specifically the most "bodily" form of discourse in the poem. Thus, the most time-bound aspect of Milton's epic, within the poem's own fictional coordinates, *is* the most corporeal level stylistically in the poem and serves partly to establish precisely that middle world of human names through which alone fallen men may pierce to the "meaning"—in this poem. It is a world only ostensibly outside the poem, and the poem can only pretend to abjure it entirely.

6

The Contexts of Simile

Eighteenth-century critics of *Paradise Lost,* whose value Christopher Ricks has recently demonstrated, thought of the poem's similes as moments where poet stepped in for narrator.[1] Addison mentioned the characteristic focuses of analysis when he wrote in effect that in the similes the poet quit his fable, often wandering into an "unresembling Circumstance" and sometimes rising to a "great Idea."[2] Such readings did not distinguish poet from narrator *as* poet, but at their best they did focus on the presence of the poet throughout the poem, whether he was a more-or-less transparent medium for his fable or the irrelevant, erring lyricist.

More recent commentary, taking the poem as the primary focus, has neglected such distinctions to concentrate instead on the poem's world or (in the case of the most complete study of Milton's similes) on the relation of the poem to classical precedents). Thus the extent of correspondence between details of context and those within the simile—homologation—was Milton's prime contribution to the epic heritage. Another, harking back to the eighteenth-century distinctions, was the use of simile as more than merely decoration, something apart from narrative and placed (as in Statius) at the end of a verse-paragraph for the sake of epic bravura (see above, chap. 5, n. 18). Concerned more with the general nature of that context, B. Rajan wrote in 1947 that by his count "2,140 lines of *Paradise Lost* are set in Heaven. Yet in all these lines there is not a single complex or multiple simile, only one simile which involves a literary allusion, and only one place name, Biblical or classical."[3]

1. Christopher Ricks, *Milton's Grand Style* (Oxford: Clarendon, 1963), esp. chap. 4.

2. *Spectator,* no. 303, 16 February 1712.

3. B. Rajan, *"Paradise Lost" and the Seventeenth Century Reader* (London: Chatto & Windus, 1947), p. 163.

The observations of Whaler and Rajan suggest two different but related questions: (1) the relation between the different settings of *Paradise Lost* and the use of formal simile, and (2) the relation between this most conventional (and poetic) kind of imagery and narrative. To anticipate our conclusions: (1) I believe that a close reading of the similes themselves forces us to recognize them not as formal ornament but as perceptual crises displaying the narrator/poet in his most informal, "lowest" guise, that of maker and expositor of images—one of the very men to whom the ways of God are to be justified. (2) The similes pretend to refer; they take us outside the poem, to a world presumably recognizable, in order to explain—or to establish—details of the realm within the poem. (3) We may speak of a "world" to which simile refers because of its coherence. Ostensibly, this world is outside the poem; it belongs to us, both as men and as readers. But it also is given a mythic origin within *Paradise Lost,* in the imaginations of the "Sons of Eve," historically "long after" the action of the narrative itself but presented early in the poem, notably in the catalogue.

The similes, then, are part of the way in which the poem as a whole is framed or articulated; they resemble the invocations in calling attention to its presenter, whose difficulties, and primary techniques, in getting at "the meaning, not the name" they so clearly project. We can be more specific about those difficulties. The narrator uses the world of simile to clarify certain details in the worlds of his narrative fable, notably Hell and Eden. We know Milton's Hell, because we are supposed to know the arguments which establish it; but our "superior" knowledge is of a world itself "mingled and involved" with Hell. Moreover, Milton further uses simile in a dramatic or rhetorical way, so as to absorb our response into the narrative one of Satan. Frequently the frame for a particularly intense passage of such poetry serves to disentangle narrative from dramatic or rhetorical responses—to distinguish, that is, reader from the poem's Satan. Clearly, at such moments, a lucidly defined aesthetic scene has been corrupted, and audience, poet, and character become indistinguishable. Where the poet does go on to distinguish, he betrays an extraordinary scrupulousness about his poem's world and its "visibility." And I would suggest that at such moments he calls attention to the status, the validity as it were, of his own poem.

Such a count as Rajan's—and some recent studies have shown that this is a fruitful approach to Milton's poetry, given a healthy dash of skepticism—inevitably suggests a connection between the use of simile (even metaphor) and certain settings. The definition of what precisely constitutes setting may affect such a statistic; and the War in Heaven, for example, *is* a simile, the implications of which we shall develop in chapter 8. But at the very least, there is a sense in which simile is used to present the Hell and Eden of *Paradise Lost,* and we may turn first to the function of simile in that presentation and how, in particular, it involves the function of the poet.

First, then, how is simile used to present Hell, in the description of which so many of the memorable similes occur? If we consider only their most immediate kind of context—their threshold, or what James Whaler called their "grammatical nexus"[4]—we can already account to some degree for the idea that Milton's best poetry was written in the first two books, located as they are in that region of "darkness visible." We may properly doubt that Milton would have comprehended or agreed with the assumptions of readers like Eliot or Waldock that poetry was concerned with rendering a particular concrete reality or even, in Eliot's terms, the processes of a sensibility submerged in experience. But nevertheless, many of the similes take off from an initial term of comparison which is indeed sensuous in a sense remarkably close to Eliot's (and others') postromantic criteria. Angel forms lying "thick as Autumnal Leaves" (*PL* I. 302); Satan's broad shield hanging "like the Moon" (I. 287); Satan viewing the order, visages, and stature of his army and then reacting (I. 573 ff.); Satan standing "in shape and gesture . . . like a Tow'r . . . As when the Sun . . . (I. 590 ff.); all of these and numerous other similes occur precisely in immediate contexts of visualization in some form. In all of them an initial purpose seems quite clearly to be the concrete representation of particular appearances. And it does

4. Whaler, "Grammatical *Nexus* of the Miltonic Simile."

seem that many of these similes contain passages of Milton's best poetry, like the oft-quoted description of Mulciber (I. 740–46).

In most such passages, however, there are immediate complications. As a general strategy, it would seem, Milton forces the distinction between logical and more passionate appeals, as though we cannot be trusted to see the pattern of argument, the "great Idea" in the particular "shapes and forms of things" to which simile usually refers us.[5] As many readers have noticed, there is often a shift in what we would like to call the threshold of simile—an actual change in the ostensible point of comparison.[6] Thinking of Longinus, some eighteenth-century readers saw this as a *loss,* not a shift in threshold, a moment when the poet could leave mere grammar behind as he soared toward the unresembling "great Idea" that was the real function of comparison.[7] But in the following example, describing the land on which Satan first alights, we are clearly dealing with a shift which forces a reexamination of the relation between the poem's facts and the protagonist's feelings. It is a pretended revision, moreover, implying rather unusual scruples about the details of a poem's world:

5. See the letter to Charles Diodati, *CPW,* 1 : 326.

6. See, for example, Ferry, *Milton's Epic Voice,* pp. 66–87, and the critics quoted by Ricks, *Milton's Grand Style.*

7. "When Milton alludes either to Things or Persons, he never quits his Simile till it rises to some very great Idea, which is often foreign to the Occasion that gave Birth to it. The Resemblance does not, perhaps, last above a line or two, but the Poet runs on with the Hint, till he has raised out of it some glorious Image or Sentiment, proper to inflame the Mind of the Reader, and to give it that sublime kind of Entertainment, which is suitable to the Nature of an Heroick Poem" (*Spectator,* no. 303, 16 February 1712). See the discussion by Christopher Ricks (*Milton's Grand Style,* pp. 120–21). Addison anticipates later commentators in suggesting that the nobility of a simile is something distinct from its rhetorical occasion, the initial point of likeness; roughly half of the passage quoted implies a conscious control over the presentation of the "glorious Image or Sentiment." Addison allows that "the *Poet* runs on with the Hint, till he has raised out of it" the glorious image; but he has previously suggested that the simile *itself* "rises to some very great Idea," and his metaphor of the occasion *giving birth* to the sublime image all but cuts the tie between poetry and rhetoric. In short, the rhetorical conception of epic simile is submerged in an account which emphasizes the "poetic" imagination; "poetry" and the imaginative process are on the way to that assumed fusion which came to underlie so much literary criticism. Addison's account is at once somewhat confused and more to the point than Ricks's discussion suggests.

on dry Land
He lights, if it were Land that ever burn'd
With solid, as the Lake with liquid fire
And such appear'd in hue; as when the force
Of subterranean wind transports a Hill
Torn from *Pelorus,* or the shatter'd side
Of thund'ring *Aetna,* whose combustible
And fuell'd entrails thence conceiving Fire,
Sublim'd with Mineral fury, aid the Winds,
And leave a singed bottom all involv'd
With stench and smoke: such resting found the Sole
Of unblest feet.

[I. 227–38] [8]

Moreover, Milton throughout the poem worries the connections between similes merely *referring* to nature and the more definitive "actual" nature of the poem's world, both fallen and unfallen. What are we to say, for example, of the kind of phrase used to describe Satan at the ear of Eve, "Squat like a Toad" (IV. 800)? Certainly we have similitude of a sort. But it defies the old school saw about the limits of analogy; this likeness does *not* limp. A few lines later we are told that Satan resumes his own shape, and the transformation is like a "nitrous" explosion (814–19). Furthermore, immediately following the formal simile likening Satan to the "prowling Wolf . . . or Thief" (IV. 185 ff.), he is not only described metaphorically or typologically as "this first grand Thief" but actually flies up onto the Tree of Life, there to sit "like a Cormorant," watching Adam and Eve.[9] Milton uses

8. In this quotation I have followed the punctuation of the MS. Although Shawcross and Wright among modern editors accept the text of the first edition here, Helen Darbishire argues convincingly for the authority of the MS, and Hughes accepts her reading. See Shawcross, *Complete Poetry of Milton;* B. A. Wright, ed., *Milton's Poems* (London: Dent, 1956); and Helen Darbishire, ed., *The Poetical Works of John Milton* (Oxford: Clarendon, 1952), vol. 1. The evidence, though slight, suggests that Milton intended a fuller stop at line 230 than the comma, perhaps to indicate a more involved elaboration within the comparison, a more extensive pattern of likeness than that initially designated.

9. Whaler calls this "quasisimile" ("The Miltonic Simile," p. 1039). See William Madsen, "'Earth the Shadow of Heaven': Typological Symbolism in *Paradise Lost,*" *PMLA* 75 (1960): 519–26.

simile so self-consciously here (as in book I) that he exploits even the syntactical joints of the formal device, carrying us at times beyond metaphoric likeness, limited and merely pragmatic, to a kind of magic metamorphosis:

> Then from his lofty stand on that high Tree
> Down he alights among the sportful Herd
> Of those fourfooted kinds, himself now one
> Now other, as thir shape serv'd best his end
> Nearer to view his prey, and unespi'd
> To mark what of thir state he more might learn
> By word or action markt: about them round
> A Lion now he stalks with fiery glare,
> Then as a Tiger, who by chance hath spi'd
> In some Purlieu two gentle Fawns at play,
> Straight couches close, then rising changes oft
> His couchant watch, as one who chose his ground
> Whence rushing he might surest seize them both
> Gript in each paw.
>
> [IV. 396–408]

This precise manipulation of simile's ordinary connectives, along with the use of a narrative present tense, allows Milton to mix fallen and unfallen nature in an unexpected way, to say the least. The word *as* here yields to a clause which is in form the usual elaboration of Milton's heroic simile, complete with the formula "by chance" and the pretended casualness of "some Purlieu"; but with the second *as* Milton literally verifies what had seemed to be mere metaphor.

The best recent commentary on such passages has taken the position that the ironic undercutting of poetry is an integral part of its consciously intended meaning, whatever its relation to the psychic repression with which J. B. Broadbent and others are concerned.[10] What happens at such points—the questioning of the poem's presentation, the substitution of verse in its least premeditated, least definitive form—does not necessarily take us outside the poem, it would seem; more immediately, it helps to establish

10. J. B. Broadbent, *Some Graver Subject: An Essay on "Paradise Lost"* (London: Chatto & Windus, 1960), pp. 92–95.

the perceptual difficulties in the poem's world. With other material, it suggests that what seems to us—and to Satan—most real because most concrete, is poetry or "poetic" precisely because it is *merely* an appearance—an image, and as such an "ordinance of man." Something like this is at times explicitly stated; sometimes the difficulty of perspective is suggested at greater distance, though still imaging a crisis in the poem's rhetorical situation. Normally (to the delight of most readers) we are made the viewers of scenes in Hell, and the narrator calls our attention, as above, to the disparity between visual appearances and merely asserted but definitive meanings:

> Before the Gates there sat
> On either side a formidable shape;
> The one seem'd Woman to the waist, and fair,
> But ended foul.
>
> [II. 648–51]

In many similes, however, Milton seems to add a detail apparently extraneous to the images' normal schematic patterns of homologation: a dramatized viewer for the very scene the poet has himself quite concretely "rendered." It is at such points in *Paradise Lost,* I believe, that both fallen audience and poet are most closely engaged: one might even say that here they are identified and most clearly *located* in the poem's implied scheme of things. Of all Milton's rhetorical strategies, the similes most clearly identify our vision as fallen at the same time that they dramatize narrative difficulties; as an important part of the essentially descriptive organic art with which we can partly "repair the ruins of our first parents," they also epitomize the poem's attempt to correct that vision.[11]

It is hardly necessary to add, however, that the narrator is generally more active than we have indicated and that he takes on functions in his poem which range from emotional response to almost magical efficacy, as in book III. At one point in book II,

11. In my discussion of Miltonic simile in its relation to vision and "visual concreteness," I am indebted to Irma Brandeis, *The Ladder of Vision: A Study of Dante's Comedy* (Garden City: Doubleday, 1962).

the narrator interrupts the council of devils with the following words:

> whence
> But from the Author of all ill could spring
> So deep a malice, to confound the race
> Of mankind in one root, and Earth with Hell
> To mingle and involve, done all to spite
> The great Creator?
>
> [II. 380–85]

The form of this intrusion, like its content, is designed to punctuate the moment, to signal a crux in a collective history that belongs to all readers. This is the official plan of action, the projected campaign against *us*. But Milton splits the visions of reader and man; we are dealing with "*another* World, the happy seat / Of some new Race call'd Man" (II. 347–48; my italics). Given luck, the devils will be able

> with Hell fire
> To waste his whole Creation, or possess
> All as our own, and drive as we were driven,
> The puny inhabitants, or if not drive,
> Seduce them to our party.
>
> [II. 364–68]

At the very center of *Paradise Lost* in its 1667 version, the War in Heaven—Raphael's great similitude—works with a similarly rhetorical context easily missed, one which we may describe as involving a discrepancy between the dramatized response of wonder (established by Raphael's and Adam's repeated designation of the spiritual war as "strange" and "hard") and the quite different attitude inevitable for the poem's implied readers. In much the same way, the argument of Milton's more ordinary similes seems to establish an external context, in that they refer to a realm of familiar or (in the seventeenth-century sense) modern experience. But by the time we reach the War in Heaven, we are likely to recall the aims quoted above, precisely by virtue of the commentary surrounding it. If we remember the council, and the urgency with which Milton frames it in the closing lines of book I, we shall not quite laugh at Satan's otherwise ludicrous boast that he will turn Heaven into "the Hell / Thou fabl'st" (VI. 291–92), because we have perceived the primary setting of Milton's own fable, mainly through the very similes which seem to take us outside the poem. Indeed, the interrupted speaker, Beelzebub, is distinguished from previous contributors by his impression (later to be virtually shared by Adam himself) that Adam and the race of man are part of a created pattern of "likeness," already established, between Paradise and an archetypal Hell: man is "like to us, though less / In power and excellence, but favor'd more / Of him who rules above" (II. 349–51).[12] By the time he speaks, of course, the fully cooperating reader will play at agreeing. For Milton himself has not only used "likeness" to render the visual "excellence" of the devils as they gather for the council, he has used the likeness, thus by now doubly familiar, of a wasted creation:

> they stood,
> Thir Glory wither'd. As when Heaven's Fire
> Hath scath'd the Forest Oaks, or Mountain Pines,
> With singed top thir stately growth though bare
> Stands on the blasted Heath.
>
> [I. 611–15]

A major part of Milton's problem initially in *Paradise Lost,* then, is to make a convincing (or decorous) case for a historical, social, and perceptual context in which Adam is almost absolutely *not* of the devil's party, in which earth is not yet mingled and involved with Hell. Inevitably, for the most cooperative readers, Hell is the imaginative or sensuous archetype; the world as it were outside the poem, the mere stuff of simile, is used only to establish the demonic archetype, with which, we are gradually brought to discover, it is "mingled and involved." To put it another way, the action of *Paradise Lost*'s fable, conveys the progressive stages in the mingling and images the tragic extent of

12. For a general discussion of the pattern of analogy, see Douglas Bush, "Ironic and Ambiguous Allusion in *Paradise Lost,*" *Milton Studies in Honor of H. F. Fletcher* (Urbana, Ill.: University of Illinois Press, 1961), pp. 23–32.

Satan's successes in achieving his purposes: the reality—and the poetic if not the "real" primacy—of Satan's anticreation.[13] But as the deliberate use of "Heaven's Fire" in the above passage suggests, another part of the problem is to define the limits of that reality, to develop just as convincingly the sense in which Adam and Eve were neither simply driven from Eden "as we were driven" (II. 366) nor simply seduced to the devil's party: to render, in short, the joy in the "Great Creator," an ultimate providential reality and thus a perspective from which Satan's entire quest, together with all its accomplishments, is seen ironically. It is the root function of simile in solving these partly technical problems that I shall examine in this chapter, the complex and individual handling of a traditional heroic "device." As long as metaphor or "Image" is central in our definition of poetry, it is illuminating to examine the fruits (as well as the blossoms) of a poetic which relied like ours on figurative conceptions, but without our implicit bias against discourse. Such an inquiry is particularly interesting if we recall that ultimately Milton's poetic was in some ways more suspicious of its linguistic and metaphoric bases than our own.

Expository Simile: Presentation and Reference

In the sense that many of Milton's formal images are apparently concerned with the problem of seeing, they are similar to those of Dante; occurring most frequently in the presentation of Hell, they often seem primarily to serve the purpose of concrete visualization, as T. S. Eliot believed was true in the *Inferno*. What escaped Eliot, as Irma Brandeis has shown, is that the imagery of the *Inferno* is in some sense logical even where it seems most purely visual; we see in a more complicated way than we do, say, in an impressionist painting, or an imagist poem.[14]

13. The "Nature" of Hell, in a possible quote from Burton's description of the "phantasy" mentioned above, breeds "Perverse, all monstrous, all prodigious things" (II. 625). See *Anatomy*, p. 140.

14. Brandeis, *Ladder of Vision*, pp. 143–51. On Milton's relation to Dante generally, see Irene Samuel, *Dante and Milton: The "Commedia" and "Paradise Lost"* (Ithaca: Cornell University Press, 1965).

Even more evident in *Paradise Lost* than in the *Commedia,* moreover, is the significance of the form of imagery itself, as a level in the discursive economy of the poem—notably in the sense that it signals a perceptual crisis. The similes reveal how closely integrated the organic arts remained in Milton's thought, and even the kind of pressure he was willing to place on poetry.

To be more specific, we may turn to the relation between visualization and logical argument in a single simile of book I. The first simile of the poem follows one of Satan's first speeches to Beelzebub, his exhortation to rise from the fiery lake. Satan himself is lying prone, "With Head up-lift above the wave, and Eyes / That sparkling blaz'd" (193–94); his "other Parts" also float up on the surface, extended "many a rood." Milton has thus already visualized Satan in the usual sense of that word *before we arrive* at the simile—we already have the sparkling eyes that served Satan's descendants so well through the nineteenth century, for instance. As for the simile itself, the poet is prompted first to convey some sense of Satan's great bulk; he is

as huge
As whom the Fables name of monstrous size,
Titanian, or *Earth-born,* that warr'd on *Jove,*
Briareos or *Typhon,* whom the Den
By ancient *Tarsus* held, or that Sea-beast
Leviathan, which God of all his works
Created hugest that swim th'Ocean stream.
Him haply slumb'ring on the *Norway* foam
The Pilot of some small night-founder'd Skiff,
Deeming some Island, oft, as Seamen tell,
With fixed Anchor in his scaly rind
Moors by his side under the Lee, while Night
Invests the Sea, and wished Morn delays:
So stretcht out huge in length the Arch-fiend lay
Chain'd

[I. 196–210]

The initial point of the comparison is specified both before and after the simile; and the implication is quite clear that we know more about fabled monsters and the biblical Leviathan than we do about the size of Satan in Hell just after the fall from Heaven. But what is striking about this simile, and it is characteristic of many in *Paradise Lost,* is the discrepancy between what the simile claims to do and what actually happens within it.[15] Of the simile's twelve lines, about one and one-half specify the huge referents, the fabled monsters and Leviathan respectively; the rest, we might say, are amplification. Are they mere digression? In Addison's terms, Milton does indeed seem to quit his fable entirely for the moment—though he has done so in favor of the description, not exclusively for the simile's sake. What "happens" in the simile, its digression, however, is patently *staged;* that is the point. It is the narrator, or poet, and not Milton, who is confronted with a crisis in the poem's community of knowledge; it is he who pretends to cast about for appropriate alternative likenesses. And what emerges as it were spontaneously from this improvised performance is an emblematic scene which clearly has little to do with size. Whatever its relation to the poem's fable, though, the simile has definite structure, movement, and even tone. In its shifts of tense, and in what would seem to be a dramatized mood or response to a detail *in the poem,* it reveals the ironies of the present scene in Hell; at the very least, then, the simile complicates our response to the archfiend.

Clearly we must speak of alternative appeals which progress in both time and space. The image moves from fabled monsters warring against a patently classical deity (material from Hesiod and Ovid) to the true, and rather more complicated, situation of the biblical Leviathan, one of God's works which yet wars against mankind. The poet does not labor the distinction between true and feigned narrative here as he does elsewhere in the poem. Instead, in his sequence of reference, he develops an unobtrusive movement from fabled, vaguely "literary" experience toward the hugest of God's "real" created works; and the nature of this rhythm is clear from what now happens. Milton borrows an old story, available in encyclopedic literature anywhere from the Old

15. I do not mean to suggest a gap between conscious and unconscious meaning at this point.

English *Physiologus* to Olaus Magnus and Caxton, and presents it faithfully enough as a "seaman's tale." [16] But the story is dovetailed with the biblical comparison, and despite the fact that the beast is Eastern in its literary origin, Milton gives it a north European setting. Knowing already that Leviathan is the hugest of God's creatures, we encounter Milton's version of the old story, set in a pathetic and emotionally immediate world of random disaster. Its tone is almost one of naïve bewilderment at the frequency of this mishap; it occurs "oft, as Seamen tell." Against the gloomy background of "hap," bad weather (making the lee particularly desirable) and the blackness of night, are projected the pathetic wishes of the pilot on the small boat, with whom we partly sympathize. As told in the *Physiologus,* the story ends, of course, with the plunge and the inevitable doom of those who have deemed him some island. Milton omits the conclusion —at least it is not rehearsed—but the ending, like the meaning of the simile, is hardly in doubt, once we learn of a "fixed Anchor in his scaly rind," a detail at once emblematic and particular. The pilot represents those who place faith in Leviathan or the appearances of power or false security in this world, whatever their intentions or feelings, whatever the dangers involved.

Consider, however, the location of this simile; a near ending placed so close to a poetic beginning both highly literary and "original." Since the pioneering work of James Whaler, the proper question at this point has been the relation of the simile to its immediate context (see above, chap. 5, n. 18). If the most

16. Hughes cites versions of this tale from Olaus Magnus, Caxton's illustrated encyclopedia *Mirrour of the World,* and Bartholomew; Todd cites Hakluyt (*Voyages,* 1 : 568) and Ariosto (*Orlando Furioso,* canto 6, stanza 37). Caxton's version is as follows: "In this see of Ynde is another fysshe so huge and grete that on his backe groweth erth and grasse; and semeth properly that it is a grete Ile. Wherof it happeth somtyme that the maronners saylling by this see ben gretly deceyved and abused; for they wene certaynly that it be ferme londe; wherfor they goo out of their shippes theron, and lyghted their fyre, and made it to brenne after their nede, wenyng it to be on a ferme londe, [but] incontinent as this merueyllous fysshe feleth the hete of the fyre, he meveth hym sodenly and devaleth doun in to the water as depe as he may. And thus all that is uppon hym is lost in the see. And by this moyen, many shippes ben drowned and perisshed, and the peple, when they supposed to be in savete" (Caxton, *Mirrour of the World,* ed. Oliver H. Prior, Early English Text Society O.S. [London, 1913], pp. 88–89).

carefully wrought and emotionally immediate part of the simile has virtually nothing to do with "hugeness" (ostensibly the "idea" of the comparison), what *is* its function? As though anticipating the question, Milton appends an extensive commentary:

> So stretcht out huge in length the Arch-fiend lay
> Chain'd on the burning Lake, nor ever thence
> Had ris'n or heav'd his head, but that the will
> And high permission of all-ruling Heaven
> Left him at large to his own dark designs,
> That with reiterated crimes he might
> Heap on himself damnation, while he sought
> Evil to others, and enrag'd might see
> How all his malice serv'd but to bring forth
> Infinite goodness, grace and mercy shown
> On Man by him seduc't, but on himself
> Treble confusion, wrath and vengeance pour'd.
>
> [I. 209–20][17]

Here and elsewhere the commentary can be read as a definitive explanation, one mode of the assertion mentioned by the poet in the opening invocation. Medieval and Renaissance allegorizers were fond of saying quite explicitly that "the whale is the Devil, who . . ."; and modern scholars have continued the tradition in noting detailed points of correspondence between simile and context. Whaler's word for this schematic tightness, unique in the epic tradition, was "homologation." As the poet's own commentary makes clear, however, *Satan* is chained to the lake in Hell, while in the simile it is the pilot who fixes his anchor in the scaly rind of Leviathan. Milton's Ramist training, and that odd view of imagery expounded so copiously and tediously in his handbook on logic, undoubtedly forced an interest in correspondence or homologation, as we have seen. But judging from this and other images, it would seem that in *Paradise Lost* he deliberately blurs any static pattern we might discover, pretending to discover instead multiple or ambiguous correspondences, and even an entire world of analogy. The "poet's own" com-

17. In lines 790–91 we are told that the devils "*were* at large, / . . . amidst the Hall / Of that infernal Court" (my italics).

mentary we have quoted above certainly suggests that the primary interest of the similes must lie in the implications its own small scene clarifies in the immediate situation of the fable. The irony of the devils' position in Hell, the paradoxical involvement of the simile's human figure at once in heaping damnation on Satan and bringing forth "infinite goodness"; the commentary of the poem's first simile serves to clarify what may be called the poetic moment's historical outcome, its "event," and suggests that the function of Miltonic simile is to do so, even where it pretends to amplify such simpler (and more sensuous) likenesses as the hugeness or magnificence of Satan.

As we might expect, the early similes, like other details, serve to establish the poem's world as well as suggest the nature of our relation to it. Though the examples we have examined are not confined to book I, they have dramatized a relatively neutral narrator or presenter. They represent moments when our relation to Hell becomes more self-conscious, more critical or problematic; and they do so by making the presentation unusually scrupulous or merely more discursive. Eliot could well be speaking of such moments as well as Satan's speeches in saying that Milton "writes English like a dead language." The poet at such times, we might say, is a public man, sharing with the reader his difficulties in the face of the poem's mysteries. No vision or flight of fancy cuts him off from his audience, taking him either into himself or (alternatively) above the poles and toward the Holy Light. He is most clearly one of us; and as a stylist he is most clearly time-bound, most evidently at the mercy of his own unpremeditated process of speech.

All of this, however, is less complicated than the facts of the poem itself. As we have seen, the umpremeditated "error" of simile often wanders into a circumstance which establishes the ironies of a narrative scene; "low" as they may seem stylistically, *as forms of perception* they bring us closer than does the "purer" narrative (narrative without the directive commentary) to the highest kind of awareness in the poem, contained ultimately in God's "prospect high" (see *PL* III. 77). Furthermore, if we read them closely, we discover to our surprise the practical difficulty even of distinguishing the "what happens" of narrative from the built-in apparatus of perception which we call drama. Unaware of Locke and Wordsworth, and seemingly mistrustful of collective or "racial" experience, Milton provides *both* narrative and drama in this sense virtually throughout his poem, for the most part absorbing one into another. Though it is true also of the earliest parts of the poem, it seems particularly clear in the presentation of Eden that the narrator's perspective is hardly the neutral medium we might expect. For many readers, one feels, Eden is hardly made mysterious *enough;* although they rarely examined the source of their response, the anti-Miltonists in particular seemed to recognize Milton's Paradise all too easily.

C. S. Lewis's reading of *Paradise Lost* reminds us that the antagonists did not speak for all modern readers in failing to respond sympathetically to Milton's description of Paradise.[18] But if we are not as immediately engaged as Lewis, there is an important warrant to be found in Milton's frequent reminders about the nature of our relation to Eden. As in the portrayal of Heaven, Milton's account serves almost always to recall the inevitable gap in perception separating us from the immediate vitality of unfallen Eden. The reason a re-creation of Comus's libertine Nature would not be appropriate here, as J. B. Broadbent suggests, is that Eden is represented in the poem as still existing, but as a dream from which we have just awakened.[19] For us, as for Satan, the earthly Paradise is an object of desire; but while Milton can present Eden with great appeal, we are forced to recognize that our nostalgia is directed at the very object of Satan's destructive will. To a great extent, indeed, it is with Satan that we view, and sometimes covet, Milton's unfallen Eden.[20]

It is primarily because Eden is seen simultaneously through Satan's eyes and through our (or the poet's) imaginative "art" that Milton's Paradise seems corrupted, and on the verge of history, almost at once. The presentation of Eden exactly suits—

18. C. S. Lewis, *A Preface to "Paradise Lost"* (London: Oxford University Press, 1942).

19. Broadbent, *Some Graver Subject,* pp. 176–77.

20. Frank Kermode, "Adam Unparadiz'd," in *The Living Milton: Essays by Various Hands,* ed. Frank Kermode (London: Routledge & Kegan Paul, 1960), pp. 106–13.

in fact, taken as a whole, it serves largely to create—the fallen reader's distance from God's Garden; and once again, the heroic similes contribute solidly to the impression that the poet's art has fundamental rhetorical connections with Satan's essential vision. Their distribution alone suggests that simile has to do not merely with mingling and involving earth with Hell but (at least initially) with the way in which Eden is actually seen in the poem, at once by Satan and by the reader. As Satan approaches the earth, he lingers at the now empty Limbo of Vanity, not entirely out of idle curiosity: the delay is likened (at III. 431 ff.) to a vulture loitering on the plains of Sericana while en route to better regions for prey. One hundred lines later, high in flight, Satan "looks down with wonder at the sudden view / Of all this world at once" (III. 542–43); the wondrous view and Satan's reaction are presented in a simile suggesting that Satan sees "this world" almost exactly as he has just seen Heaven. A simile once again involving Galileo gives us a human perspective on Satan at this point (III. 588 ff.). As Satan approaches more closely (IV. 131 ff.), we begin to get the kind of description which is partly qualified or dramatized; significantly, we also get a whole cluster of extended similes, many of them specifically including reminders of Satan's gazing presence.[21] With the mythological similes and their inevitable prolepsis, the temporal formulas ("not yet," "since") become much more frequent and open, reminding us that prolepsis is quite different from the novelist's devices of anticipation. The necessity of comparisons involving time, fabled places, and their stories seems to arise the moment Satan enters the Garden.

How does simile function in the presentation of unfallen Eden? It now appears that we cannot ask the question in this form, since the Garden itself can never be presented outside the context of the very art which is so much a vehicle for Satan's own interests. Since Eden is presented, indeed, partly through Satan's eyes, we can come close only to such ambiguous details as "vegetable gold," like the work of the kingly palace gate in Heaven itself.

21. See *PL* IV. 159 ff., 168 ff., 183 ff. (in which Satan actually leaps into "God's fold" like animals of prey and an exploiter of "metropolis"), and the mythological similes beginning at line 268.

The additional irony, that Satan's entrance into Eden and his "gestures fierce" are also observed from a higher viewpoint, is suggested indirectly but firmly; we have seen this kind of irony at work in the similes for Hell as a kind of ironic optic glass.[22] Throughout the poem, as I have suggested, Milton does not limit himself to a single consistent perspective; he employs rather multiple viewpoints and calls our attention sometimes to one of these, sometimes to another. As Satan approaches Eden, we are subjected first to his view:

> So on he fares, and to the border comes
> Of *Eden,* where delicious Paradise,
> Now nearer, crowns with her enclosure green,
> As with a rural mound the champaign head
> Of a steep wilderness, whose hairy sides
> With thicket overgrown, grotesque and wild,
> Access deni'd
>
> [IV. 131–37]

But just as we appear to pan in on the Garden's vegetation, Milton shifts abruptly to the viewpoint of Adam, attributing to him virtually the same view, if not the same vision, that Satan will enjoy once inside a few lines later (205 ff.) and, at the same time, with ambiguous pronouns confusing us as to who really *is* seeing all this:

> The verdurous wall of Paradise up sprung:
> Which to our general Sire gave prospect large
> Into his nether Empire neighboring round.
> And higher than that Wall a circling row
> Of goodliest Trees at once of golden hue
> Appear'd, with gay enamell'd colors mixt:
> On which the Sun more glad impress'd his beams
> Than in fair Evening Cloud, or humid Bow,

22. IV. 117, 125 ff. Though Satan's hypocrisy is "the only evil that walks / Invisible, except to God alone" (III. 683–84), the angels (which are called God's "eyes," III. 650) can see the other sins. Uriel, as "the sharpest-sighted Spirit of all in Heav'n" (III. 691), can distinguish this world from the other shining "Globes" and points to Paradise for Satan; it is Uriel who sees Satan's "gestures fierce and mad demeanor, then alone, / As he suppos'd, all unobserv'd, unseen" (IV. 128–29).

When God hath show'r'd the Earth; so lovely seem'd
That Lantskip: and of pure now purer air
Meets his approach, and to the heart inspires
Vernal delight and joy, able to drive
All sadness but despair.

[IV. 143–56] [23]

Only with the last line, perhaps, can we be sure we are getting back to Satan, and even here we are given only a statement about the *general* power of the spectacle. By such shifts and ambiguities, Milton suggests the great beauty of the place almost regardless of viewer. He gets back to Satan's particular reaction in a pair of similes which ironically foreshadow the ultimate defeat:

As when to them who sail
Beyond the *Cape of Hope,* and now are past
Mozambic, off at Sea North-East winds blow
Sabean odors from the spicy shore
Of Araby the blest, with such delay
Well pleas'd they slack thir course, and many a League
Cheer'd with the grateful smell old Ocean smiles.
So entertain'd those odorous sweets the Fiend
Who came thir bane, though with them better pleas'd
Than *Asmodeus* with the fishy fume,
That drove him, though enamor'd from the Spouse
Of *Tobit's* Son, and with a vengeance sent
From *Media* post to *Egypt,* there fast bound.

[IV. 159–71]

Even as Milton's highly artful presentation of Paradise implies a world of organic richness, then, it also insists on Eden's remoteness. Like Raphael's elaborate discourses in books V–VI, it is often apparently framed with apology; it emphasizes its own artifice and at times even fuses with Satan's vision, which itself is remarkably *independent* in projecting the Hell within him.[24] The man-

23. Compare with this shift the more purely visual change in perspective of II. 629–44.

24. See in particular *PL* VI. 472 for the kind of vision involved in Satan's doctrine of invention.

ner of such fusion is by no means always clear-cut, especially if we forget the complications of attitude in which Milton seems to delight. Given the passages we have just examined, we might be hard pressed to identify the speaker of the following lines, for instance. It is Raphael, warning Adam against disobedience, but the passage is characteristic of Milton's art in describing the unfallen Garden, the similitude of Heaven:

> that Earth now
> Seem'd like to Heaven, a seat where Gods might dwell,
> Or wander with delight, and love to haunt
> Her sacred shades: though God had not yet rain'd
> Upon the Earth, and man to till the ground
> None was, but from the Earth a dewy Mist
> Went up and water'd all the ground, and each
> Plant of the field, which ere it was in the Earth
> God made, and every Herb before it grew
> On the green stem.
>
> [VII. 328–37]

Even as Raphael addresses Adam, with what may be an allusion to his own pivotal symbol of the bright consummate flower, we know that "Gods" in this poem are likely to be human inventions—the waiting devils at this point are "godlike shapes and forms"—and that even now there is no man precisely specialized "to till the ground" (I. 358). The hint of awe and even apology at the lack of progress, indeed, sounds suspiciously demonic for readers, even though in context the speech works decorously enough as the kind of warning to which Adam does respond.

More characteristically, however, Milton is careful to introduce us to Eden as Satan's companion, and potentially even as an "archetypally" fallen participant in what we see. At several points our own nostalgia is used to amplify or explain Satan's reactions; whether in the Garden or at the foot of Heaven's stairs, we are most like Satan precisely at the moments when he is "stupidly good." Satan's initial view of Heaven's stairs is precisely identified with Jacob's dream-vision (the poem, after all, concerns itself with the origin of all such heavenly visions), but in this instance, Satan is apparently more interested in the facade:

> Far distant he descries
> Ascending by degrees magnificent
> Up to the wall of Heaven a Structure high,
> At top whereof, but far more rich appear'd
> The work as of a Kingly Palace Gate
> With Frontispiece of Diamonds and Gold
> Imbellisht
>
> [III. 501–7] [25]

Clearly we respond to the rich appearance of the palace gates with Satan; and if we are forgetful we do so less critically than, say, the second time we encounter the rich "structure" of Pandemonium. Satan rightly stands in awe of this wondrous sight, but he is more impressed by the magnificent artifice of the gate than the fact that it belongs to *Heaven's* king. When he "looks down with wonder" at the universe a few lines later, the analogy for his response is the enthusiastic wonder of the explorer first confronting one of the New World's golden cities:

> As when a Scout
> Through dark and desert ways with peril gone
> All night; at last by break of cheerful dawn
> Obtains the brow of some high-climbing Hill,
> Which to his eye discovers unaware
> The goodly prospect of some foreign land
> First seen, or some renown'd Metropolis
> With glistering spires and Pinnacles adorn'd,
> Which now the Rising Sun gilds with his beams.
>
> [III. 543–51]

It is a mistake to identify the scout's prospect too precisely with Satan's here, or at least with that of a purely malignant Satan; this scout, like the pathetic mariner or the fatigued "Seafaring men o'erwatcht" of II. 288, welcomes the wished morn with a relief we can share. If we miss the real cheer of this dawn, we have only to recall the invocation framing this segment of the poem, mentioning the poet in his most pathetic and lowest

25. The sight, Milton goes on, is in effect another "Lantskip," a work of art "inimitable on Earth / By model, or by shading Pencil drawn" (508–09).

aspect: rolling his eyes in vain for the return of day itself. Both the responses of the simile have to do with an eye which is unaware of certain possibilities in the scene; but it is necessary to add that they are comprehensible because they are images for wonder to a degree abstracted from its essential evil.[26]

At this point, then, Milton unravels a generalized, unassigned response, in which his own narrator would seem to share, as though to split rhetorical from narrative responses:

> Such wonder seiz'd, though after Heaven seen,
> The Spirit malign, but much more envy seiz'd
> At sight of all this World beheld so fair.
>
> [552–54]

In another example, Milton complicates the narrative response with catalogue and finally with the definitive commentary of the narrator:

> Beneath him with new wonder now he views
> To all delight of human sense expos'd
> In narrow room Nature's whole wealth, yea more,
> Heaven on Earth; for blissful Paradise
> Of God the Garden was, by him in the East
> Of *Eden* planted; *Eden* stretch'd her line
> From *Auran* Eastward to the Royal Tow'rs
> Of Great *Seleucia* built by *Grecian* Kings
> Or where the Sons of *Eden* long before
> Dwelt in *Telassar:* in this pleasant soil
> His far more pleasant Garden God ordain'd;
> Out of the fertile ground he caus'd to grow
> All Trees of noblest kind for sight, smell, taste;
> And all amid them stood the Tree of Life,
> High eminent, blooming, Ambrosial Fruit
> Of vegetable Gold; and next to Life
> Our Death the Tree of Knowledge grew fast by
> Knowledge of Good bought dear by knowing ill.
>
> [IV. 205–22]

26. "Essential" here because located outside the reader's ken in this poem; in such moments Satan is abstracted from the kind of vision described at VI. 472 ff.

Our own knowledge and history here are used not only to explain but even to justify Satan's "new wonder." With Satan we see nature's whole wealth first as expansive space, measured in the extent of historical kingdoms extinct only to us, then (moving backward in time) in one kingdom established by our predecessors the fallen "Sons of Eden," then within the Garden itself. Temporarily our eye follows, *is,* Satan's, not merely from the farthest reaches of Eden's geography to the tree next to the one Satan occupies "like a Cormorant" (IV. 194–96) but perhaps even from the bloom to the "vegetable Gold"—a phrase perfectly suggesting the ambiguity of "that life-giving plant" depending on its use (IV. 199–201). The way in which such a collective glance seems to light, with genuine wonder, on the "vegetable Gold" in this passage is like Satan's earlier responses to Heaven and the first prospect of "all this world at once" (III. 543), a view distinguished from God's chiefly, it would seem, by its lack of historical or providential perspective.

Milton emphasizes both the transience of our glimpse of unfallen Eden here and the ambiguous, even dangerous, possibilities of a description which itself is patently a word of "art." What Satan, together with the reader of this poem, inevitably sees in Eden is the substance also found underground in Hell—and even in Heaven, for those angels whose vision is not superficial: "Groves, whose rich Trees wept odorous Gums and Balm, / Others whose fruit burnisht with Golden Rind / Hung amiable" (IV. 247–49). There is no need of a heroic account of the kingdoms visited by the rivers of Paradise,

> But rather to tell how, if Art could tell,
> How from the Sapphire fount the crisped Brooks,
> Rolling on Orient Pearl and sands of Gold,
> With mazy error under pendant shades
> Ran Nectar
>
> [236–40]

We need not worry that Milton means to apologize for those final two words, which so powerfully image the "enormous bliss" of the poem's Eden. The point of such qualification is neither merely that Paradise is the archetype of all luxury nor even that all this really transcends art somehow. More nearly it would seem to be the opposite; by including the program, as it were—the imaginative matrix of the poetry—the poet alerts us to the status of the proceeding fiction and even, perhaps, to the way in which its own mazy error may serve to recall the "base originals" of those riches in Milton's Hell.

Expository Simile:
The Basis of Reference

It now seems clear that any complete account of the structural significance of simile involves not merely a world of reference apparently outside the poem but a narrative origin, mythic in its nature, for that world within the poem's confines. For the account of that origin, perhaps surprisingly, we must turn to Milton's use of another conventional device, the epic catalogue, and to the way in which it serves to establish in part the world of *Paradise Lost.*

When Satan has arrived at the shore of the burning lake and calls to his legions, Milton's narrative again becomes enmeshed with a well-known simile, this one used somewhat differently:

> he stood and call'd
> His Legions, Angel Forms, who lay intrans't
> Thick as Autumnall Leaves that strow the Brooks
> In *Vallombrosa,* where th'Etrurian shades
> High overarch't imbow'r; or scatter'd sedge
> Afloat, when with fierce Winds *Orion* arm'd
> Hath vext the Red-Sea Coast, whose waves o'erthrew
> *Busiris* and his *Memphian* Chivalry,
> While with perfidious hatred they pursu'd
> The Sojourners of *Goshen,* who beheld
> From the safe shore thir floating Carcasses
> And broken Chariot Wheels; so thick bestrown
> Abject and lost lay these, covering the flood,
> Under amazement of thir hideous change.
>
> [I. 300—13] [27]

27. The initial comparison of multitudes to leaves, as Todd observed, occurs without elaboration in Homer and Virgil. Among modern writers it oc-

Even more clearly than in previous examples, the poet designates an apparently sensuous point of comparison, the way the devils are "thick bestrown." He then goes on to dramatize both logic and its limits in suggesting that any comparative argument inevitably involves complication; although that initial, intended point of comparison is twice indicated (in references to the leaves and the scattered sedge), a third and more appropriate likeness in the "floating Carcasses / And broken Chariot Wheels" appears as an accidental ramification of the second.

But although the simile thus pretends to concern the physical situation of the fallen angels in Hell, the logical aspect of the simile is closely related with the irony that is its primary effect. Presented though they are as an innocuous "unresembling Circumstance," the accidental ramifications of the logical comparison are all ironic in their suggestions. Even as he makes the image particular, focusing it in space and time, Milton also hints at the design which contains, and places, the devils' evil. The autumnal leaves at Vallombrosa paradoxically fall from evergreen trees, and the entire scene is surrounded spatially (imbowered) by the Etrurian shades. The historical and moral irony of the devils' situation is even clearer, though Milton moves into it unobtrusively. Though the devils' bodies are likened throughout to the floating sedge, the subordinate clause provides an incidental likeness of another sort. Milton moves from a timeless present verb form describing the sedge on the Red Sea in storms to a particular notable *instance,* the biblical crossing of the Red Sea, in which the winds and waves of a somewhat obviously typological "Orion arm'd / . . . o'erthrew / Busiris and his Memphian Chivalry" (305–7). More important in this pretense of digression is the suggested historical "event" to the pursuit of men. We are reminded that the devils are ultimately doomed to the same kind of divine overthrow experienced by Pharaoh's army.

---

curs in Dante, Tasso (*Gerusalemme Liberata,* canto 9, stanza 66), and Ariosto. In Dante (*L'Inferno,* canto 3, stanza 112), the leaves are in heaps upon the ground. Ariosto has a simile of autumn foliage in *Orlando Furioso* (canto 14, stanza 75); at canto 22, stanza 36, he also describes Vallombrosa, the renowned vale (eighteen miles from Florence) perhaps actually visited by Milton. The trees at Vallombrosa are evergreen but (like many evergreens) shed abundantly.

What distinguishes this passage from Dante's use of a similar image (in the first canto of *L'Inferno*) is the way in which Milton makes the reader of the poem, not merely the poet/reporter, part of the miniature narrative analogue.[28] In attempting to convey a visual sense of this scene, the speaker moves easily from natural observation to biblical geography and then, quite casually, to a notable instance of God's care for man in Judeo-Christian history. Even more foreshortened is the sense of time within the historical episode alone. To our surprise, the sojourners of Goshen appear to watch their *own* exodus and the defeat of the pursuing armies. But by virtue of the poem's way of presenting scenes, *we become* those sojourners as our eyes move from the leaves to the sedge (half biblical, half geographical) and then all the way back to the carcasses and broken chariot wheels of the Memphian chivalry. If we read the image correctly, the analogy reminds us that the narrative scene in Hell is the archetypal origin for an even more ultimate defeat as well as for the loss of an earthly Paradise.

It is this simultaneous presence of reader and poet which enables us to balance our response between the poetic wonders of the narrative and the less simple assurance of the clarifying commentary and irony. The point emerges most clearly when we ask how the carcasses and broken chariot wheels of those soldiers can provide a "more appropriate" likeness for the way the devils are lying on the burning lake: an important consideration in a poem involving "anthropomorphism" so self-consciously. The narrative line in this section (I. 331–615) follows the devils from the moment they first awaken from the "amazement of thir hideous change" and their flight to the shore of the burning lake to the formation into squadrons, the parade in front of Satan and the reader—all of this a narrative action implied in details of the epic catalogue—Satan's own dramatized reaction to his "embodied

28. E come quei che con lena affannata
uscito fuor del pelago alla riva
si volge all'acqua perigliosa e guata,
cosi l'animo mio, ch'ancor fuggiva,
si volse a retro a rimirar lo passo
che non lascio gia mai persona viva.
[*l'Inferno,* canto I, stanzas 22–27]

force," and finally the spectacle of his own physical appearance. More than any other extended passage in *Paradise Lost,* this is saturated with the kind of clarifying shifts, particularly within the catalogue itself, from which we cannot rightly dissociate simile in the poem.

The narrative passage leading into the catalogue itself is indistinguishable structurally from the previous simile, which serves in part to visualize the amazed prostration of the devils. Part of its purpose is to convey some sense of their flight to the shore. It is in fact the first time the devils are compared directly to men:

> They heard, and were abasht, and up they sprung
> Upon the wing; as when men wont to watch
> On duty, sleeping found by whom they dread,
> Rouse and bestir themselves ere well awake.
> Nor did they not perceive the evil plight
> In which they were, or the fierce pains not feel;
> Yet to thir General's Voice they soon obey'd;
> Innumerable. As when the potent Rod
> Of *Amram's* Son in *Egypt's* evil day
> Wav'd round the Coast, up call'd a pitchy
> Cloud of *Locusts,* warping on the Eastern Wind,
> That o'er the Realm of impious *Pharaoh* hung
> Like Night, and darken'd all the Land of *Nile.*
> So numberless were those bad Angels seen
> Hovering on wing under the Cope of Hell
> 'Twixt upper, nether, and surrounding Fires;
> Till, as a signal giv'n, th'uplifted Spear
> Of thir great Sultan waving to direct
> Thir course, in even balance down they light
> On the firm brimstone, and fill all the Plain;
> A multitude like which the populous North
> Pour'd never from her frozen loins, to pass
> *Rhene* or the *Danaw,* when her barbarous Sons
> Came like a Deluge on the South, and spread
> Beneath *Gibraltar* to the *Lybian* sands.
> Forthwith from every Squadron and each Band
> The Heads and Leaders thither haste where stood

Thir great Commander; Godlike shapes and forms
Excelling human, Princely Dignities,
And Powers that erst in Heaven sat on Thrones.
[I. 331–60] [29]

The frenzied bestirring of the men in the first simile tells us much more about the devils than that they heard and sprang up —pointed up by the paradoxical "Yet," it expands and clarifies a neglected ingredient of their existence, their abashment. The *motion* of the devils in the narrative context, a motion implied throughout the simile, is made to image the psychology of the situation, the question of motivation. Milton clearly gives us the devils' point of view—or that of anyone who, like the pilot of the first simile, follows Satan—by appealing to a kind of knowledge we all possess: of the confused state between consciousness and unconsciousness, of the horror of consciously neglecting duties and being found out by a feared superior. With utmost economy, Milton sketches the complicated psychology behind the very phenomenon we are watching, the painful but nevertheless prompt obedience to a dreaded and mistaken commander.

The second simile is even more complicated, although at the level of logic it pretends to be more precise, an image of innumerability. Like the comparison to the leaves at Vallombrosa, this one ends with a "prospect"; we become the beholders of the hovering "bad Angels." Once, again, the *innumerability* of the angels, ostensibly the simile's raison d'être, is kept in mind throughout; the final reminder, "so numberless," simply names the quality suggested by the cloud of locusts and further developed later in the passage. But more significant here is the fact that the comparison adduces many more analogies than it pretends to; the logical argument, seemingly by its very nature (its

29. In the MS at line 338, there is an apparently authoritative correction from "Innumerable, as when . . ." to "Innumerable. As when . . ." (see Helen Darbishire, ed., *The Manuscript of Milton's "Paradise Lost" Book I* [Oxford: Clarendon, 1931], pp. xxxix–xl, MS p. 15). The disjunct simile would be a favorite bit of evidence for those (following Addison) who claim that Milton's mind wanders in the similes "into some unresembling Circumstances" (Zachary Pearce, quoted in Ricks, *Milton's Grand Style,* p. 122); but it is an unusual connection for Milton, and has more than once raised problems of punctuation in textual editing. See above, n. 8.

ratio, Milton might say), *cannot help* involving the likeness in a context of historical event. If discursive reason invents a concrete image or sketches a scene in a simile, the analogous scene is inevitably more significant as a whole than the narrative situation it is meant to illuminate in but one concrete respect. Here, for example, we are reminded of the likeness between the devils' "evil plight" (335) and "Egypt's evil day," in which another impious ruler *met defeat.* Furthermore, the disparity of the simile here is equally important, and Milton emphasizes it. Milton does not give us the likeness for the devils' innumerability until we learn who *summoned* the locusts—Moses ("Amram's Son"), who bears the office of Christ "in figure," as Michael tells Adam in book XII (240–41).[30] The irony of providential control is clear enough without the additional homologous detail, gratuitously and self-consciously added after the fact: "th'uplifted Spear / Of *thir* great Sultan."

Brilliant as all this may be, it is so tidily enclosed within the simile, as it were—the connections so neatly made—that we may well have lost the wonder so essential in that balance of the reader's attitude, the wonder at represented origins of his own experience and history. As the catalogue illustrates, to say that the primary effect of the similes is to widen the implications and suggest the ironies of the immediate narrative action at any given point is by no means to imply that in them Milton "lets his fable stand still"—that favorite bias about the similes of all epics, it would seem. Like Waldock, Addison thought of the poem as essentially a narrative; when he praised a rhetorical figure, he did so because it seemed to underline the importance of a particular incident. If we look carefully at the separate visual points of likeness in the similes of book I, however, we might well argue that, even as Milton clarifies the action in the rhetorical figures, he implies an evolving phantasmagory (to use T. S. Eliot's word) on a virtually independent narrative level (Eliot, p. 156). The fable thus appears to continue, as it were imagistically, via the impressions

30. The narrative in book XII describing the "figures" of Christ has the effect of dramatizing material which before the Fall appears only in simile. Rhetorically, this has the effect of dramatically *identifying* Adam with the reader, whom (we may recall) Adam *includes.* For a discussion of this aspect of simile, see below, chap. 7.

that are poetry's peculiar contribution to knowing, at the same time that we are coming to know in other, subtler, ways.

It is in this sense that the floating carcasses and chariot wheels of Pharaoh's army provide an incidental visual likeness to the "Angel forms" which is more appropriate than the original comparisons to leaves or sedge. Milton's language, however, refers at once to the *psychological* state of the angels and to the fact that they are physically "strait'n'd" (as Milton words it later in book I); scene is metaphor for psyche. The angels do not merely lie "as thick as"—Milton tells us that they lie "intrans't thick as . . ." The words framing the simile, as well as those within it, point to an image both about the appearances in Hell and the devils' state of mind: ". . . so thick bestrown / Abject and lost lay these, covering the flood, / Under amazement of thir hideous change" (311–13). What Milton seems to suggest in the mere sequence of visual impressions is that the "hideous change" continues, as it were, before our very eyes.

It is precisely because we think too quickly of anthropomorphic meanings here for the word "form" that we may miss the progression. These are spiritual "Angel forms," recently "spirits of purest light" (we learn later in the poem, VI. 660)—spirits "now gross by sinning grown" (VI. 660–61). A crucial element in their hideous change, then, is the transformation from souls of pure light to visible forms, or "figures." The "incidental" progression of visual impressions, then (from vegetable to human and even "godlike" forms), can perhaps be taken to suggest a gradual accommodation to our own experience, a gradual corporealization of the angel forms, reversed and only gradually humanized in Hell.

The word "form" is significantly used throughout the poem; but it is crucial especially from the Vallombrosa simile through the catalogue. In the series of similes presented during the devils' flight to the shore, the fallen angels are initially compared to men; finally, after landing, they are referred to as having "Godlike *shapes and* forms," a phrase significantly different from angel forms. Later Milton makes much of the brutish form worshiped early in human history (I. 481). Throughout the book Milton is concerned to emphasize the brevity of the devils' stay in Hell and to accentuate their rising and quick passage to an earthly career in the figures of men—a career, it would seem, which is implied throughout the poem and responsible for its poet's occasional passionate outbursts. It is for this reason, I believe, that form and likeness—as well as the names to which we have already alluded—continue to be emphasized as we pass into the epic catalogue itself and, beyond it, to the construction of that very palpable temple of Pandemonium.

Whether or not Milton means to imply the gradual corporealization I have suggested, such an effect does seem to fit his purpose of suggesting an imaginative movement of evil *toward the reader* in book I. We can be somewhat more definite regarding the narrative "implied behind" the simile involving Amram's son. Even as we begin to visualize the devils *as men* or (later in this passage) as pagan "Godlike shapes and forms," we are told that the devils sprang "upon the wing." In what follows, the narrative is mixed with incidental impressions visually appropriate for the devils' flight safe to the shore and for their massing on the plain —as well as "logically" suggesting the ultimate defeat of the devils in history. In the final simile of three in this passage, we still "see" only the "multitude" far greater than the barbarians who overcame Rome in human history; and Milton's use of visual perspective, if that is what is suggested by the metaphor of spreading liquid, puts us at a great distance from them. But then we view "every Squadron and each Band" and finally the individual leaders themselves, moving toward the great commander.

The catalogue of devils represents the introduction of these individual devils: "Godlike shapes and forms / Excelling human"; more than simply a list of names, it implies an action, a progression of leaders who come "singly where he stood on the bare strand, / While the promiscuous crowd stood yet aloof" (I. 379–80). Beyond this, however, the catalogue's basic strategy—and in particular the kind of temporal reference it employs as its mode of argument—is that of the similes writ large. As readers we can know these devils only through their later exploits against humanity, as partly recorded in biblical history. The accounts of the exploits, in turn, serve to explain further the devils' evolving godlike shapes and forms, for our fallen knowledge of gods is actually embodied in the likeness of them which we create—and this in a quite literal sense actually recapitulated in reading the poem. In the present scene, as "later" at the gates of Hell, the devils *themselves* seem to have no true shape or even existence—no form, at least in any anthropomorphic sense.[31] Without names in Heaven, they have as yet no "new names" given them by the sons of Eve:

> till wandering o'er the Earth,
> Through God's high sufferance for the trial of man,
> By falsities and lies the greatest part
> Of Mankind they corrupted to forsake
> God thir Creator, and th'invisible
> Glory of him that made them, to transform
> Oft to the Image of a Brute, adorn'd
> With gay Religions full of Pomp and Gold,
> And Devils to adore for Deities:
> Then were they known to men by various Names,
> And various Idols through the Heathen World.
>
> [I. 365–75]

Needless to say, this bit of history describes a pattern or sequence in human experience much later than the Fall. But for Milton, "immediate are the acts of God"; the seeds of latter-day history are contained in the original catastrophe, a prime aspect of which—especially for readers of poetry—he here defines at the outset of his poem. The focus here is on a crucial moment at once in the life of individual men and of whole civilizations. Milton believed that the origin of "human Names" was inseparable from the origin of *human* religions, and inevitably, of human (only sometimes anthropomorphic) *likeness*. Thus, fallen human language, originating with "names," is for our purposes one of the most important subjects of the Muse's catalogue; the account of brutish idolatries is a fitting stage in the gradual corporealization of the devils in Hell, not to mention the ultimate incorpora-

31. Joseph H. Summers makes a similar observation with regard to Sin and Death. See *The Muse's Method: An Introduction to "Paradise Lost"* (Cambridge: Harvard University Press, and London: Chatto & Windus, 1962), pp. 32–70.

tion of them in Pandemonium. The origin of names and of communal languages is, within the poem's fictional coordinates, located in the realm of visible, corporeal shapes and is alien to (or rather, in degree *beneath*) the realm of spirits and "th'invisible / Glory of Him that made them" (369–70). We are not far removed, in the way in which we are educated to read the catalogue, from Milton's theory of logic and the attempt, embodied in the very style of *Paradise Lost,* to recover a truly spiritual (as opposed to merely verbal) poetic language.

As a whole, then, Milton's scene presents such "Angel forms" as we can understand only by the historical careers of the devils; the leaders coming singly toward Satan and reader from the "promiscuous crowd" in the background are those "who from the Pit of Hell / [Roam] to seek their prey on earth" (381–82). The history of their careers "long after" is presented chiefly as the corruption of the individual soul (or "temple not made with hands") and thus a chronicle of assaults against the "house of God" (470) or the church. Thus, while the devils are presented as individual names, we can perceive them only as the institutions and particular idols or "godlike forms" to which the poem's narrative will gradually introduce us. Thus the catalogue represents a link between the comparison with those fabled individuals of the first simile who "warr'd on Jove" (198) and the elaborate institutionalization of Satan's "imbodied force" which culminates visually in the poem with the dreamlike emergence of Pandemonium.

The catalogue embodies the dynamics of the first book—and of the poem as a whole—in other ways too. In introducing the devils *via* the signs of their historical careers, Milton partly avoids different kinds of "history" later incorporated into books V–VII and XI–XII by concentrating our attention, as I have suggested, on names.[32] Taken by themselves, however, simultaneously as references and impressions, the names suggest rapid movement in space and time:

> Next *Chemos,* th'obscene dread of *Moab's* Sons,
> From *Aroar* to *Nebo,* and the wild

32. Two single heroes, one a seer, do resemble Abdiel and the heroic figures of books XI and XII; Josiah, who drove the followers of Chemos to Hell (I. 418), and Ezekiel, who saw the wanton passions of "the Syrian damsels" in the "dark Idolatries of alienated Judah" (455 ff.).

Of Southmost *Abarim;* in *Hesebon*
And *Horonaim, Seon's* Realm, beyond
The flow'ry Dale of *Sibma,* clad with Vines
And *Eleale,* to th'*Asphaltic* Pool.

[I. 406–11] [33]

Almost exclusively of the geographic detail, the lines enact a movement spreading outward past flowery dales, bounded in one direction by a "wild," in another by an equally well-known "Asphaltic Pool."

At another point, this kind of exotic and alien effect works together with a peculiarly native diction that is perhaps parodic to suggest explicitly the spread of evil toward the reader himself in both space and time:

Thammuz came next behind,
Whose annual wound in *Lebanon* allur'd
The *Syrian* Damsels to lament his fate
In amorous ditties all of a Summer's Day,
While smooth *Adonis* from his native Rock
Ran purple to the Sea, suppos'd with blood
Of *Thammuz* yearly wounded: the Love-tale
Infected *Sion's* daughters with like heat,
Whose wanton passions on the sacred Porch
Ezekiel saw, when by the Vision led
His eye survey'd the dark Idolatries
Of alienated *Judah.*

[446–57]

The verbal effect here serves to merge immediate linguistic and literary experience (at the least) with the "original" spread of alienation in history, following the fable we ourselves are about to rehearse.

The rhetorical or poetic movement of the devils in geography and history in this passage, then, parallels and helps to realize

33. See William K. Wimsatt, Jr., *The Verbal Icon* (1954; rpt. New York: Noonday, 1962), pp. 209–10. In his illuminating discussion of the relation between consonants and tone in this passage, Wimsatt omits the final line, obscuring the full achievement. The soft labials of Eleale are bypassed, like the flowery dale of Sibma, as we progress to those volcanic consonants of "th'Asphaltic Pool."

the first stirrings of the narrative, in Hell and from Hell toward the unfallen Eden. And we need not invoke Milton's belief in the possible renewal of the English revolution to respond to the multiple movement in history and poem toward the contemporary English reader of any age. More than simply a catalogue of names and idolatries, the parade of chiefs who "sought their prey on earth" is comprehended through persistent reference to a progression, both historical and poetic, moving closer to the reader in each stage. After Dagon and Rimmon appear a group of devils who in history abused Egypt and then Israel "with monstrous shapes and sorceries" (479); their reign extends to Bethel and Dan in the idolatries instituted by Jeroboam, who likened his Maker to the "Grazed Ox,"

> *Jehovah,* who in one night when he pass'd
> From *Egypt* marching, equall'd with one stroke
> Both her first born and all her bleating Gods.
>
> [487–89]

Characteristically, Milton concludes each account with a grimly ironic setback. The last of these sequences, however, is both the most sweeping in space and time and the most unalleviated in the progress it traces; it recalls the myth behind Herbert's "Church Militant," though without passing beyond the utmost isles "To the American strand":

> The rest were long to tell, though far renown'd,
> Th'*Ionian* Gods, of *Javan's* Issue held
> Gods, yet confest later than Heav'n and Earth
> Thir boasted Parents; *Titan* Heav'n's first born
> With his enormous brood, and birthright seiz'd
> By younger *Saturn,* he from mightier *Jove*
> His own and *Rhea's* Son like measure found;
> So *Jove* usurping reign'd: the first in *Crete*
> And *Ida* known, thence on the Snowy top
> Of cold *Olympus,* rul'd the middle Air
> Thir highest Heav'n; or on the *Delphian* Cliff,
> Or in *Dodona,* and through all the bounds
> Of *Doric* Land; or who with *Saturn* old

Fled over *Adria* to th'*Hesperian* Fields,
And o'er the *Celtic* roam'd the utmost Isles.

[507–21]

It is in this context, with the poem's origin for the gods and other merely imaginative forms of the "middle Air / Thir highest Heav'n" as immediate background, that we can most profitably examine mythology as a prime material for the similes of *Paradise Lost*.[34] If as a formal epitome of discourse in *Paradise Lost* they reveal how difficult it is at times to divorce narrative from drama, they also epitomize the proximity of human sense and that secular Heaven of the middle air to divine concerns of various kinds. In considering simile as a radical strategy in *Paradise Lost,* we have thus far neglected the *material* of simile and the extent to which its reference, its way of taking us outside the poem in order to locate us within it, is consistent. And of course, it is the catalogue that provides the poem's origin for that material. With the possible exception of geography, it is the poem's mythological reference which, more than any other kind, invites undergraduate impatience with Milton's "pedantry." As one form of human sense in the poem, however—one realm of human names to which the poem's meaning is superior—it further clarifies the effective continuity in *Paradise Lost* of poetry with poem. It also provides a fascinating illustration of the extent to which Milton's own poem participates joyfully in the very middle air of which he seems so suspicious; and it does so primarily by joining the poem's most skeptically viewed thematic material to its most discursive form of "procedure."

As a group, it is the mythological similes in *Paradise Lost* which have received the highest praise, although, as we have seen, the mythological material ("whom the fables name") cannot for the most part be dissociated from other literary or historical experience as a frame of reference. Because this material forms part of a larger element in the design of *Paradise Lost*—the mythic or imaginative element in all its various manifestations—I believe it is misleading to stress a pagan-Christian pattern (whether it be

34. See Jonathan H. Collett, "Milton's Use of Classical Mythology in *Paradise Lost,*" *PMLA* 85 (1970): 88–96.

a simple antithesis or typological in nature) or to say, as Frank Kermode does, that the mythological parallels are "inserted only to be denied" (*The Living Milton,* p. 113).

More than one of the similes which has seemed to psychologizing readers merely "competitive" specifically recalls the lore of book I and in particular the way in which the description of Pandemonium is framed. If we read without prejudice against what we assume are puritan hostilities, these passages call attention more to the make-believe of the comparisons than their mere falsity—to the inevitably "erring" but wondrous quality of human relation:

> In shadier Bower
> More sacred and sequester'd, though but feign'd,
> *Pan* or *Silvanus* never slept, nor *Nymph,*
> Nor *Faunus* hunted.
>
> [IV. 705–8]

Beginning as in the similes of book I with a simple occasion, the amplification moves inevitably into history for its clarifying analogy; and the erring poet even exclaims at an unpremeditated likeness in the historical complications of Pandora's loveliness:

> More lovely than *Pandora,* whom the Gods
> Endow'd with all thir gifts, and O too like
> In sad event, when to the unwise Son
> Of *Japhet* brought by *Hermes,* she ensnar'd
> Mankind with her fair looks, to be aveng'd
> On him who had stole *Jove's* authentic fire.
>
> [IV. 714–19]

Quite clearly it is the disparity between the present Eve and the future corrupter of mankind that is more important here than the comparable loveliness of Eve and Pandora; Milton is his own best expositor in defining the prime likeness in terms of event. But the full effect of the simile, even as a reference, is lost if we do not remember the great catalogue of human names for the devils in their earthly careers—those names with which Javan, the son of Japhet and founder of the Greek race, is associated so closely.[35] Milton's twentieth-century readers are sometimes less learned in these matters than, say, Milton's own schoolmates at St. Paul's; and they are certainly unfamiliar with the syncretic view of mythology sketched out in Isabel MacCaffrey's helpful study.[36] All this really means, though, is that we need, more than did Milton's original audience, the kind of help with which Milton is so free in initially establishing the nature of his poem and its references—the help Milton offers particularly in the catalogue of book I, with its recapitulation of myth's nature.

Thus, whether in or out of similes, the use of mythological material is inseparable from the implied attitudes toward it. And the MacCaffrey study makes it clear why it is most important not to attribute these entirely to Milton's personal biases. In a passage like the following, the poet can clearly rely on an audience which is willing to associate "Love" (or Cupid) with decadence and artifice:

> Here Love his golden shafts imploys, here lights
> His constant Lamp, and waves his purple wings,
> Reigns here and revels: not in the bought smile
> Of Harlots, loveless, joyless, unindear'd,
> Casual fruition, nor in Court Amours,
> Mixt Dance, or wanton Mask, or Midnight Ball,
> Or Serenate, which the starv'd Lover sings
> To his proud fair, best quitted with disdain.
> These lull'd by Nightingales imbracing slept,
> And on thir naked limbs the flow'ry roof
> Show'r'd Roses, which the Morn repair'd. Sleep on,
> Blest pair; and O yet happiest if ye seek
> No happier state, and know to know no more.
>
> [IV. 763–75] [37]

35. These historical complications include "Th'Ionian Gods, of *Javan's* Issue held / Gods" (I. 508–9). Javan was the son of Japhet and the grandson of Noah. The brothers Epimetheus and Prometheus were sons of the Titan Iapetos, often identified with Japhet. See Hughes, p. 295.

36. *"Paradise Lost" as "Myth,"* pp. 1–43.

37. Clearly, simile cannot be dissociated from such passages; for part of Milton's effect in using mythological and related material is to show that

In these lines we are as close as we ever get to the original Paradise, and we begin with a figure like the "Universal Pan" of line 266. Yet the impulse of the simile moves again toward corruption and a world in which falling flowers or leaves are not repaired by the morn: the libidinous atmosphere of court entertainment. If we have read closely, the juxtaposition recalls and heightens an earlier suggestion that the present bower is a "silvan Scene" and a "woody Theatre" (140–41), a more particular *kind* of "Lantskip." From the "serenate" and midnight ball, the poet moves abruptly back to the exquisite scene of the embracing and the flowers; but as if we are unable to keep the picture of "eternal Spring" in focus, an agonized voice breaks in to stop the poem's action, only half mindful that the Fall has long since taken place —and forgetful of his own origins. Located late in human history, and surrounded by the forms of myth, it could be the voice of either poet or reader.

At times in the presentation of Eden, moreover, the reminder that the Garden too has a story, is fragile and ultimately inaccessible, is coupled with the suggestion that Satan too is watching what we imaginatively see. Enna and the series of places fabled and real which could not "strive" with "this Paradise" are known to us only by stories analogous to the present, true fable—or are located as geographical distances easily negotiable by the devil. Exactly paralleling the clauses reminding us of these stories is the circumstance of "this Assyrian Garden, where the Fiend / Saw

---

these moments in Eden immediately precede both the realm of "unreal" myth and the vulgar surfaces of virtually contemporary "history." Adam is

> . . . without more train
> Accompanied than with his own complete
> Perfections; in himself was all his state,
> More solemn than the tedious pomp that waits
> On Princes, when thir rich Retinue long
> Of Horses led, and Grooms besmear'd with Gold
> Dazzles the crowd, and sets them all agape.
> [v. 351–57]

The analogous simile for Eve's "undeckt" beauty is virtually echoed when she leaves Adam in book IX—except that there it is presented as a "like": she is "more lovely fair / Than Wood-Nymph, or the fairest Goddess feign'd / Of three that in Mount *Ida* naked strove . . ." (v. 380–82). For a discussion of the change in form, see below, chap. 7.

undelighted all delight" (IV. 285–86). Similarly, the long passage describing Adam and Eve, their repast and their entertainment, concludes at sunset, "when Satan still in gaze, as first he stood / Scarce thus at length fail'd speech recover'd sad" (356–57).

In these passages, the use of mythology is added to the convergence of perspective we have already noticed between reader and Satan, though one particularly illuminating example has been noted chiefly for its unidiomatic "Greek" syntax and its "anachronism":

> So hand in hand they pass'd, the loveliest pair
> That ever since in love's imbraces met,
> *Adam* the goodliest of men since born
> His sons, the fairest of her Daughters *Eve*.
>
> [IV. 321–24]

As Frank Kermode has observed, the rationale for the word order here is to make "Adam and Eve here literally include us all." [38] We need not follow Kermode in his insistence that this "distortion" is among the poem's "counterlogical elements" to share his conclusion that the syntax in such places serves a general purpose similar to the mythological parallels and to the similes. Milton uses virtually the same construction in book IX, when the reader is sharing Eve's gaze at the "imbruted" devil:

> Pleasing was his shape,
> And lovely, never since of Serpent kind
> Lovelier, not those that in *Illyria* chang'd
> *Hermione*
>
> [IX. 503–6]

In all such passages, as in the catalogue explaining Satan's pride in his "imbodied force," the reader has the advantage of knowing more than the poem's characters.

What mythology provides, then, is appropriate likenesses only for what modern readers know is a *result* of the Garden's story (its "sad event"); usually part of the similes' effect depends on the contrast between Eden's "Eternal Spring" and the endless

38. *The Living Milton*, p. 113. Douglas Bush notes English precedents in *Complete Poetical Works*, p. 282.

complications of history and fable. Certainly this is the dominant impression in one of the poem's longest comparisons, which begins with a fragile but literal description of Eden:

> The Birds thir choir apply; airs, vernal airs,
> Breathing the smell of field and grove attune
> The trembling leaves, while Universal *Pan*
> Knit with the *Graces* and the *Hours* in dance
> Led on th'Eternal Spring. Not that fair field
> Of *Enna,* where *Proserpin* gath'ring flow'rs
> Herself a fairer Flow'r by glooming *Dis*
> Was gather'd, which cost *Ceres* all that pain
> To seek her through the world; nor that sweet Grove
> Of *Daphne* by *Orontes,* and th'inspir'd
> *Castalian* Spring might with this Paradise
> Of *Eden* strive; nor that *Nyseian* Isle
> Girt with the River *Triton,* where old *Cham,*
> Whom Gentiles *Ammon* call and *Lybian Jove,*
> Hid *Amalthea,* and her florid Son,
> Young *Bacchus,* from his Stepdame *Rhea's* eye;
> Nor where *Abassin* Kings thir issue Guard,
> Mount *Amara,* though this by some suppos'd
> True Paradise under the *Ethiop* Line
> By *Nilus* head, enclos'd with shining Rock,
> A whole day's journey high, but wide remote
> From this *Assyrian* Garden, where the Fiend
> Saw undelighted all delight, all kind
> Of living Creature new to sight and strange.
>
> [IV. 264–87] [39]

39. In searching for the animal to enter, Satan actually travels "West from *Orontes* to the Ocean barr'd / At *Darien*" (IX. 80–81). In *Milton and the Literature of Travel* (Princeton: Princeton University Press, 1951), pp. 69–70, R. C. Cawley has shown that here (and generally in the poem) Milton drew chiefly from Peter Heylyn's *Cosmographie . . . Containing the chorographie and historie of the whole world* (1652). In Heylyn's map of Africa, the equator passes through Mount Amara, which "some have taken (but mistaken) for the place of Paradise." Amara is "the greatest Ornament of this province, and indeed of the whole Empire of Aethiopia, . . . situate in a large and delightful Plain: the bottom of the Hill in circuit 90 miles, and a day's journey high; the Rock so smooth and even (but lesser and lesser toward the top) that no wall can be more evenly polished (*Cosmographie,* book 4, p. 64;

The passage is the climax of Satan's long approach to Eden and this universe; but Milton reminds us of his gazing presence only at the end of the enormous complication of his simple description, which initially involves only the mighty Pan of the *Nativity,* "Knit with the *Graces* and the *Hours* in dance." As C. S. Lewis notes, the relevance of the first analogy is that "in both these places the young and beautiful while gathering flowers was ravished by a dark power risen up from the underworld." [40] But the ironic pathos of the metaphor "Herself a fairer Flow'r . . . / Was gather'd" links the simile even more tightly with the literal description immediately preceding, by recalling that Eve is herself part of the eternal spring of God's creation.[41] The analogies that follow continue the large shift in visual focus from nature and nature's flowers to our first parents—from the "shadow" of nature mirrored in the lake (IV. 261–63) to the image of the Creator shining in Adam and Eve's "looks Divine." The "fair field" of Enna, the grove of Daphne, the Nyseian Isle, and Mount Amara are initially presented as places which cannot "strive" with Eden. But by the time we get to the Nyseian Isle, the initial point of comparison is virtually forgotten in favor of the history involved in each place: the hiding of Amalthea and Bacchus and the guarding of the "issue" of the insecure Abyssinian kings for the purpose of avoiding sedition. Once again, in the context of quasilogical comparison, there is no distinction to be made between the mythic history of gods "Ionian" or Roman and contemporary political lore, available in books like Heylyn's *Cosmographie* of 1652. In fact, to stress the rapid movement as it were *toward the reader* in time and to unify all experience within his fable, Milton closes the compound simile by putting the entire progression in the context of travel and by the dark suggestion that, although we do not even know where the earthly Paradise was, after his voyage through Chaos Satan has somehow come to precisely the right place—once again, we glimpse the

quoted by Cawley, p. 70, with Cawley's italics omitted here). Heylyn also mentions the detail of the guard, which is intended "to avoid sedition."

40. Lewis, *Preface to "Paradise Lost,"* p. 142.

41. In the general movement of the poem from "figure" to "fact," discussed in chap. 7, this simile is recalled when Satan spies the "fairest unsupported flow'r" alone (IX. 432 ff.).

positive value of "error" in its primal sense. It is here that we are reminded of Satan's watchful presence, and our eye follows his from the picture of general delight to the godlike inhabitants placed, as Satan never was, "in true filial freedom" (294).

The way in which Milton rapidly shifts his references toward the reader in this passage resembles the geographical progression in the catalogue. In fact, by focusing attention so precisely on what the Gentiles *call* Cham, and by reminding us of human supposition in general, Milton seems to recall the catalogue quite deliberately, at least as a basic framework for our knowledge in the poem. Certainly Ammon is by now a most familiar figure,[42] and although Milton does not include many mythological figures among the devils' immediate offspring, he does specifically name Jove and Rhea's son among the rapid final survey of myth and idolatry from the Ionian gods on out to the "utmost Isles" of northwest Europe, the poem's natural habitat for Leviathan. But more important, that progression of devils introduced us to godlike shapes and forms as yet without names, stories, earthly careers, or idolatries—though they are known to us only in those stories. By multiplying names in *Paradise Lost,* Milton reminds us, then, of etymological uncertainty and the difficulty of true "notation," described in such detail in his *Art of Logic.* He makes it quite clear in introducing the catalogue that originally the stories, myths, and idolatries often associated with the devils in their earthly forms are in effect equivalent to fallen angels' new names; once "blotted out and ras'd" from the records of Heaven [43] —like the very knowledge for which the arts are a mere vehicle —they become the proper and indeed inevitable material of poetry.

Similarly, the multiple form of simile itself reminds us that we are getting a bit of logical "argument" with roughly the same effect as the new names given the fallen angels by "the greatest part / Of mankind." The similes, in fact, actually contain many of these names, which work somewhat like the meticulous detail of geographic references, in and out of the formal images, calling attention to modern uncertainty about the location of the earthly Paradise. Both kinds of argument—similitude and notation—

42. See *PL* I. 396, where the Ammonites are said to worship Moloch.
43. See *PL* I. 364–75; quoted above in this chapter.

originate in the very realm which has produced the mythology, idolatry, and the implied politics that the similes themselves must adduce as the ground of all our knowledge. In sum, then, by calling attention throughout the passage (and poem) to different names and by incorporating so much human conjecture—as well as in the actual forms of rhetoric—Milton reminds us of more general uncertainties and the need for instruments like the organic arts. A major motif in the poem, this kind of reminder is available either in such submerged formulas as "they say," "as some suppose," or in more fully imaged forms, like that of the belated peasant who "sees / Or dreams he sees" (I. 783–84).

In turning to the second of the poem's ways of originating our poetic knowledge, we must qualify somewhat. "Literal" in the passage of description which we have just examined means something like "in one sense irreducible," as distinct from the frankly imaginative mythology into which the vision of Eden fragments. Milton recapitulates the experience of imaginatively recovering the earthly Paradise; though he establishes Eden as it seems *negatively*, the ineffability of the glimpse and the artifice of what succeeds it (to sustain it) are almost realistic—given the nature of the project.

But we must clearly distinguish this kind of literal description from another form of irreducible metaphor: the language with which Milton portrays the abyss within poet and poem's cosmos, and which mythically "originates" the very world into which Milton's description of Eden fragments, to us "reduces." We may as well admit that the poem is legitimately responsible for scholarly and lesser efforts to peer behind its orthodoxies into obscure doctrines of, say, the Creation. But rather than conclude prematurely with speculation about Milton's theological beliefs, we should go on to recognize the proper function of poetry's fiction in such a context: it serves precisely to create the tension, to which so many apologists and antagonists succumb, between a doctrinal primacy (such as C. A. Patrides has so effectively described[44]) and the "sensuous" primacy which is poetry's unique contribution to the epistemological and (thus) discursive arts. Hence, our mere exposure to Hell makes it in some temporary

44. C. A. Patrides, *Milton and the Christian Tradition* (Oxford: Clarendon, 1966).

and quite imaginary way archetypal. But even Hell in the early portions of *Paradise Lost* is reducible, if only because it must be argued into our consciousness—for the most part, "comparatively" argued, as we have seen. If there is a single realm in the poem which is *ir*reducible in this sense, however, it is Chaos, related to Comus's fantastic shapes and (in the prose) to the "babblements and ragged notions" of those whose predominantly verbal education may produce an "ignorantly zealous divinity." Though it is portrayed in the second book—perhaps to establish a "poetic memory" and to ground within it further epic references—Chaos is, with the epic catalogue, one of the poem's two major sources of reference.

Early in the poem, the narrator passionately—and, we may say, knowingly—clarifies Beelzebub's "devilish Counsel," the official plan of action for the fallen angels:

> for whence
> But from the Author of all ill could spring
> So deep a malice, to confound the race
> Of mankind in one root, and Earth with Hell
> To mingle and involve, done all to spite
> The great Creator? But thir spite still serves
> His glory to augment.
>
> [II. 380–86]

The lines constitute one of those clarifying intrusions by the author to which many modern readers object. But far from simply embodying an author's didactic preaching, they express a level of vision only occasionally attained by the poet; and in this instance they introduce a crucial theme in *Paradise Lost,* the changes, both apparent and real, in the poem's cosmos.

What I wish to suggest in this matter is, first, that the world of natural change—or chance—is available to us at first only in the world of simile, as what L. D. Lerner has called the "sense of context," [45] emblematically but not vaguely evoked in the expansion of referent which we have already noticed. These "natural" similes, used either to describe Hell (perhaps dramatically) or Satan's journey toward this world, often appear in close se-

45. L. D. Lerner, "The Miltonic Simile," *Essays in Criticism* 4 (1954): 297.

quence, perhaps partly to suggest the flickering change of appearances in Hell; more basically, however, they adduce as "likenesses" conventional images for a world apparently governed by chance, a world usually illumined by moon and lightning, full of astronomical wonders once associated with tragedy, now with fear of change.

First, then, our idea of Hell's appearance (its landscape, its inhabitants) depends upon a series of analogies assuming familiarity (both literary and everyday) with an earth already ravaged by tempest, in which knowledge and survival itself are uncertain. The first two books, of course, are full of similes of this kind. But at the end of the second book, when Sin opens the gates of Hell, we experience a kind of recognition with which we shall have more to do in the poem: a kind of extended and as it were *retroactive* homologation at the point when Satan ventures into the "dark / Illimitable Ocean" and seems almost to become the night voyager we encounter so frequently in the poem.

As we reread the description of Chaos and of Satan's encounter with the "Anarch old," several features of its metaphoric language are particularly interesting in connection with the speaker's invectives, with Satan's view of his "imbodied force," and especially with the visions of books XI–XII. The prospect of Chaos is a "dark / Illimitable Ocean" through which Satan makes the poem's first "voyage"; Milton's imagery here links Satan deliberately with the pilots—or rather the vessels—in previous *similes;* his wings are "Sail-broad vans" (II. 927); he makes his way

> on the calmer wave by dubious light
> And like a weather-beaten Vessel holds
> Gladly the Port, though Shrouds and Tackle torn.
>
> [II. 1042–44]

The voyage itself is

> more endanger'd than when *Argo* pass'd
> Through *Bosporus* betwixt the justling Rocks:
> Or when *Ulysses* on the larboard shunn'd
> *Charybdis,* and by th'other steer'd.
>
> [II. 1017–20]

It is no accident that the analogy from epic voyage occurs at this point, in the description of Satan's informal trip through this abyss called the "Illimitable Ocean." For it is the language of heroic combat that most immediately describes a world of warring atoms, the unmeasured matter of Chaos—in fact, the atoms themselves are described much like the devils' "bannered host":

> Before thir eyes in sudden view appear
> The secrets of the hoary deep, a dark
> Illimitable Ocean without bound,
> Without dimension, where length, breadth, and highth,
> And time and place are lost; where eldest *Night*
> And *Chaos,* Ancestors of Nature, hold
> Eternal Anarchy, amidst the noise
> Of endless wars, and by confusion stand.
> For hot, cold, moist, and dry, four Champions fierce
> Strive here for Maistry, and to Battle bring
> Thir embryon Atoms; they around the flag
> Of each his Faction, in thir several Clans,
> Light-arm'd or heavy, sharp, smooth, swift or slow
> Swarm populous, unnumber'd as the Sands
> Of *Barca* or *Cyrene*'s torrid soil,
> Levied to side with warring Winds, and poise
> Thir lighter wings. To whom these most adhere,
> Hee rules a moment; *Chaos* Umpire sits,
> And by decision more imbroils the fray
> By which he Reigns: next him high Arbiter
> *Chance* governs all. Into this wild Abyss,
> The Womb of nature and perhaps her Grave,
> Of neither Sea, nor shore, nor Air, nor Fire,
> But all these in thir pregnant causes mixt
> Confus'dly, and which thus must ever fight,
> Unless th'Almighty Maker them ordain
> His dark materials to create more Worlds,
> Into this wild Abyss the wary fiend
> Stood on the brink of Hell and look'd a while,
> Pondering his Voyage: for no narrow frith
> He had to cross.
>
> [II. 890–920]

It is significant that we have in this passage the relatively smooth texture of metaphoric description rather than the elaborate involutions of simile with which Milton partially describes Hell.[46] It is a kind of primary descriptive language which links nonentity itself with decadent chivalric tournament and political intrigue.[47] Satan claims he comes no spy; he wishes safe-conduct through this nether "Empire," he claims to be constrained to wander this "darksome Desert." Beyond the metaphoric coupling of royalism and "anarchy old," the two most noteworthy features of Chaos are the noise ("the universal hubbub wild / Of stunning sounds and voices all confus'd," 951–52) and the countenance of the Emperor himself, who replies to Satan's queries "with faltering speech and visage incompos'd" (989). Milton's inclusion of the builders of Babel among later inhabitants in the Limbo of Vanity and in the sequence of fallen artifice in the plain constitutes two of his important reminders of Satan's vow to reduce Earth to her "original darkness" and the sway of Chaos (II. 984; see above, n. 26, and *PL* VI. 472–81).

It would seem, indeed, that something like Chaos is what Satan sees beneath the gilt surfaces of Heaven itself. Though Raphael points to the similarity between the "entrails" of "this [unfallen?] Earth" and Heaven, both are like the "Womb of Nature and perhaps her Grave" (II. 911). But more important, Milton's Chaos provides the first extended literal description of an ocean-abyss, crossed in a voyage. Thus, it embodies an internal archetype—though, clearly, no *doctrinal* substratum—for the world of the travel similes, helping particularly to explain such details, for example, as the often present formula "by chance." Associated primarily with the similes, it is this realm which eventually links the poem's Hell with our earth. By introducing it primarily as an "Illimitable Ocean," Milton redefines—indeed, he poetically originates—the world we may previously have thought of as a merely natural context.

46. See my comments on the more literal Hell, however, in n. 13 above.

47. Compare *PL* IX. 1–41 and the passage from *Ref* quoted and discussed above in chap. 2.

7

Process and Structure in *Paradise Lost*

At this point in our discussion, we may widen our perspective to take into consideration that larger question of structural coherence in *Paradise Lost*. It seems clear enough that how we conceive of a relatively minor detail like an epic simile may both reflect and determine the way in which we *think* of a poem's structure, that most difficult of critical terms to unpack and one for which quite different metaphors—notably "pattern" and "progression" —have been proposed in Milton studies of recent years. In many of these discussions—particularly in those adopting spatial metaphors for a poem's largest modes of coherence—the place of the reader's experience has been especially difficult to define (see above, chap. 5). Yet Milton's poem is singularly disconcerting in its insistence on that experience, and especially on the temporal dimension it necessarily involves. Milton's large arrangement of materials in *Paradise Lost* certainly images the extratemporal immediacy of God's acts, at least relative to the mortal men who are the poem's readers. The students of the poem's metaphoric design have been most helpful here, even if they have too narrowly confined their analysis to questions of effect. But Raphael's emphasis in discussing the difficulties of his narration, we may remember, falls upon the arresting phrase "process of speech," a phrase recalling the ironic vehicle of the uncouth swain in *Lycidas*. "But now my Oat proceeds, / And listens to the Herald of the Sea / That came in Neptune's plea" (*L,* 88–90). Even more than Milton's Adam, we need—or at any rate we are encouraged to *use*—this poem's linear procedure. It is significant and even necessary in our pursuit of the poem's structure, analogous to the poem's intention, and to the pursuit emphasized so clearly in its opening lines.

A moment in book IX, near the conclusion of the satanic plot in *Paradise Lost,* may serve to illuminate the structural richness provided, sometimes unexpectedly, by what I have called the poem's process of speech. With the poet we discover a clarifying analogy for the moment when Satan "imbruted" leads Eve to the Tree of Knowledge:

> Hope elevates, and joy
> Bright'ns his Crest, as when a wand'ring Fire,
> Compact of unctuous vapor, which the Night
> Condenses, and the cold invirons round,
> Kindl'd through agitation to a Flame,
> Which oft, they say, some evil Spirit attends,
> Hovering and blazing with delusive light,
> Misleads th'amaz'd Night-wanderer from his way
> To Bogs and Mires, and oft through Pond or Pool,
> There swallow'd up and lost, from succor far,
> So glister'd the dire snake, and into fraud
> Led Eve, our credulous Mother, to the Tree
> Of prohibition, root of all our woe.
>
> [IX. 633–45]

In such formal images James Whaler has taught us to detect the rigorous pattern of correspondences likely to be at work: Satan—or at any rate the glistering dire snake—is to Eve as the wandering fire is to the night-wanderer. But even though Milton himself exercises this manner of reading in the *Art of Logic,* we have by no means exhausted the argument of the simile, even at this level (see above, pp. 125–27). For to be precise, the image *begins* by focusing on the relation between the hope and joy of Satan on the one hand and the physical appearance of the snake's elevated and brightened crest on the other—the same kind of comparison as the "thick" amazement of the devils' first awakening in Hell. That is, the initial discovery made here is that the delusive wandering fire has the same relation to the night-wanderer that Satan's hope does to the wily adder, his "shape." Finally, as if to clinch the point that we cannot read such images statically, as a set of mere correspondences divorced from the poem's own process of speech, Milton once again turns in on his own epic by recalling the very landscape of *Satan's* difficult "way" through

Chaos to this world: "O'er bog or steep, through strait, rough, dense, or rare" (II. 948).[1]

Like Eve, the night-wanderer is a viewer of rather odd phenomena. But Milton drenches the description of what he sees with a kind of scientific language—it is only "unctuous vapor" condensed and kindled—and he does so in such a way that no reader, at least, could be amazed by the *ignis fatuus* until he discovers the real strength of that delusive light and the credulity of a wanderer apparently warned by both science and superstition—the power, in short, of mere sense experience. The incongruity created by such casual detail goes far to make Eve more than the innocent victim she later pretends to be, in the manner of that pilot imprudent enough to fix his anchor in a "scaly rind." In moments such as this, I have suggested, Milton opens the poem out, in developing the discovery made available through a process of speech. The poet involves our world with his own archetypal fable, and particularly with Satan's own voyage of discovery. The point here is that an "evil Spirit" is attending *both* realms, as the parodic diction helps to remind us. Just as the whole poem is necessary, at least in theory, to "say . . . what cause / Mov'd our Grand Parents in that happy State" (I. 27–28), so the simile must be read as an evolving process of dramatized discovery. In this instance, Milton moves us from Satan's feelings to their effects on that shape in which he deceived mankind (the shape from which he is later so anxious to distinguish his own "form") and finally to the effects of that visible prospect on Eve. Involved in the cumulative discovery—in the realization that his hope and joy are as misleading to Satan as his shape and brightness are to Eve—is the lesson so often repeated in *Paradise Lost,* that we cannot separate the phenomena of earthly existence from their potential for evil use.

This example may remind us that the similes only pretend to take us outside the poem, even if they open the poem out in something like the way I have proposed in chapter 5. The world

1. See CE 12 : 274–76 for a commonplace ground for such navigational reference, the passage over the "sea of knowledge"; in the seventh Prolusion, Milton contrasts a true knowledge with "a kind of Lernian swamp of sophisms."

they reveal in moments of rhetorical argument or appeal is itself fictionally originated within the poem, mythically created on a level we must suppose to be more definitive than the merely argumentative one: the level of the poem's fictional narrative. As we have seen, two passages early in the poem point to this origin with special clarity: the catalogue, which reveals the origin of "human names," divinities, and even politics; and Chaos, which, in a somewhat different context of quasiscientific description, reveals the "base originals" of our own world—or what we might more accurately call the poem's norm of reference. Thus, if the similes pretend only to refer, they actually epitomize the poem's *mimesis* in the particular sense that they shape the reader's experience by locating him within the archetypal coordinates of the poem's fable.

In turning to the problem of structure at this point, then, we are in effect asking how the similes are more than arguments that somehow take us outside the poem in order to clarify a situation within it. To generalize, while still distinguishing the poem's related aspects of an argumentative (or procedural) drama and a definitive confirming narrative, we might say that the reader's experience, as portrayed within *Paradise Lost,* is somewhat as follows:

Established as it is in the catalogue and in the poet's quasiscientific description of Satan's visit to Chaos, the poem's norm of reference appears otherwise only in the argument of simile until the moment of the Fall itself, when it begins to invade the phenomena of Eden itself. Now deprived of the comparative apparatus which makes it explicitly argumentative, this realm becomes the very atmosphere surrounding Adam and Eve. Thus, in book IX, the *energy* of simile diminishes sharply, even if the form does not quite disappear altogether. At this point we lose the sense of analogy's limitations. We are less impressed with the incongruities implicit in the arguments of similes. In short, there is a relatively distinct point within the poem at which the mere argument of simile is actually verified on the narrative level.

Similarly, until book IX we see ourselves in the poem (if at all) only as belated and usually benighted travelers on an ocean or plain, as weary and "amazed" laborers. The poet himself is cut off, not from reality but from "sight of vernal bloom, or Summer's Rose, / Or flocks, or herds, or human face divine" (III. 43–44). His kind of blindness figures our own fallen perception, though for the poet the visual compensations "shine inward." Before the Fall, we are for the most part distant spectators; to a remarkable extent we are forced to share Satan's perspective throughout. But in book IX and subsequently, Adam and Eve virtually become the figures in the precarious but providential world of the similes, figures that have previously served to enact some part of the reader's response. The last such figure, indeed—the laborer, "homeward returning" less than twenty lines from the end of the poem—appears to confirm what other features of the poem suggest, that the reader is ultimately made another Adam in *Paradise Lost*. It is he who in concluding the poem most clearly returns homeward, back to the familiar creatural realm now also about to receive Adam and Eve.[2] Like the individual similes, the poem as a whole opens out.

Simile and Narrative: The Uses of Argument in Book IX

If we are right in saying that the similes of book I are closely associated with what I have called the poem's drama and at times merely imply the action of the narrative level, it is difficult to escape the impression that book IX brings narrative into phase with drama, in a manner virtually peculiar to *Paradise Lost*. It is here, where simile actually conveys important shifts in the narrative fable, that epic convention rises most clearly above the fate of decoration or digression; the strategic location of similes in this crucial book of the poem reflects Milton's attitude toward the burdens to be placed on a rhetorical convention,[3] as two examples may serve to illustrate.

If we remember the importance of Adam and Eve's joined hands in imaging the "rational delight" of unfallen Eden, it is highly significant that Milton begins a long mythological simile in

2. Erich Auerbach, *Mimesis* (Berne, 1946; rpt. Garden City: Doubleday, 1953), pp. 216–19.

3. See Whaler, "Grammatical *Nexus* of the Miltonic Simile."

the very line in which Eve withdraws her hand. If we further recall the belated peasant and the revels he seems to see at the end of book I, the situation is singularly ominous:

> from her Husband's hand her hand
> Soft she withdrew, and like a Wood-Nymph light,
> *Oread* or *Dryad,* or of *Delia's* Train,
> Betook her to the Groves, but *Delia's* self
> In gait surpass'd and Goddess-like deport,
> Though not as shee with Bow and Quiver arm'd,
> But with such Gard'ning Tools as Art yet rude,
> Guiltless of fire had form'd, or Angels brought.
> To *Pales* or *Pomona,* thus adorn'd,
> Likest she seem'd, *Pomona* when she fled
> *Vertumnus,* or to *Ceres* in her Prime,
> Yet Virgin of *Proserpina* from *Jove.*
> Her long with ardent look his Eye pursu'd
> Delighted, but desiring more her stay.
>
> [IX. 385–98]

As the frequent shifts from argument to narrative suggest, the simile actually contains the action following Adam's final—and most discursive—speech to the unfallen Eve. Several features of the image are different from previous comparisons, mythological and otherwise. In the first place there is the simple fact that Eve's departure is *like* the "Wood-Nymph light"—no favorable comparison, as the comment submerged in the adjective "light" suggests; in previous similes, on the other hand, the *unlikeness* has been stressed. The shift in the facts of the poem's world is manifested in the shift of simile's syntactic connections. Furthermore, while previous similes generally digress with a separate clause or sentence related only to the referent (thus emphasizing disparateness, contrast, the inadequacy or error of logical comparison), it is the narrative that breaks in on the comparison here, emphasizing the real analogy. Even the terms of comparison are different. Already it is implied that Eve is in someone's "train." She does surpass Delia herself, in gait and in "Goddess-like deport." The qualifying clauses notwithstanding, Eve is now for the first time *literally* armed with "such Gard'ning Tools as Art yet rude, / Guiltless of fire had form'd, or Angels brought" (IX. 391–92). The qualifying clauses, in fact, function in much the same way as the temporal formulas (chiefly "yet") which cluster in this passage. What we seem to perceive is the entrance of Eve into a world of art and vaguely urban "agriculture" which Paradise has until now barely managed to exclude. At the same time, we are given the distinct impression that the speaker's discursive instruments are now more appropriate for talking about Eve, that there are more real points of likeness "in fact"; logically she is more accessible, in a sense, than at any previous moment in the poem. As the logical tool of comparison becomes more and more appropriate, open to more ramifications somehow answerable, we are reminded, through the cumulative weight of significance given to creatures like nymphs, that Eve, too, has a story now about to be rehearsed. The whole mood is one of anticipation; we are viewing the moments of Eve's "prime" just before the poem's great crisis. Milton is able to draw on several figures, "Ovidian" figures variously armed and associated with agriculture —Pomona, usually depicted with a pruning hook, and Ceres, who first taught men the use of the plow. Everything points to the fact that Eve's great (and true) story, in all its implications— including refinements in art of all kinds—is now about to begin. Ceres in this simile is not the mother seeking Proserpina through the world but is "yet Virgin of *Proserpina* from *Jove*"—a remarkably suggestive compression of time and of the hierarchy of perspectives as well. Eve is still in her prime, the simile suggests; but as a wood nymph she is liable to pursuit, and the moment immediately precedes a genealogy of "gods."

A second example brings us closer to the climactic encounter between Satan and Eve. Here again, simile is virtually inseparable from the narrative of the fateful scene. Because the passage in effect rehearses the first entrance of Satan into Eden, it is worth quoting at some length:

> For now, and since first break of dawn the Fiend,
> Mere Serpent in appearance, forth was come,
> And on his Quest, where likeliest he might find
> The only two of Mankind, but in them

The whole included Race, his purpos'd prey.
In Bow'r and Field he sought, where any tuft
Of Grove or Garden-Plot more pleasant lay,
Their tendance or Plantation for delight,
By Fountain or by shady Rivulet,
He sought them both, but wish'd his hap might find
Eve separate, he wish'd, but not with hope
Of what so seldom chanc'd, when to his wish,
Beyond his hope, Eve separate he spies,
Veil'd in a Cloud of Fragrance, where she stood,
Half spi'd, so thick the Roses bushing round
About her glow'd, oft stooping to support
Each Flow'r of slender stalk, whose head though gay,
Carnation, Purple, Azure, or speckt with Gold,
Hung drooping unsustain'd, them she upstays
Gently with Myrtle band, mindless the while,
Herself, though fairest unsupported Flow'r,
From her best prop so far, and storm so nigh.
Nearer he drew, and many a walk travers'd
Of stateliest Covert, Cedar, Pine, or Palm,
Then voluble and bold, now hid, now seen
Among thick-wov'n Arborets and Flow'rs
Imborder'd on each Bank, the hand of Eve:
Spot more delicious than those Gardens feign'd
Or of reviv'd *Adonis,* or renown'd
Alcinous, host of old *Laertes'* Son,
Or that, not Mystic, where the Sapient King
Held dalliance with his fair *Egyptian* Spouse.
Much hee the Place admir'd, the Person more.

[IX. 412–44]

We see almost everything here through the eyes of Satan, and it is a curious experience, appropriate to the Hell he brings within him. Following Eve's departure from the Garden and the speaker's explanation (which calls attention, like the simile, to "that moment"), Satan's quest is simply narrated in the past tense—until "Eve separate he spies." What follows conveys the expanding movement of his vision (at first "earthbound,") from place to person. He glimpses Eve "Veil'd in a Cloud of Fragrance, . . . / Half spi'd," hardly visible in the thick growth of flowers.[4] There are suggestions that, at least in Satan's eyes, Eden and Eve are changing; Satan sees a flower "speckt with Gold," and Eve too is seen as a flower. Stylistically and otherwise, we are in different circumstances from those in which the Proserpina of an earlier simile, "herself a fairer Flow'r by gloomy *Dis* / Was gather'd" (IV. 279–80). That simile, indeed, is not merely recalled; *its metaphor is becoming narrative fact.*[5]

Quite different is the vision in book IV, where Satan first leaps into the Garden like a wolf or thief (IV. 183–91). Although the mythological and geographical comparison explains what, and partly how, Satan sees, the vision is not immediate, certainly not sensuous or concrete, as in the passage just quoted. Nor can we say that it is entirely dramatized, internalized within the fable: we, as well as Satan, see (for the first time in the poem, we may recall) at once the images and the true meanings inherent *in* the images of Eden. If we notice those golden tresses, we also observe the curling tendrils of the vine, "which implied / Subjection, but requir'd with gentle sway" (IV. 305–6). The fiend sees "undelighted, all delight," including the following:

> Two of far nobler shape, erect and tall,
> Godlike erect, with native Honor clad
> In naked Majesty seem'd Lords of all,
> And worthy seem'd, for in thir looks Divine
> The image of thir glorious Maker shone,
> Truth, Wisdom, Sanctitude, severe and pure,
> Severe, but in true filial freedom plac't.
>
> [IV. 288–94]

Strange as it may seem to readers accustomed to more recent modes in poetry, it is perhaps the most literal description of the

4. The flowers do not merely grow "gladlier" at her coming as in VIII. 47 ff.; the "Roses bushing round" all but obscure Eve from Satan.

5. To take one instance, the unusual first participle of "Roses bushing round / About her glow'd, oft stooping to support / Each Flow'r" makes the second, "stooping," momentarily ambiguous in its reference, briefly suggesting that the temporarily "mindless" Eve is weaker than the flowers with which Satan's gaze identifies her.

unfallen parents that we get (see above, pp. 179–83). As in other descriptions of book IV, this is presented and not merely "told." If the image of "Universal Pan" and the "Hours in dance" seems overly fragile, and Love's "purple wings" followed too closely by the abuse of the starved lover's "serenate," the meaning of what we see *is* inherent in the image.[6] Like Satan, we are being introduced to Adam and Eve in book IV, and we must conclude that mythological comparisons in the poem (especially references to particular fabled gods) serve to explicate evil possibilities, among them the possibility that appearance will part company with essence.[7]

The use of simile at this point in book IX is not as consistently dramatic throughout the passage as some readers familiar with Jamesian techniques might wish. We clearly view Satan from outside, for example, when he makes his way toward Eve, "now hid, now seen" (436), though the ambiguities of this passage are more evident than is usual in Milton's verse. And it is the poet, more than Satan, whose emotion charges the lines "Herself, though fairest unsupported Flow'r, / From her best prop so far, and storm so nigh" (432–33). But one thing is clear throughout the entire passage: the perfect beauty of Paradise and of Eve's "Heav'nly form." The mythological comparison here serves to amplify the fiend's reaction to "the hand of Eve"—her decorative touches in the Garden; and to judge from the analogues, the reaction is nearly devoid of malevolence at this point. At the prospect of the Garden and Eve herself, Satan stands temporarily abstracted from his own evil intentions:

> As one who long in populous City pent,
> Where Houses thick and Sewers annoy the Air,
> Forth issuing on a Summer's Morn to breathe
> Among the pleasant Villages and Farms
> Adjoin'd, from each thing met conceives delight,
> The smell of Grain, or tedded Grass, or Kine,
> Or Dairy, each rural sight, each rural sound;

6. See Isabel MacCaffrey's helpful distinctions between myth, metaphor, and allegory in *"Paradise Lost" as "Myth"*, pp. 38–39.

7. This is the opposite of Adam's "real" vision, imparted by Michael in books XI–XII. See below, in this chapter.

> If chance with Nymphlike step fair Virgin pass,
> What pleasing seem'd for her now pleases more,
> She most, and in her look sums all Delight.
> Such pleasure took the Serpent to behold
> This Flow'ry Plat, the sweet recess of Eve
> Thus early, thus alone; her Heav'nly form
> Angelic, but more soft, and Feminine,
> Her graceful Innocence, her every Air
> Of Gesture or least action overaw'd
> His malice
>
> [IX. 445–62]

It is at points like this that we can best understand Satan. He is most like us in moments when his malice is "overaw'd" and he temporarily rejoins the community from which he and, for quite different reasons, the poet are normally removed: the "sight of vernal bloom, or Summer's Rose, / Or flocks, or herds, or human face divine" (III. 43–44). Milton is careful to avoid the satiric portraiture of the "starv'd lover"; indeed he re-creates the situation of the *pastourelle* in a surprisingly sympathetic and immediate way, suspending moral judgment and appealing deliberately to impulses most readers will share. In describing so richly the conception of delight, Milton seems to rehearse in little the movement of the entire passage, from the smells of vegetable and animal nature to the other elemental perceptions ("each rural sight, each rural sound") and finally to the chance encounter with the maid, whose looks—suspiciously like those of Eve in those bad moments related to Raphael—sum *all* delight. Almost everything in the simile is both immediate (as part of an everyday context) and recognizably homologous—particularly the fair virgin with the "Nymphlike step." She is *both* the country maid in whom everyone simply (and innocently) joys (with perhaps the touch of a leer at her femininity) and Eve herself, who, as an *actual* wood nymph at this point, is "fit love for Gods," as Satan remarks at line 489. While Satan is abstracted from his veil, in fact, his reactions to Eve closely parallel Adam's anxious submission to Eve's "absolute" loveliness (VIII. 546–47).[8]

8. Particularly interesting, in light of the poem's procedural displacement of doctrinal priorities, is Adam's remark that Eve seems "As one intended first, not after made / Occasionally" (VIII. 555–56).

The movement of the entire passage we have examined is multiple in its nature; we progress toward things "not Mystic," in many senses of that difficult word, toward the immediately comprehensible experience of the final comparison and even a factual realm where signs (or similes) are verified.[9] Milton uses a series of similes to convey Satan's reaction first to the Garden, then to Eve's "person" when she "chances" to appear alone, exactly as he has wished. The comparisons themselves have an order like other sequences we have observed—from such fabled places as the gardens of "reviv'd Adonis" and "renown'd Alcinous" we move to a reference "not Mystic" in the biblical garden of Solomon.[10] And it is a testimony both to the architectonic function of simile in *Paradise Lost* and to the coherence of its "norm" that we move to a natural or creatural realm as well. In the last lines of the passage, Milton confirms the impression that we are on the threshold of the poem's (and our own) history by virtually bridging the gap between metaphor and fact. Here, as previously, imagery involves *view,* this one an expanding prospect from flowers to Eve's "Heav'nly form." But now, the circumstance of the simile's apparently random world of "hap" (and of the devil's wishes) seems to match almost exactly with those of the fable's real world: "If chance with Nymphlike step fair Virgin pass."

9. The meaning of "not Mystic" has been variously interpreted: (1) not symbolic or allegorical and (2) not mythical or mythological (Hughes, p. 388); see Douglas Bush, *Mythology and the Renaissance Tradition in English Poetry,* rev. ed. (New York: Norton, 1963), pp. 269–70. Judging from the structure of this passage, Milton would not have made quite the same distinction, since mythology is related to "feigned" metaphor. The most important considerations here seem to be, first, the fact that the "not Mystic" introduces the shift to "person" and, secondly, that it is followed by one of the most sympathetic "creatural" similes in the poem. Since mythological references in the poem after this point are drastically cut, I am inclined to agree with Hughes that "not Mystic" means "historical," if by historical we mean the procession of figures or "persons" which makes up so much of books XI and XII. This is a difficult phrase, and one cannot be sure that it has any reference to a new kind of significance in what follows. Milton uses "mystic" elsewhere, sometimes favorably, in a technical sense ("Mystic dance," V. 178), sometimes abusively, to mean only "obscure." He may simply be rejecting the commonplace "mystic" interpretations of the Song of Songs. One must never rule out the possible artistic integrity of such a reference, however. At X. 173, Satan's doom is put "in mysterious terms, judg'd as then best."

10. "Reviv'd Adonis" is linked in the catalogue of book I with the cult of Thammuz. See also *Mask,* 976–1011, *N,* 204.

What is happening here, it would seem, is that (in Whaler's terms) Miltonic simile homologates most perfectly in these moments of the Fall; in the language of Milton's *Logic,* the likenesses hobble less at this point in *Paradise Lost,* because the poem's entire fable is entering the realm of what Raphael calls human sense. Thanks to the recollection of specific similes near and far, and of the catalogue, it is difficult to escape the sense that experience in Eden has radically changed—is changing, indeed, even as we read. We are virtually entering another world when the comparisons need no longer be mystic.

As an argumentative "drama," *Paradise Lost* in its entirety mirrors the progression of the passage we have just discussed, and that of the poem's earliest multiple similes. From the reader's point of view, the poem's fable moves from metaphoric or figurative to a real manner of presentation. Varied though the speaker's posture may be, the rhetorical situation implied by the conditions of the poem's world undergoes a single basic shift from figure to fact, a shift in the direction of things "not Mystic." The simile itself does not disappear once it has served its several functions. But characteristically, its *material* continues to appear frequently, without the clarifying apparatus. In particular, the poem's "nature" after the narration of the Fall is made recognizable as the natural context of the earlier similes—even as we recall that this poetic nature is a fabric of signs. From here to the end of the poem, Milton recalls particular similes to verify them, whether in the literal description of fallen nature or in the visions of history explained and interpreted by Michael in books XI and XII. There is a "real Eclipse" (X. 413) to match, and to verify, the much earlier figurative one (I. 594 ff.). And in book XII, Moses "once more his potent Rod extends," in a passage which recalls the arresting vision of the poem's earliest "sojourners" (I. 309). More generally, the Fall in nature and the subsequent narrative are specifically linked with the similes used much earlier to describe Hell and Satan's journey through the original night of Chaos. Here in book IX, moreover, Milton's mythological references cluster more integrally with the kinds of idolatry archetypally—in this case, initially in the poem—associated with the historical careers of the devils, as foretold in the catalogue. And all this follows the poet's most explicit wish that his poem transcend the world implied by this very cluster, in the invocation to book IX.

It is clear, then, that to describe the larger effects of Milton's similes, we cannot confine ourselves to discussions of local neatness or the novelistic foreshadowing implied by terms like *homologation* and *prolepsis*—even if these are the effects usually considered to be Milton's chief contribution to an art of epic simile. The first lines of *Paradise Lost,* after all, tell us something of how the poem will end; and the epic's manner is characteristically one of rehearsal, more resembling liturgy than the novel. There is, it seems, an important connection to be made between Milton's norm of reference—the very existence of which is perhaps uniquely Miltonic—and the largest rhythms of the poem's fable, including its great movement from figure toward fact, from shadowy types to truth. The similes are successful in answering the overarching idea of the epic, because they carry us *on into* the poem as well as outside it.

Michael and the Issues of Books XI–XII

The final two books of *Paradise Lost* yield an important and somewhat neglected measure of this fundamental unity. Michael's mission, like Raphael's, is sometimes dismissed as a high-flown pedagogy—it is precisely these sections which have provoked the most abundant and vehement critical complaints about *Paradise Lost*—but the different normative purposes and quite distinct methods of each "teacher" have yet to be discussed in adequate detail. In particular, a somewhat neglected key to their function is in the way the two books are framed as the education of Adam. As Michael amplifies the mysterious doom enunciated in X. 175–81, he continues to offer us, in effect, the world of Miltonic simile without the apparatus of comparative argument. Together with Adam, moreover, we also view the first great epic catalogue's literal fulfillment, in history, its "verification" on the narrative level. But Milton also connects the final two books with such "heroes" of the figural similes as the belated peasant, the reaper, the plowman—all outside the early narrative of the poem; and there is an unmistakable link between Abdiel, the central figure of the War in Heaven, and the series of heroes in the "braver fortitude": that procession of figures in a more technical sense of the word, bearing the office of Christ.[11] It is because these books are so *resonant* that they may seem to lack energy. Because poem and Scripture alike are verified, we may well anticipate Adam and Michael in identifying the visions of book XI with the devils' continuing efforts to mingle Earth with Hell and Chaos. Nor are we likely to forget the ominous irony more clearly explicated earlier in the poem: the apocalyptic framework implied by Raphael's narrative in its typological aspect—and still earlier in the poem, by the logical patterns of the expository similes. In general, I would submit that what we are encouraged to see at the outset of the poem turns out to be the end point, and ideal, of Michael's reeducation of Adam in the poem's concluding books.

About one hundred lines from the end of the poem, Michael hints obliquely at the function of books XI and XII by relating them to the doom delivered by the Son in "mysterious terms." His narration has proceeded to "the day / . . . of respiration to the just, / And vengeance to the wicked, at return / Of him so lately promis'd to thy aid, / The Woman's seed, obscurely then foretold, / Now amplier known thy Saviour and thy Lord" (XII. 541–44). Like the Great Argument of *Paradise Lost* itself, the passage to which he thus refers is in its essence a messianic gloss upon Gen. 3 : 14, the judgment pronounced "in mysterious terms, judg'd as then best":

11. All of these figures confront a "world"; all of them make a free decision. They are used in the similes for explaining the feelings of the devils, usually with a clear distinction from the devils, suggested by giving the men of the referent a separate sentence, as we have seen. Milton's emphasis on free will makes the men potential heroes in history, provided they actually confront the world with their willed choice. It is because so many of them are seers like Ezekiel and Jacob that I link them with Abdiel, Adam, and Christ—and, outside the narrative, with both poet and reader of *Paradise Lost*. These figures bring out the significance of the similes' sequential effect, an effect we might call historical or (with William Madsen) typological; see "Earth the Shadow of Heaven," pp. 519–26.

> Between Thee and the Woman I will put
> Enmity, and between thine and her Seed;
> Her Seed shall bruise thy head, thou bruise his heel.
> So spake this Oracle, then verifi'd
> When *Jesus* son of *Mary* second *Eve*
> Saw Satan fall like Lightning down from Heav'n,
> Prince of the Air; then rising from his Grave
> Spoil'd Principalities and Powers, triumpht
> In open show, and with ascension bright
> Captivity led captive through the Air,
> The Realm itself of Satan long usurpt,
> Whom he shall tread at last under our feet;
> Even he who now foretold his fatal bruise,
> And to the Woman thus his Sentence turn'd.
>
> [x. 179–92]

Here and elsewhere in *Paradise Lost,* Milton verges on the kind of language we recognize as liturgical; the substance of the scriptural gloss closely parallels the Apostles' Creed. The lines make clear the radical connections of his final two books and help to explain their use of time. We will be involved with connections involving identity ("*Jesus* son of *Mary* second *Eve*") and verifying "event"—in which Milton telescopes together, for example, the fall of Satan and the ultimate apocalyptic triumph of the Son "in open show." [12] The concluding two books frequently recall the doom—Adam must come to know all this more "amply"—and they are filled with the "technical" signposts which enable Milton to get at the scriptural intention: "mental sight" (XI. 418), the "shapes" of Death (XI. 467), human and divine similitude (XI. 512), human names (XI. 683–99), "types and shadows" (XII. 232–33), "figure" (XII. 241); "shadowy" expiations and "types" (XII. 291, 303), and finally "truth" (XII. 303).

It is essential to notice, however, that the final books of *Paradise Lost* (like its middle ones) are also generated at the human level, in the questions which Adam poses for Michael, the second of the poem's "divine instructors." In avoiding all preliminaries

12. "Whom he shall tread . . . / Ev'n he who now foretold" (x. 190–91).

to his initial "sentence," of course, Michael is faithfully carrying out God's charge, quite as precisely as Raphael does in books v–VIII.[13] But the Father fails to prescribe the manner in which Michael is actually to intermix the covenant of renewal "lest they faint / At the sad Sentence rigorously urg'd" (XI. 108–09). Adam must be enlightned lest he "live for ever, dream at least to live / For ever" (XI. 94–95). When he actually requests this enlightenment, he does so mainly in perceptual terms: once driven from Eden, the human parents will be cut off from the places where God "voutsaf'd Presence Divine," in the immediate appearances of unfallen life—the sights, sounds, and smells of Eden:

> This most afflicts me, that departing hence,
> As from his face I shall be hid, depriv'd
> His blessed count'nance; here I could frequent
> With worship, place by place where he voutsaf'd
> Presence Divine, . . .
> . . . .
> In yonder nether World where shall I seek
> His bright appearances, or footstep trace?
> For though I fled him angry, yet recall'd
> To life prolong'd and promis'd Race, I now
> Gladly behold though but his utmost skirts
> Of glory, and far off his steps adore.
>
> [XI. 313–33]

Michael's response, too, suggests that the poem here deals with a necessary and conscious change in vision; it is to this fundamental question that Michael's amplification of the doom must serve as response.[14] He virtually repeats God's charge, specifying the second part of his purpose, the "history" of future days, both of

13. If patiently thy bidding they obey,
Dismiss them not disconsolate; reveal
To *Adam* what shall come in future days,
As I shall thee enlighten, intermix
My Cov'nant in the woman's seed renew'd;
So send them forth, though sorrowing, yet in peace.
[XI. 112–17]

14. Among studies of the final books, see especially Prince, "Last Two Books of *Paradise Lost*."

Adam and of the race he literally includes. In doing so he frames it quite specifically as a confirmation of God's visible presence in the "lower world, to this obscure and wild" (283–84). Reminding Adam of God's continuing omnipresence and the gift of all the earth, Michael thus suggests that the last two books of the poem are the handing down of an art of interpretation:

> Yet doubt not but in Valley and in Plain
> God is as here, and will be found alike
> Present, and of his presence many a sign
> Still following thee, still compassing thee round
> With goodness and paternal Love, his Face
> Express, and of his steps the track Divine.
> [XI. 349–54] [15]

In the way he initiates books XI and XII, then, Milton seems to imply that Adam's fallen vision is symbolic in the Platonic sense that essences are no longer accessible in the phenomena. Surrounded "in spirit" by a world of chaotic and hellish appearances —from our point of view by a world apparently of Satan's manufacture—Adam must learn what the poem's commentator has already taught the reader logically: to read these appearances as an entirely new mode of divine signification, as typological rather than merely symbolic signs.[16] The terms of Adam's initial question hint at the new way of reading the appearances of nature, as in the phrase "appearances, or footstep" (XI. 329). And previously, he has glimpsed the possibility that natural signs might now be "forerunners" of God's provident purpose, including a temporal dimension formerly incidental. But the last major movement in the poem is clearly designed to expound and amplify the new historical relationship between fallen experience or vision and the kingdom of God. Books XI and XII recount the translation of a symbolic into an essentially mythic vision. The terms we have called technical gradually replace the language for the unfallen

15. We may recall that the Son is the "image express" of the Father, the divine similitude (III. 384).

16. In Heaven, God's skirts appear "dark with excessive bright, / Yet dazzle Heav'n, that brightest Seraphim / Approach not, but with both wings veil thir eyes" (III. 380–82).

perception of presence, because the revelation of Scripture's "mysterious terms" is the only answer now available to Adam's original question about the relation between "Presence Divine" and the perception of ordinary experience. We can be specific about this large shift in vision, because Adam actually seems to experience it.

Nor is the reader quite excluded from the experience of our first parent. A major element in this section of *Paradise Lost* has to do with what we have been calling the poem's rhetoric; it consists in the complicated and shifting relations between dramatized figures, the speaker of the poem (himself an active character at times), and the reader. Adam's general predicament here recalls the position of the poet in the invocation to book III—that visitor to Heaven who "finds no dawn," excluded as he is from

> the sweet approach of Ev'n or Morn,
> Or sight of vernal bloom, or Summer's Rose,
> Or flocks, or herds, or human face divine;
> But clouds instead, and ever-during dark
> Surrounds me, from the cheerful ways of men
> Cut off, and for the Book of knowledge fair
> Presented with an Universal blanc
> Of Nature's works to me expung'd and ras'd,
> And wisdom at one entrance quite shut out.
>
> [III. 42–50]

In book III the Bard goes on to pray for the inward mental vision necessary to "see and tell of things invisible to mortal sight"; and his prayer is answered by the Father's bending down his eye, "His own works and thir works at once to view" (III. 59; see below, chap. 8). Here Adam and Michael together "ascend / In the Visions of God," and the film is removed from Adam's eye by ingredients which pierce "ev'n to the inmost seat of mental sight." Like the poet, Adam is physically blinded and "intrans't"; but our first parent, as promised, awakens to foresight, a condition Milton had long associated with the completion of human learning (see especially Prol VII, CPW, 1 : 296).

The reader is thus carefully located for the poem's final two books. Throughout the poem, like so many of the characters both human and divine, he has been a viewer of prospects. Milton makes the ascent into a present dramatic scene by shifting into the present tense and then by superimposing space and time:

> So both ascend
> In the Visions of God: It was a Hill
> Of Paradise the highest, from whose top
> The Hemisphere of Earth in clearest Ken
> Stretcht out to the amplest reach of prospect lay.
> . . . .
> His Eye might there command wherever stood
> City of old or modern Fame, . . .
> . . . .
> . . . in Spirit perhaps he also saw
> Rich *Mexico,* the seat of *Montezume*
> And *Cusco* in *Peru,* the richer seat
> Of *Atabalipa,* and yet unspoil'd
> *Guiana,* . . .
> . . . but to nobler sights
> Michael from Adam's eyes the Film remov'd
> Which that false Fruit that promis'd clearer sight
> Had bred.
>
> [XI. 376–414]

While keeping our eye focused on the present scene, Milton moves in history and space at once, scanning places and successive rulers of places, reminding us of the catalogue both by specifying thrones for particular locales and by alluding once again to the motif of human conjecture ("*Sofala* thought *Ophir,*" 400).[17] He suggests the fusion of dramatic moments in alluding to the hill of "speculation" where Satan tempted Jesus, as well as by glancing ahead to the "Capital seats" later to tempt Adam's progeny (including Rome and the "richer seats" of the New World), and implicitly he includes the reader who has previously joined the narrator in turning away from "riches" of Hell (I. 691).[18]

We are involved somewhat differently in the visions that fol-

17. At 1 Kings 9 : 28; Job 22 : 24, 28 : 16; and Isa. 13 : 12.

18. Milton's first comparison is to the hill used by Satan to tempt Jesus in the wilderness; and the ambiguous "his" of XI. 385, just following the comparison, illustrates this conjunction of moments.

low. In them Milton first displays the apparent extension of Satan's kingdom, in a manner strikingly "neutral." As in the catalogue, the survey is interrupted periodically by the appearance of a prophetic figure. Michael then forges the link between Adam and victim or villain—and, too, the tie connecting the realm of unreal shapes and corrupt empires with human will. But throughout all this, Milton confronts the problem of perceiving "Divine similitude." To a great extent the sequence of visions and interpretations deals with the relation between perceived appearance and reality, or between "forms" human and divine. In each of the scenes Adam beholds first a place, starkly furnished with emblematic scenery, then human figures. These are unnamed until Abraham at XII. 152, and thereafter, Michael emphasizes, only as a concession. Milton presents these scenes as tableaux, draining history from them by keeping narrative verbs to a minimum and sometimes aiming at impersonal sense impressions in such a way as to make the reader as much a viewer and recorrected hearer as Adam—quite as he does, indeed, in the similes and scenes of Hell. In the action which follows the introduction of the figures, the carnage is presented directly to eye and ear (particularly in book XI), as in the killing of the just brother: "he fell, and deadly pale / Groan'd out his soul with gushing blood effus'd" (446–47).[19] Finally, in each of these scenes, we have Adam's "natural" reaction, followed by the instructor's corrective interpretation.

It is the relation of the "official" interpretation to the style of presentation in these scenes that is our main concern here. Adam opens his eyes to the first effects of the original crime and beholds a field half "arable and tilth" and half sheepfolds, with a central altar (XI. 432). He watches one brother kill the other in a manner so immediate and graphic that we are likely to share his shock at the "mischief" done to the "meek man who well had sacrificed; / Is piety thus and pure devotion paid?" (451–52). Michael explains and promises eventual justice, in a passage which successfully

19. Here as elsewhere Milton conveys the sense of change, rather than giving us a static picture; we literally follow the progress of Abel's fall to his countenance and groaning, to the pouring-out of his soul-blood, gushing and then finally "effus'd."

conveys the double emphasis that the Father's charge has led us to expect:

> the bloody fact
> Will be aveng'd, and th'others faith approv'd
> Lose no reward, though there thou see him die
> Rolling in dust and gore.
>
> [457–60]

What Adam has seen, Michael goes on to say, is the first *shape* of Death "on man," not Death itself; Michael seeks to display death in all possible sensuous horror, at the same time asserting that Adam's "natural horror" is directed at what is really an "entrance." As Adam's reaction moves from sight toward an ultimate criterion of sense, Michael insists authoritatively that this response—to injustice and to the horror of death—must yield to a higher vision which sees death and injustice both as a kind of "outside." No longer continuous with eternity, the immediate moment (like the immediate perceptions of fallen sense) must be seen in relation to inner meanings, now yielded only by history.

In the second vision, Milton dwells on bodily disorder, in 1674 adding mental disease as well as pestilence to the original catalogue of the first edition. But we should notice that if we "see" anything here it is only "numbers of all diseas'd," a catalogue which verges on a procession of allegorical figures. "Moping Melancholy" is tended by Despair, threatened but not relieved by Death. The interpretation which follows is mainly a discussion of similitude; Adam mistakenly identifies divine similitude with visible human form, which he complains is undergoing debasement in the "unsightly suffering" of the scene. The truth about "image" here, as Michael tells Adam, is that men "took / His Image whom they serv'd, a brutish vice" (XI. 517–18), a sentence implying that men do indeed approach the unreality of medieval allegory and of Sin and Death themselves—"once actual, now in body" (X. 587).

The pattern is similar as Michael proceeds through biblical history. The third scene is presented virtually as immediate sights and sounds; Milton's details suggest both indiscriminate impersonal artifice and the rich surfaces of fleshly corruption. Although *as readers* we may sense the irony in the speaker's designation of this as "happy interview and fair event," Adam's heart is understandably "soon inclin'd to admit delight;" and we too, with the poet, have had similar lapses. The lesson here once again is the necessity that Adam must recognize the allegorical surfaces for what they are: "Those tents thou saw'st so pleasant, were the Tents / Of wickedness" (XI. 607–8). Adam is told that he must see the full development of what we have observed already in the fall of the poem's heroine:

> that fair female Troop thou saw'st, that seem'd
> Of Goddesses, so blithe, so smooth, so gay,
> Yet empty of all good wherein consists
> Woman's domestic honor and chief praise;
> Bred only and completed to the taste
> Of lustful appetence, to sing, to dance,
> To dress, and troll the Tongue, and roll the Eye,
> [XI. 614–20]

Adam's "natural" mistake in this sequence of visions is to confuse what is immediately apparent in the vision with its ultimate meaning. The vision of feasts and music—of the sort to which conventional epic poetry habitually exposes us—is seen as a portent of "peaceful days"; wishing history to stop, Adam is tempted to see this as Nature's fulfillment "in all her ends."

The vision of the "heroic age" which follows recalls both the devils' games in Hell and the attack on heroism in the invocation to book IX. Adam concludes mistakenly that the warriors are "death's Ministers, not Men." The phrase underscores once again Milton's use of allegory as imagery; men *are* the ministers of death in the new world, the living vices are also Adam's own progeny. But in this scene, Adam's vision has begun to change in a way which helps to explain the subsequent decrease in actual instruction, as well as the shift to narration in book XII. For it is Adam, as well as the reader, who sees the upward motion of recovery: "one rising, eminent / In wise deport" who "spake much of right and wrong, / Of justice, of religion, truth and peace / And judgment from above" (XI. 665–68). In asking about this prophetic figure, Adam reveals an outlook (and vocabulary) quite different from his earlier reactions; a vocabulary Michael himself had applied to Abel: "But who was that Just Man whom had not Heav'n / Rescu'd, had in his Righteousness been lost?" (681–82). That is, Adam rightly describes the figure later to be known as Enoch, and Michael can now discuss finer distinctions than he could previously: between fame and earthly "styling," on the one hand, and the true names, "Plagues," "destroyers," rather than "patrons" and "gods."

The change in Adam's vision is even more evident when Adam is directed to behold the punishments of the "rest"; he sees "the face of things quite chang'd" from the roaring of the "brazen Throat of War" (712–13): a shift which he hailed as the fulfillment of "Nature in all her ends." Indeed, the scene is quite the same as the corruption of the apparently "just men" (577), except that Adam and reader alike see it foreshortened, as the crucial sin it is:

> All now was turn'd to jollity and game,
> To luxury and riot, feast and dance,
> Marrying or prostituting as befell,
> Rape or adultery, where passing fair
> Allur'd them; thence from cups to civil broils.
>
> [713–17]

In marked contrast is the detailed attention given to the "wonder strange" beheld by Adam at this point: the miraculous escape of the figure "of God observ'd / The one just Man alive" (817–18).

At this point Milton divided the final book of the 1667 edition into what became books XI and XII in 1674, adding only the lines which open book XII by marking a "transition sweet":

> As one who in his journey bates at Noon,
> Though bent on speed, so here the Arch-Angel paus'd
> Betwixt the world destroy'd and world restor'd,
> If *Adam* aught perhaps might interpose;
> Then with transition sweet new Speech resumes.
>
> [XII. 1–5]

The figures whose story marks the shift in Adam's vision is Noah, the "reverend sire" who testifies against the ways of the bellicose and corrupt society and who, like the righteous Enoch, barely manages to escape the wrath of the mob. Noah is not one of those who bear the office of Christ "in figure," but his survival of the Deluge does end the eleventh book—as well as the sequence of visions. How does Noah fit in? [20]

In the context of Adam's education in book XI, Noah is a most congenial figure; for a prime concern here, as we have seen, is the perception of form in the ambiguous sense of that word: the distinction of the divine similitude as seen in the naked majesty of Adam and Eve from other kinds of likeness created by fallen men or by Satan in men:

> Can thus
> Th'Image of God in man created once
> So goodly and erect, though faulty since,
> To such unsightly sufferings be debas't
> Under inhuman pains? Why should not Man,
> Retaining still Divine similitude
> In part, from such deformities be free,
> And for his Maker's Image sake exempt?
>
> [XI. 507–14]

Adam's question here links divine similitude mistakenly with human form in the visible sense—that realm of "outsides" from which Milton's *Art of Logic* is so careful to distinguish form properly conceived. Milton's handbook, we recall, in effect anticipates Michael (and earlier the narrator) in its insistence that in the fallen world we can see "visibly" only the forms of artificial things:

> To know the internal form of anything, because it is usually very remote from the senses, is especially difficult. In artificial things, however, the form, as being external and exposed to the senses, is more easily observed. . . . But there is no true distribution of form. For the distribution of [i.e., the distinction between] internal or external which some hold will . . . apply . . . merely to the corporeal; and the external is not

20. See D. C. Allen, *The Legend of Noah* (Urbana: University of Illinois Press, 1949).

> less essential to each artificial thing than the internal to each natural thing. [CE 11 : 61–63]

On the other hand, the first historical "just Man" in the poem bears a striking resemblance to that lady of *A Mask* who had threatened Comus's magic structures with her "sacred Vehemence." What he denounces is the scene of "arts that polish life" and the spectacle of a Hobbesian "Sword-law / Through all the Plain," both prospects which Milton presents as impersonal, if not "allegorical," tableaux. If Milton largely followed Genesis in his account of the Flood, his Noah is the visionary patriarch of Paul's Epistle to the Hebrews: the "reverend sire" declaring great dislike of the society's ways and in the assemblies preaching "Conversion and Repentance, as to Souls / In Prison under Judgments imminent" (XI. 724–25), before building the gigantic ark.[21] As with Enoch, Milton emphasizes his preaching—here, as in Milton's educational thought, the art which above all others makes Noah "the only Son of Light / In a dark age," an image of God in a world of unreal, even artificial imitations.[22]

Noah is thus one member in a procession of figures, just and unjust, heroic and typically fallen, whose connectedness—with each other and with Adam—it is Michael's purpose to establish. Adam has been told that the death of the meek Abel is in fact the murder of the just by the unjust brother. The fruits of the

21. See Hughes, p. 449, and Heb. 11 : 7: "By faith Noah, being warned of things not seen as yet, moved with fear, prepared an ark to the saving of his house; by the which he condemned the world, and became heir of the righteousness which is by faith."

22. D. C. Allen has argued that Milton's extended use of the Noah story has as its purpose the affirmation of the literal and, by Milton's time, generally suspect story of the Flood. It is true that Milton follows closely with one of the important formulas of the poem: "Lo a wonder strange!" (XI. 733). The context of the story in book XI, however, is also significant and has interesting connections with certain emphases given to the story. As we have seen, the book as a whole begins as an answer to Adam's question about the presence of God. More particularly it concerns the image of God in men, obscured by the Fall. By emphasizing Noah's *speech,* Milton focuses on that "art" which above all makes Noah a "Son of Light"; he even hints at the kind of prophetic voice he attributes also to Enoch. As Merritt Hughes has observed, the phrasing comes directly from Paul's first Epistle to Peter, where the preacher is Christ and where the ark is viewed as a "figure" of baptism, a connection accepted in *CD* I. 28. See CE 16 : 191.

lesson in the third scene, one of civil war and "council," are presented in a way verbally recalling the heroic games of Hell. In the midst of "factious opposition," Adam sees the single heroic figure rising "eminent / In wise deport" speaking of judgment, hooted down, and barely saved from the crowd by being snatched up in a cloud. And he recognizes him as the just man—a near "equal in fate" with Abel. This recognition is crucial. The Flood marks the violent end of the First Covenant, and of "one world." Here as in the middle of the poem Milton emphasized the triumph of divine creativity over evil in the way he redivided the books for the edition of 1674. Man now proceeds, as Michael says with an appropriate figure, "as from a second stock." But the division also emphasizes a shift away from vision which occurs within the Noah story itself: a shift, at any rate, away from the immediate and sensuous kind of vision which is a staple for Adam in book XI (and for the reader in the poem's first two books). From this point, Adam will continue to be taught, of course; and Michael carefully punctuates the new kind of perception that comes with the narration of the Second Covenant: "I perceive / Thy mortal sight to fail; objects divine / Must needs impair and weary human sense" (XII. 8–10). Michael's words clearly recall Adam's initial question in this final section of the poem, his request for some knowledge of the mode of God's presence in the subjected plain. And they serve to redirect attention to the new method of signification, as well as to the somewhat different function of book XII.

In general, the final book of *Paradise Lost* is more political, more historical, as well as more "intellectual" than book XI. The unnamed "City and Tow'r" of Babel is the culmination of the gradual movement toward a crowded and urbanized prospect, and it is succeeded by several projections of institutional order. Adam's education proceeds in a manner strikingly similar to Milton's own curriculum in *Of Education,* which similarly postponed the study of politics and theology. The book begins with the story of Nimrod and Babel, with a discussion of rational liberty and the Fall. In book XII the long line of nations sprung from "one faithful man" becomes central. Along with the archetypal tyrant and secular "architect" in Nimrod, we are told of the line descending from Abraham, Moses, and Aaron, Joshua ("whom the Gentiles *Jesus* call"), David, and Christ. At the same time, Milton is at some pains to stress that we are moving from a realm of shapes into a world of names and figures. Milton describes Adam's reaction to the Flood which ends the whole era by comparing him to a father mourning "His children, all in view destroy'd at once" (XI. 61). Although the discrepancy is crucial, the concluding simile of the passage is almost totally appropriate, and it implies a sharp difference between our experience of book XI's material and Adam's. It suggests that while we have viewed a sequence of visions as readers, Adam's and Michael's ascent "in the Visions of God" has involved a prospect of "one world." In their eyes, if not in ours, the view in time is equivalent to the view in space (Cope, pp. 50–71). In effect—to Adam's way of seeing—the visions of the eleventh book have all taken place at once. Even the absence of biblical proper names serves here to make Adam's vision of things future seem an archetypal, as well as a particularized, historical future.[23] The reintroduction of biblical names in book XII serves to distinguish, to individuate, and as it were to rehistorify the poem, precisely as Michael introduces to Adam the apparatus (by this time familiar enough to the poem's reader) of typology.

This is by no means to say that we leave archetypal recurrence behind as we move into history. Pharaoh, a traditional figure of Satan, is *the* lawless tyrant who must be compelled by "signs and judgments dire." These characters in the poem have a double existence, of the kind Milton gives Belial much earlier:

> To him no Temple stood
> Or Altar smok'd; yet who more oft than he
> In Temples and at Altars, when the Priest
> Turns Atheist, as did *Ely's* Sons, who fill'd
> With lust and violence the house of God.
> In Courts and Palaces he also reigns
> And in luxurious Cities
>
> [I. 492–98]

23. Abraham too must leave his "native Soil,"

Perhaps the supreme instance of this ambivalence is the way in which Milton treats the origin of the Mosaic Law. Milton moves us in time, without surrendering his overarching pattern of loss and recovery, to the point where "Law appears imperfet." Though the passage renders a discrete historical moment, its context clearly includes all the pressures of the poem, from the "One Greater Man" of the opening lines to the doom based upon Gen. 3 : 14 f.:

> God from the mount of *Sinai,* whose gray top
> Shall tremble, he descending, will himself
> In Thunder, Lightning and loud Trumpet's sound
> Ordain them Laws; part such as appertain
> To civil Justice, part religious Rites
> Of sacrifice, informing them, by types
> And shadows, of that destin'd Seed to bruise
> The Serpent, by what means he shall achieve
> Mankind's deliverance. . . .
> . . . .
> [But] to God is no access
> Without Mediator, whose high Office now
> *Moses* in figure bears, to introduce
> One greater, of whose day he shall foretell,
> And all the Prophets in thir age the times
> Of great *Messiah* shall sing. . . .
> . . . .
> So Law appears imperfet, and but giv'n
> With purpose to resign them in full time
> Up to a better Cov'nant, disciplin'd
> From shadowy Types to Truth, from Flesh to Spirit,
> From imposition of strict Laws, to free
> Acceptance of large Grace, from servile fear
> To filial, works of Law to works of Faith.
> And therefore shall not *Moses,* though of God
> High belov'd, being but the Minister
> Of Law, his people into *Canaan* lead;
> But *Joshua* whom the Gentiles *Jesus* call,
> His Name and Office bearing, who shall quell

> The adversary Serpent, and bring back
> Through the world's wilderness long wander'd man
> Safe to eternal Paradise of rest.
>
> [XII. 227–314]

To a remarkable extent, Milton holds the parallel between the Mount of Sinai and the Hill of Paradise ("this Mount of Speculation"), while engaging with the original question that prompts the final two books. Throughout the passage it is difficult to miss the historical dimension of "shadow," partly because it is an appropriate part of Adam's rediscovery of Providence. To recall what is surely the most striking of the poem's pressures on these lines is to see at once the essential departure in Michael's lesson: "what if Earth / Be but the shadow of Heav'n, and things therein / Each to other like, more than on Earth is thought?" (*v.* 574–76). Though Milton is clearly articulating the temporal symbolism so ably explained by William Madsen, Raphael's distinction here is primarily atemporal—it is atemporal, at any rate, for his unfallen "dramatic" audience, if not for the poem's implied reader.[24] An *exclusively* typological reading of "shadow" becomes possible, then, only if we recognize the great difference between dramatic and rhetorical audiences in the poem. In Michael's presentation, of course, these audiences are more at one. Indeed, the readers in any way susceptible to metrical and syntactic emphasis will sense the motions of recovery and completion as Milton concludes the account.

By nearly two hundred lines, all this anticipates Adam's final hymn of joy in the "goodness immense," and by still more the poem's ultimate vision, promised in its opening lines, of "New Heav'ns, new Earth, Ages of endless date" (XII. 549). But it clearly shows how Michael's mission engages throughout with Adam's initial question about reading the now "mute signs" in nature. The terms we have called technical occur precisely at those points in the poem when Milton is *at once* reading the "mysterious terms" of Gen. 3 messianically *and* explicitly answering Adam's query about God's "bright appearances" in the plain which con-

24. See Madsen, "Earth the Shadow of Heaven," and see my discussion in chap. 8.

tains most fallen human existence in the poem. In such passages, moreover—dry though they often seem—we never quite lose the impassioned claim of Raphael, in different ways valid alike for fallen and unfallen experience, that "one Almighty is, from whom / All things proceed, and up to him return" (v. 469).

The reason books XI and XII do not just rehearse a vision of history previously programmed is that the poet who has previously rectified our own vision has now in effect entered the poem's narrative as yet another of Milton's literary "daemons," to do something like the same thing for Adam. In part the fun of the poem's final books is thus in seeing the poem's narrative Adam gain the reader's perspective. It is thanks to the poet of *Paradise Lost* and his commentary, we may recall, that we are enabled to see the angel forms at all in Hell, or indeed to visualize the poem's action at the sensuous level traditionally appropriate to the domain of poetry. Of his continuous presence the argumentative form of simile is one frequent reminder; and no full account of the poem's largest modes of coherence can afford to omit him as a prime character. The perspective offered us by the poet (and here by Michael to Adam) may be called definitive in the *Art of Logic*'s rather specific sense that it takes us beyond poetry because it must take us beyond the ken of mere description. In *Paradise Lost,* as in the early *Mask at Ludlow Castle,* we are offered a vision of forms, and those not merely of a nominal or artificial world—that realm of the middle air which the poem as a whole rejects. It is from this vision of "artificials" that Michael successfully rescues Adam in books XI and XII, enabling him to perceive the ultimate joy in the ways of God. The final books have seemed dead even to perceptive readers of the poem perhaps because the gradual shift in Adam's vision is not easily kept in mind by readers used to "purer" forms of narrative. Reading carefully, however, we discover in XI and XII a kind of momentary superiority to Adam which is a measure of the poem's success—and the success of its wholeness.

Argument and Structure

The final books of *Paradise Lost* show that even the materials of simile imply a presenter and thus some degree of argument, beyond the emblematic value they may have brought to the poem —so suspicious does Milton seem to be of "automatic" archetypes and images. As arguments, the similes epitomize a speaker's attempts at secondary definition, through description and necessarily through "names." At the same time, they reveal the speaker as a poet verging on definer and even carry the poem as a whole part way into the realm of what the *Art of Logic* calls the inartificial argument of "divine testimony," the kind of vision possessed by Ezekiel and other prophets of the poem's narrative, and of Milton's prose. Thus we may view the corporealization of the angel forms in Hell as a temporary accommodation to "human sense"—a shift, as it were, in the location of "form" which can occur only as the angels (1) revive in Hell, and (2) ipso facto become artificial in the sense of the *Art of Logic* and thus controllable by a narrator himself "godlike" at times. Theologically, of course, the fallen angels are controlled, though "actually" they still possess power. Within the poem's narrative (as within Providence clearly seen) they are similarly controllable. We might even say, perhaps, that to the extent that we fix on the narrative of *Paradise Lost* (and in particular on the demise of Satan or the mere tragedy of the Fall) we are engaging only with the poem as object whereas the poem itself—in its widest aspect—offers more, in attempting to offer us the freedom from "art" that is in part Michael's contribution to Adam's perception. How far this preoccupation went in Milton's thinking is clear even in a relatively early passage like the following, from the *Areopagitica:*

> If every action which is good, or evil in man at ripe years, were to be under pittance, and prescription, and compulsion, what were vertue but a name, what praise could be then due to well-doing, what gramercy to be sober, just, or continent?
> Many there be that complain of divine Providence for suffering Adam to transcend. Foolish tongues! when God gave him reason, he gave him freedom to choose, for reason is but choosing; he had been else a mere artificial Adam, such as Adam as he is in the motions. [Hughes, p. 733A]

Within *Paradise Lost* itself, it is the similes, along with the invocations, that most clearly reflect this essential Miltonic concern, a preoccupation neither purely formal nor thematic. In part, Milton's formal images serve to emphasize the patent artifice of his work, and thus the secondary status of the poem itself.[25] If we now return to the poem's beginning, and to the poet's scrupulousness in establishing his poem's world, we may further clarify the structural value of Miltonic simile.

In recognizing what happens in books XI and XII as in part a rehearsal, we are referring back to a kind of logical education which takes place for the reader largely in the first books of the poem. Here, as we have seen, Milton reforges his fable's connections with the poem's true "utmost isle," articulating it with our experience in what we have called an argumentative fashion. Milton reverses this movement, I believe, toward the end of book I. Just after he has completed the poem's rhetorical orientation by grounding the poem's mythological, literary, and historical allusions in the catalogue, he begins to distinguish the realities of the poem's effects from the artifice of his poem's narrative. If the function of the catalogue is to provide a fictional genesis of the reader's knowledge in *Paradise Lost,* we might say that the balance of book I serves in part to sort out some elements in his moral and literary experience. Throughout *Paradise Lost,* the similes actually discover the largest wonder of God's causes even as they pretend only to accommodate the wondrous fable to "human sense." Our own experience dovetails with the poem's story most clearly in these moments, and often we seem to *become* the conventionally heroic protagonist. At this point—the beginning of the large unraveling of responses which occupies the balance of book I—Milton employs conventional epic simile dramatically, actually to project the vision of Hell's monarch. The image also overlaps with the implied narrative action of the catalogue in such a way as to suggest that the poet too is involved in this collective survey and self-congratulation. Turning ironically on the machinery of epic itself, Milton reviews the Muse's catalogue of gods (here they are emphatically literary) in a corrupt calculation of "thir number": [26]

25. On the distinction between arguments "artificial" and "inartificial," see *Art of Logic,* CE 11 : 279–83.

26. See the treatment of "number" (or "numerability"), for example, at III. 346 and in the presentation of Eden, briefly discussed below, chap. 8, n. 10.

> He through the armed Files
> Darts his experienc't eye, and soon traverse
> The whole Battalion views, thir order due,
> Thir visages and stature as of Gods;
> Thir number last he sums. And now his heart
> Distends with pride, and hard'ning in his strength
> Glories: for never since created man
> Met such imbodied force as nam'd with these
> Could merit more than that small infantry
> Warr'd on by Cranes: though all the Giant brood
> Of *Phlegra* with th'heroic Race were join'd
> That fought at *Thebes* and *Ilium,* on each side
> Mixt with auxiliar Gods: and what resounds
> In Fable or *Romance* of *Uther's* Son
> Begirt with *British* and *Armoric* Knights;
> And all who since, Baptiz'd or Infidel
> Jousted in Aspramont, or *Montalban,*
> *Damasco,* or *Marocco,* or *Trebisond,*
> Or whom *Biserta* sent from *Afric* shore
> When *Charlemain* with all his peerage fell
> By *Fontarrabia.* Thus far these beyond
> Compare of mortal prowess, yet observ'd
> Thir dread Commander.
>
> [I. 567–89]

The passage beautifully illustrates Milton's detailed and scrupulous attempt to include aesthetic "contingencies" within his poem's bounds. Here as elsewhere, simile is intimately meshed with its context; and this section both begins and ends with acts of beholding, first by Satan—or by Satan, poet-as-Satan, and reader.

Formally, the caesura at line 573 marks the shift from a conventional description of Satan's feelings to an ironic recollection of epic battles. If it reads like an irrelevant flyting at all previous epic performances (the kind of attack so often ascribed to Milton the man), the poet has made it architecturally successful by framing it as though it were the dramatized reaction of Satan to what he sees. The apparent anachronism of "for never since created man / Met such imbodied force" follows and amplifies the striking shift to the present tense and an almost physiological reference to Satan's distending heart. The lines which follow ironically display an extraordinary ideological toleration; given the assistance of "auxiliar Gods" on *each* side in conventional epic, he is willing to include "Baptiz'd or Infidel" in mustering the pure power necessary for the appropriate comparison; this is the reaction of almost anyone but Milton—specifically it is the poet or reader who would admire the pure power of "imbodied force." Its primarily narrative dimension is explicitly recalled only when we are told a few lines later that Satan "yet observ'd" the assembling army (588–89).

If we must speak of Milton's dramatic technique, it is at points like this that we must be particularly careful. The drama in a line like "for never since created man . . . ," as in "Adam the goodliest of men since born / His Sons" (IV. 323–24),[27] consists precisely in the apparent *disregard* for decorum, in the way it is Satan who seems to make his army contemporary with the armies of history and legend. Milton's anachronisms involve the reader as well as Satan and what Satan is seeing; this one is dramatic in the sense that it seems to include the reader *within* what Satan sees. The poem's rhetoric locates even the reader of *Paradise Lost,* or at least the alter egos we now and then encounter in the poem, within the purview of both God and Satan. "Adam the goodliest of men since born / His Sons" may be the logical comparison of a rather discursive poet late in human history; but like the passage we have been discussing it occurs in a context of Satan's supervision and should be seen as the dramatized perception of Satan, who is gleeful at being able so easily to "confound the race / Of mankind in one root" (II. 382–83). Since that root *in the poem*—as the speeches of book IX or the War in Heaven make clear—also becomes the reader in whom both Adams meet, the use of anachronism in *Paradise Lost* has the double effect of locating the reader within the poem and locating Satan outside it.

It would be a mistake to insist, however, that Milton is writing a Jamesian novel here and consequently to focus too narrowly on Satan's perception. To an extent which may surprise us, poet

27. See also IX. 504 ff. and above, chap. 6, n. 38.

fuses with devil here; even in the detail of summing the numbers of those battalions, it is the poet who darts the experienced eye and even glories in his own production. But finally the passage reveals an art of multiple perspectives, with strategic shifts between higher and lower levels. Satan's reaction is qualified even in the fact that this is another extended catalogue, a stock routine naming all the giants and heroes who could not match the fallen angels' strength. Though the effect is perhaps concealed by the conventional mode of heroic comparison, it is related to that of the celebrated Mulciber passage, where Milton encloses deliberate and finely wrought poetry within a frame of tempered irony: "thus men relate, / Erring" (I. 746–47). Here, as in the building of Pandemonium (I. 700 ff.), any appropriate comparison to the artifacts and power of Hell must involve references to the strife of human history—if not to outright war (heroic poetry's conventional subject), at least to the analogous peacetime activity of conspicuous and competitive consumption. Thus, striving himself, the poet demonstrates that Satan's cause is "beyond compair of mortal prowess" by associating all heroes of renowned power in history and legend with his image of "created man," an image which is ultimately reduced to the stature of a band of Asian pygmies known in contemporary legend for a constant, futile battle with cranes—"that small infantry." As Satan's heart distends, created man diminishes still further by mixing with "all the Giant brood" of fable and history—the "late" embodiments of the devils, according to the recent information of the epic catalogue. Include the gigantic heroes of Aeschylus, Homer, and Ovid, Marino and Ariosto—and even the "auxiliar Gods" of Homeric epic; add, if you will, the entire world of conventional heroic poetry, and the odds would not change. Medievalizing the passage with his own peculiar "tilting furniture"—words like "brood," "begirt," and "joust"—Milton mixes all Western heroes, historical and mythical alike, in a chivalric fairyland which may be Spenser's prime contribution to *Paradise Lost:* a world, however, in which "created man" is comically and satirically reduced. Clearly enough, it is the world of Miltonic simile.

The gradual emergence of a reality partly external to the narrative is in part a function of the famous visual immediacy of

Milton's poetry generally in the first two books, and particularly in the conclusion to book I. As we have seen, the similes of book I and throughout the poem appeal to immediate and often to "concrete" visual experience as a source of argument. It is recurrent, modern experience, even in the instance of Leviathan's remarkable migration to the Norway seas. But frequently, the similes undercut epistemological certainty in the realm from which they draw such material. The analogies for certain cruxes in the narrative progression come from a world of fable, geographical conjecture, and etymological uncertainty, of human names, and inevitably (for Milton) of human religions. Milton thus uses our experience and history as an argument, but in mixing it with the realm of poetry and idolatry, especially in the catalogue and its conclusion, he calls attention to the inevitably mythic or imaginative basis—the error—of that experience. The ignorance and benightedness of human travelers in the similes, of course, are alike signs of their spiritual condition. But virtue in this poem—and perhaps only in poetry, Milton would seem to imply—recovers its primal sense of knowledge and power. The many references to the error of myth and poetry in *Paradise Lost,* in other words, are not part of a Miltonic literary petulance; they are meant to go with the poem's other suggestions about the dreamlike vision of the reader himself.

As Stanley Fish has shown, Milton is to some extent interested in inventing and correcting that condition throughout the poem.[28] But as he brings book I to a close, he seems particularly concerned to dramatize the limits of the reader's vision, in the rather special sense I have attempted to define in these pages. In portraying the moment when the devils first become recognizably human in the "subtle magic" of their artifice (727), he populates the scene in a way which appears to recapitulate book I, emphasizing both the great size of the temple and the incredible numbers of the devils. They are likened once again to "Paynim chivalry":

> thir summons call'd
> From every Band and squared Regiment

28. Fish, *Surprised by Sin.*

By place or choice with worthiest; they anon
With hunderds and with thousands trooping came
Attended; all access was throng'd, the Gates
And Porches wide, but chief the spacious Hall
(Though like a cover'd Field, where Champions bold
Wont ride in arm'd, and at the Soldan's chair
Defi'd the best of Paynim chivalry
To mortal combat or career with Lance)
Thick swarm'd, both on the ground and in the Air,
Brusht with the hiss of rustling wings. As Bees
In Spring time, when the Sun with *Taurus* rides,
Pour forth thir populous youth about the Hive
In clusters; they among fresh dews and flowers
Fly to and fro, or on the smoothed Plank,
The suburb of thir Straw-built Citadel,
New rubb'd with Balm, expatiate and confer
Thir State affairs.

[I. 757–75]

Taken imagistically, as it were, the natural figure implies great visual distance on the devils and even reduces them in size—particularly the detail of their rustling wings. But once again we are reminded that the likeness "hobbles," apt though its royalist associations may be;[29] ostensibly it is a likeness only for the thickness of the devils' swarm (775–76). At this point, Milton more literally reduces the size of the devils, at the same time calling attention to the illusory quality of the whole visual scene in Hell:

the signal giv'n,
Behold a wonder! they but now who seem'd
In bigness to surpass Earth's Giant Sons
Now less than smallest Dwarfs in narrow room
Swarm numberless, like that Pigmaean Race
Beyond the *Indian* Mount, or Faery Elves,
Whose midnight Revels, by a Forest Side

29. See Davis P. Harding, "Milton's Bee Simile," *Milton Studies in Honor of Harris Francis Fletcher,* ed. G. Blakemore Evans (Urbana: University of Illinois Press, 1961), pp. 56–61.

> Or Fountain some belated Peasant sees,
> Or dreams he sees, while overhead the Moon
> Sits Arbitress, and nearer to the Earth
> Wheels her pale course; they on thir mirth and dance
> Intent, with jocund music charm his ear;
> At once with joy and fear his heart rebounds.
>
> [776–88]

The passage epitomizes the techniques we have been examining in this chapter and seems clearly to recall once again many of the literary and other allusions of book I. At the very source of material corruption, Milton rhetorically breaks the description in an arresting way, asking the reader directly to behold a kind of miracle. Needless to say, the device is conventional, the sort of thing Chapman might gloss in the margin as "Augurium." What Milton requires us to behold, however, is the magical shrinking of the devils into the size of the very dwarfs that were previously the measure for all the armies of created man. Again in the context of beholding or seeing, we visualize through simile the apparently comic reduction of the devils who so recently seemed "in bigness to surpass Earth's Giant Sons." Once commanded to behold the wonder of the present scene, we are kept alert by the many repetitions of "sees" and "seems" in the passage. Milton first reminds us of his own catalogue (and the devils' power) by likening the shrunken devils to the "small infantry" with which we are already familiar. Then he evokes a midsummer night's dream, a quite English moonlit pastoral tableau complete with elves and a peasant viewing "revels." Readers have found in this passage a direct borrowing from the *Aeneid*—at the point where Aeneas catches a glimpse of Dido in the underworld; but the viewer of this narrative scene is no conventional epic hero. Furthermore, only the reader has accompanied Milton, as it were, on his visit to the underworld.

The presence of the elves and peasant in the simile recalls similar figures in the *Mask at Ludlow Castle*. If the aristocratic and ceremonial occasion there prevented a fully effective use of a too-democratic "rude swain," the figure is superb here, because he seems to correspond to the viewer of the wonder in Hell. The peasant, like so many other figures in the similes, represents the dramatization of a response to the moonlit scene and the narrative miracle *alike;* if indeed he is not the poet, like the uncouth swain of *Lycidas,* he would seem to be the closest thing we get in *Paradise Lost* to James's *ficelle* or "friend of the reader."[30] The world of the peasant, the one he "sees / Or dreams he sees," is illuminated like the landscapes of previous similes by the moon. Here, however, "the Moon sits Arbitress" overhead and wheels "her pale course" nearer the earth. What Milton means to suggest about the vision of the belated peasant is clarified in the lines which follow. Milton always takes into account the potentially higher level of vision as well as the lower, and the repetition of "seems" in the passage—as in the portrayal of Sin—implies that in this moment of the most vivid particularization, both in fable and in style, Milton is equating the quasicomic status of the devils precisely with the realm of deceptive poetic appearance (see *PL* 1. 648–52). In keeping with the movement of the poem toward the great destructive gesture of the devils—and toward this earth—he dismisses the importance of the devils' physical appearance, on which he has concentrated so much of his best poetry, and strikes the more ominous note of a reality "far within." The close of the first book, then, can be taken as Milton's absolute and compelling answer to the problem of representing evil in a poem pretending to be true:

> Thus incorporeal Spirits to smallest forms
> Reduc'd thir shapes immense, and were at large,
> Though without number still amidst the Hall
> Of that infernal court. But far within
> And in thir own dimensions like themselves
> The great Seraphic Lords and Cherubim
> In close recess and secret conclave sat
> A thousand demi-gods on golden seats,
> Frequent and full. After short silence then
> And summons read, the great consult began.
>
> [1. 789–98]

30. James's discussion of such matters is quoted and analyzed by Wayne Booth in *The Rhetoric of Fiction* (Chicago: University of Chicago Press, 1961), pp. 102–5.

This, in part, is the meaning of the first book's ending, then; that while myth and visual appearance can best explain or describe the nature of the devils, they are ultimately beyond the province of poetry and "likeness" altogether, "in thir own dimensions like themselves." The worst mistake of the peasant—or of the reader of *Paradise Lost* (for the duration of the poem virtually another and luckier Adam)—would be to dismiss what he has just seen as being mere figments of imagination. Milton can express the full terror of the devils only by declaring the ultimate failure of figurative or descriptive language. By thus turning in or back on his own poem, as it were—now dissolving and now emphasizing the margins of his fiction—he keeps us keenly aware of the limits of art, as well as the fallibility of our own visions. There is no real outside to this poem, he repeatedly suggests; his Adam and Eve are real enough to address directly (*PL* IV. 773–75) or artificial enough to become pageantry. Satan exists both within and without *Paradise Lost,* waiting "day and night" for man's destruction (II. 505).

Plot and Process

Such clarifications of the nature of our experience serve us well later in the poem, at those moments when Satan, Sin, and Death disappear as actualities only to reappear in body. When Satan enters the Garden for the second time, he does so literally "involved in rising mist" (IX. 75). Subsequently, in seeking out the best shape for the temptation, he proceeds through each "Thicket Dank or Dry, / Like a black mist low creeping" (179–80). The fiend's literal or metamorphic entrance into mists or such creatures as the cormorant is obviously different in effect from the kind of clarification we encounter in the animal similes—difficult though it may be at times to distinguish rhetorical from real likenesses. But all such similitudes, as Milton calls them in the *Art of Logic,* are like the commentary which elsewhere in the poem serves to illuminate the general problem of Satan's real likeness. Their function, with respect to this final part of the plot is again definitive, in the sense that they force us to confront the frankly poetic projection of Satan's form.[31]

31. "Figures" in the *Art of Logic* is a good approximation for the poem's "godlike shapes and forms."

All these metamorphic likenesses for Satan (and the fallen angels) amount to an inversion of the other kind of similitude, to be found in the kingdom of pure light where (as Raphael suggests) all things may be "each *to other* like, more than on Earth is thought" (v. 576; my italics). Indeed, we are not far from the center of Satan's character in all this. He declares at one point that his mission is partly to make "others . . . such as I," a purpose he has in part inherited from earlier "motiveless malignities." The entire project follows directly from the primal exaltation of the Son, at which Satan "thought himself impair'd." This irreducible motivation may be insufficient as an explanation of evil, but it is one he shares with Iago confronted by the "daily beauty" in Cassio's life (*Othello* 5.1.19–20). In book IV he encounters Adam and Eve "in true filial freedom plac't," as precise a description as the poem affords of where Satan has never been. Ultimately he and his cohorts are most radically opposed not to the Father but to the Son. While He is defined as divine similitude, they are presented at least implicitly throughout the poem as "in thir own dimensions like themselves" (*PL* v. 665; IV. 294; v. 576).

Satan's mistake in conception and execution alike is precisely to assume that visible form is finally separable from a reality "far within," an antipoetic or literalist view which has sometimes been confused with Milton's own. Poetry for Milton, we may recall, makes virtue delightful, largely in the sense that it brings the realm of form before our physical eyes—a function which blindness real or feigned can serve in large measure to undercut, in precisely the critical manner suggested above. For his part, Satan resembles those readers whose "hardness" might well *exclude* them from poetry's benefits. For Milton in 1642, poetry imparts delight

> to those especially of soft and delicious temper who will not so much as look upon Truth herself, unless they see her elegantly dressed, that whereas the paths of honesty and good life appear now rugged and difficult, though they be indeed easy and pleasant, they would then appear to all men both easy and pleasant, though they were rugged and difficult indeed. [Hughes, p. 670A]

It is as a result of his "character" thus conceived, then, that Satan generally operates in the poem at the level of imitation, actually transforming himself into subhuman forms on the scale of being. When we are informed that Satan is "squat like a Toad" at the ear of Eve, the image immediately expresses his nature at that point. He is, of course, attempting to "taint / The animal spirits that from pure blood arise / Like gentle breaths from Rivers pure" (IV. 804–6). For that matter, as we come to see, the grand vow to "mingle and involve" earth with Hell is also fulfilled only in the realm of appearance, the realm in which it is conceived. It has as its embodiment the world of an artificial Heaven, illumined by "light / As from a sky," or a self-enclosed Hell.

Throughout the poem, then, the devils' shapes are a focus for both comedy and pedantry. They seem to represent a physical vehicle for what Milton explains in various other ways, most notably, perhaps, in Raphael's discussion of the Almighty's oneness—that crucial passage to which we shall return in chapter 8. We are in a better position, now, to see that such ironic details as the resting-place for the sole of unblest feet or the first deceptive prospect of Sin (who "seem'd Woman to the waist, and fair, / But ended foul," II. 650–51) are the poem's way of seeming to transcend its own fable's appearances—a function, I have urged, of the poet's (though not Milton's) blindness. In the larger and more complicated sphere of the poem's plot, the same principle may be at work. It is partly for the reason of Satan's double character—as shape and essential form—that we are brought to see the poem's early heroic and tragic action so critically, even to the point of lamenting our parents' fall precisely in the manner of the foolish mouths mentioned in the *Areopagitica*. Such authorial and choric complaint is not merely inadequate, not even for Adam in book XI. It is a "fond" reaction characteristically transcended in Milton's poetry even before sonnet XIX. In *Paradise Lost,* it can be regarded as a Satanic if "natural" mode which frequently (and temporarily) infects the narrator himself, most spectacularly, perhaps, in the invocation to book III. For the poem's audience, the voice or "tone" of Satan is closer to his essence than are his various shapes. Thus, the poem inevitably fails for many readers used to reading dramatic monologues or novels of a single central perspective—readers who, in *Paradise Lost,* are likely to get trapped into following, or even accepting, the Satanic plot. Too many details of the poem, notably the similes or the survival of Satan in forms like "the River-dragon" of XI. 191, make it quite clear that he is never *essentially* degenerated in the poem—only in that lesser literary and epic aspect discussed in A. J. A. Waldock's influential chapter.[32]

Considered as a whole, indeed, the plot simply cannot be read as a "story" excluding the implied readers of *Paradise Lost* itself. For them, the poem's early similes involving mere magnitude and appearance have provided "old Ocean," for example, as their own fictional habitat, well in advance of Satan's vow to "mingle and involve" Earth with Hell. The final stage in Satan's "degeneration," moreover—the narration of the general metamorphosis in Hell—is linked with previous logical ones, in such a way as to verify them, on the more definitive level of narrative fact. The effect is similar to the way we are forced to recapitulate the early catalogue's summary of early human history:

> Thus were they plagu'd
> And worn with Famine long, and ceaseless hiss,
> Till thir lost shape, permitted, they resum'd
> Yearly enjoin'd, some say, to undergo
> This annual humbling certain number'd days,
> To dash thir pride, and joy for Man seduc't.
> However some tradition they dispers'd
> Among the Heathen of thir purchase got,
> And fabl'd how the Serpent, whom they call'd
> *Ophion* with *Eurynome,* the wide-
> Encroaching *Eve* perhaps, had first the rule
> Of high *Olympus,* thence by *Saturn* driv'n
> And *Ops,* ere yet *Dictaean Jove* was born.
>
> [X. 572–82] [33]

Milton conveys the rapid spread of sin characteristically, by glancing ahead in a manner deliberately emphasizing the *false*

32. A. J. A. Waldock, *"Paradise Lost" and Its Critics* (Cambridge: Cambridge University Press, 1947), pp. 65–96.

33. For the view that in such passages we "hear Milton thinking out loud," see Bush, *Mythology and the Renaissance Tradition,* p. 273.

conclusiveness of the "Till," followed as it is by the ironic amplification involving Ophion and that unborn shadow of the divine Son, Dictaean Jove. Recalling the historical analogues for the "lovely" serpent—Ammonian Jove and Capitoline Jupiter—Milton moves quickly into the recognizable realm of idolatry (particularly with the "annual wound" of Thammuz described in the catalogue at I. 447) and the devils' individual business of corrupting the greatest part of mankind in "gay Religions full of Pomp and Gold" (I. 372).

The devils' final transformation in the poem has proven less accessible to modern readers than other aspects of Eden's history after the Fall. We may recall, however, that Milton rarely allows his comic irony to become merely "funny." Ultimately the devils' corporeal fate never entirely excludes us, never becomes the mere mechanical automatism at which Bergson believes we laugh, partly because Milton continues to emphasize its status as a vehicle. Milton may have believed that the actual worship of idols—of "Sciential Sap," in particular—was profoundly involved with collective idolatry and imperialism, among other things, and that both were not to be dissociated from the more immediate and corporeal matters of death and evil. But finally, the best evidence that even brute forms can still captivate us is the mere existence of this poem and of poetry, whose "hovering and blazing power," we recall, Milton had associated with the pulpit, and which he even wished to institute, as a liberating communicative technology.

In some ways, Satan does resemble Milton as poet. He has a kind of antipoetics (he calls us out of our amazement at Mulciber), he thinks of himself as an essence somehow outside the figures and forms he uses to corrupt our grand parents and Eden itself. What makes his world different from Milton's in this respect, however, is the way he is ultimately "plac't." His status as epic hero in a poem transcending the heroism with which Satan so gladly associates himself—anticipating those modern literary descendants who suspect so prosaically that they are characters in a novel—is itself a kind of metaphor for his "placement" in a world not of his making, a world in which Milton himself is rather the celebrant than logos. If this is true, it would seem that Milton's purpose in appearing to mechanize the conventionally heroic portion of his plot is twofold—to shift our attention to the joy of God's profoundest "causes" and to complete the identification of reader-as-man with Adam which will make the poem true in part by depriving it of any real ending. Satan as an essence, external to the poem's mere narrative as well as magically captivated within it—like Sin and Death "once actual, now in body"—calls our attention indeed to the crucial distinction between reader and man. Since the conventional narrative, as Waldock saw, is more the storyteller's way of placing Satan than the Muse's, Milton's *forcing the distinction,* in effect, makes the scene's comedy relevant primarily as an image of our own more profound joy in "the Great Creator." It is that creativity which the poem celebrates, as the redivision of material between 1667 and 1674 makes especially clear. The poem's process of speech serves to discover and celebrate his providential design. But it is important to emphasize that the process is quite distinct from that large fable, for which the poem's "heroic" and largely conventional narrative is merely the frankly acknowledged type. If there *is* a mythic ending to that large fable within the poem, it occurs at the midpoint of the 1667 *Paradise Lost,* in Raphael's typological similitude of the great War in Heaven, whose manner of signification—at least within the poem's economy—joins the beginning and the end.[34]

34. For studies of the poem's temporal structure, see Albert R. Cirillo, "Noon-Midnight and the Temporal Structure of *Paradise Lost,*" *Journal of English Literary History* 29 (1962): 372–95, and Gunnar Qvarnstrom, *The Enchanted Palace: Some Structural Aspects of "Paradise Lost"* (Stockholm: Almqvist & Wiksell, 1967). See also Michael Fixler, "The Apocalypse within *Paradise Lost,*" in *New Essays on "Paradise Lost,"* ed. Thomas Kranidas (Berkeley and Los Angeles: University of California Press, 1969), pp. 131–78, for the claim that the Johannine apocalypse is at work cryptically throughout the poem.

8

"Discourse is oftest yours": The Situation of *Paradise Lost*

There is probably more humorous innocence in the three-book conversation between Raphael and Adam than many readers have been willing to allow. As Joseph Summers has observed, most of Adam's fanciful speculation does not spring from any immediate anxiety. Raphael furrows his brow at the speech of a first parent who has clearly transcended those interesting difficulties narrated in book VIII.[1] Undeniably, Raphael's mission to Paradise involves something of a departure from the celestial harmonies of unfallen discourse, as even the divine charge makes clear: "Go therefore, half this day as friend with friend / Converse with Adam" (v. 229–30). Raphael is told explicitly to bring on such discourse

> As may advise him of his happy state
> Happiness in his power left free to will,
> Left to his own free Will, his Will though free,
> Yet mutable; whence warn him to beware
> He swerve not too secure: tell him withal
> His danger, and from whom, what enemy
> Late fall'n himself from Heav'n, is plotting now
> The fall of others from like state of bliss;
> By violence, no, for that shall be withstood,
> But by deceit and lies; this let him know,
> Lest wilfully transgressing he pretend
> Surprisal, unadmonisht, unforewarn'd.
>
> [v. 233–45]

Mixed though it may be with the meal so useful for Raphael's warning, this conversation "as friend with friend" is of a different order, too, from the wonted discourse of Adam and Eve (see

1. See *PL* VIII. 510 ff.; Summers, *The Muse's Method,* chap. 5.

VIII. 52 ff.); we might expect as much, considering Milton's epithet for Raphael, "sociable." Yet Adam himself betrays nothing of the hostility to didactic rhetoric so common in modern readings of the poem (and in particular of Raphael's performance within it). The welcome extended to Raphael is presented, on the contrary, as the epitome of uncluttered hospitality, and Adam explicitly prefers the words of the "divine instructor" even to those occasions when "Cherubic songs by night from neighboring Hills / Aereal Music send" (v. 547 f.; see v. 350 ff.).

It is tempting, too, to follow those who seek out earlier, more irresponsible falls and to object at this point that Adam's role in listening to the divine instructor is already in part a fallen one; we remember with shakes of the head the similar pliability of Laertes. It is certainly true that Adam is too comfortably social in bidding Raphael to "oft return" at the end of book VIII. But surely the movement toward this colloquial glad-handedness is more gradual. Not until Adam seems "ent'ring on studious thoughts abstruse" do we get the departure of Eve into the gardens, so sympathetically rendered; indeed, part of the point here is the fragmentation of the primal society as the conversation becomes abstracted from gardening, from eating. If Adam comes to resemble those devils who in Hell "reason'd high . . . and found no end, in wand'ring mazes lost" (II. 558–61), his progress is well marked, as in the following passage describing the shaky moment when Adam's sensible experience fails. Here the submerged commentary suggests that knowing becomes divorced from seeing:

> Sudden mind arose
> In Adam, not to let th'occasion pass
> Given him by this great Conference to know
> Of things above his World, and of thir being
> Who dwell in Heav'n, whose excellence he saw
> Transcend his own so far, whose radiant forms
> Divine Effulgence, whose high Power so far
> Exceeded human, and his wary speech
> Thus to th'Empyreal Minister he fram'd
>
> [v. 452–60]

Even the "studious thoughts abstruse" are an effect of the "sudden mind" with which Milton so frequently signals divine motions. Although Adam's speculation seems to surround the very discourse intended to maintain him "lowly wise," he does react to the conditional forms and qualifying phrases designed to be part of the warning ("If ye be found / Obedient"). And to a large extent the conversation between Raphael and Adam remains the casual mixture it was originally intended to be.

Still, when all this is said, it remains that Adam's reactions and his questions lead into a section of *Paradise Lost* which has always been difficult for Milton's readers. Indeed, when we reexamine this centrally located visit to Eden, we find that the function of the sociable spirit is not at all a simple one. The first of the poem's two important heavenly messengers appears dressed like Mercury, the god of eloquence. Clearly enough, he is the poet, and in particular the kind we encountered in chapter 2: not so much the more purely literary one whose mind is "at home," or even "cut off," as the figure Milton himself sought actually to become, the "Interpreter and relater of the best and sagest things" (Hughes, p. 668A). Raphael's own commentary, indeed, suggests that within the economy of the epic as a whole similitude (and its formal projection, the epic simile) is less decorative than argumentative in function. But what is most impressive about Raphael as a professional communicator is the inevitable difficulties of his performance for the prime of men. Raphael defines the nature of these difficulties here and there in the long narration of the war, in passages which call attention to the nature of the delivery itself.

Itself a conventional rhetorical technique, Raphael's commentary (usually in the form of pretended narrative insufficiency) is sometimes discussed as though it were an inevitable or even adequate mode of procedure in this part of the poem. On the whole it seems more likely that the sheer abundance of commentary calls attention at once to real difficulties for the poet and complications which are deliberate and artistic. In this passage, for example, Raphael searches for a way to relate the battle between Satan and Michael:

> They ended parle, and both address'd for fight
> Unspeakable; for who, though with the tongue
> Of Angels, can relate, or to what things
> Liken on Earth conspicuous, that may lift
> Human imagination to such highth
> Of Godlike Power: for likest Gods they seem'd,
> Stood they or mov'd, in stature, motion, arms
> Fit to decide the Empire of great Heav'n.
>
> [VI. 296–303]

It may seem to us here (and of course elsewhere) that Milton offers us discussion of the problem as a solution to it. Raphael's musing, however, uses the traditional language of rhetoric, weighing his likeness with the audience in mind—he needs what "may lift / Human imagination to such highth / Of Godlike Power." And like the poem's early similes, this rhetoric refers us explicitly to the realm of appearances; the realm of "things conspicuous," to what "likest" the Angels "seem'd." In an effort to render a battle between spirits, the normal discourse of Paradise breaks down, and Raphael—or is it the poet?—must fall back on what is frankly a utilitarian resort.

This kind of qualification is frequent throughout Raphael's narration; but clearly we should consider it as a working part of the discourse designed to warn Adam. As the "critical" presenter of the War in Heaven, he even discourses at some length specifically about "likening," to the point of cautioning Adam against the confusion of shadows and things:

> High matter thou injoin'st me O prime of men,
> Sad task and hard, for how shall I relate
> To human sense th'invisible exploits
> Of warring Spirits: how without remorse
> The ruin of so many glorious once
> And perfet while they stood; how last unfold
> The secrets of another World, perhaps
> Not lawful to reveal? Yet for thy good
> This is dispens't and what surmounts the reach

Of human sense, I shall delineate so,
By lik'ning spiritual to corporal forms,
As may express them best, though what if Earth
Be but the shadow of Heav'n, and things therein
Each to other like, more than on Earth is thought?
[v. 563–76]

The tone and form of Raphael's final question here have made it easy to forget the immediate meaning of these lines, the real difficulties in Raphael's task. What makes Raphael's task hard is primarily the paradoxical nature of its matter. The "invisible exploits / Of warring Spirits" are inaccessible even to unfallen human sense.[2] The hesitancy to unfold "The secrets of another World, perhaps / Not lawful to reveal" is a direct allusion to biblical warnings.[3] But we should notice how Raphael solves the problem and what his solution implies about vision. As he says, the high matter is already "dispens't," and the remarks which follow explicitly answer the series of questions which are to this point apparently rhetorical ones: "how shall I relate / To human sense . . . ," "how without remorse . . . ," "how last unfold / The secrets . . ." The expression of his "high matter" necessarily takes him downward on the scale of spirit and substance, from an "other" world of spirit toward the realm of visible, substantial or "corporal" forms.[4] It is likening which makes this kind of expression possible.

But to what other world can Raphael be referring? The diffi-

2. See above, the second section of chap. 7. Michael narrates the history of the world restored because he perceives "Thy mortal sight to fail; objects divine / Must needs impair and weary human sense" (XII. 8–9).

3. Among numerous examples is the story of Saul and the witch of Endor, 1 Sam. 28 : 7.

4. "Lik'ning spiritual to corporal forms." Editions 1–3 read "corporal"; the fourth, which Darbishire, Wright, and others accept, reads "corporeal." Because Milton normally uses "corporal" for "relating to the body," and "corporeal" for "having a body," and for reasons of scansion, I prefer "corporal." I believe Milton has this distinction in mind at I. 301, where he likens "angel forms" to the leaves at Vallombrosa. "Form" in these passages is not merely visual "figure"; it also means "essence," or soul. See CE 11 : 59: "The rational soul is the form of man"; and *N*, 8: "That glorious Form, that Light insufferable."

culties of this three-book visit—or at least of Raphael's great similitude—seem all the more pressing for the way in which this casual talk begins. Near the beginning of the visit which has proved so troublesome, Raphael speaks the lines which Coleridge used as the epigraph to *Biographia Literaria,* chapter 13:

> O Adam, one Almighty is, from whom
> All things proceed, and up to him return,
> If not deprav'd from good, created all
> Such to perfection, one first matter all,
> Indu'd with various forms, various degrees
> Of substance, and in things that live, of life;
> But more refin'd, more spiritous, and pure,
> As nearer to him plac't or nearer tending
> Each in thir several active Spheres assign'd,
> Till body up to spirit work, in bounds
> Proportion'd to each kind. So from the root
> Springs lighter the green stalk, from thence the leaves
> More aery, last the bright consummate flow'r
> Spirits odorous breathes: flow'rs and thir fruit
> Man's nourishment, by gradual scale sublim'd
> To vital spirits aspire, to animal,
> To intellectual, give both life and sense,
> Fancy and understanding, whence the Soul
> Reason receives, and reason is her being,
> Discursive or Intuitive; discourse
> Is oftest yours, the latter most is ours,
> Differing but in degree, of kind the same.
>
> [v. 469–90]

Raphael's lines begin with the relation between the created things and the Almighty, and the floral metaphor brilliantly images the connection between substance and degrees of life with vital "spirits" and the graduated levels of spiritual life. He insists on a complete continuity of the scale in unfallen experience —even if "proportioned to each kind"; indeed the pauses and qualifications of the speech remind us that the discussion he is instructed to initiate concerns the kind most difficult to place. In moving from matter to spirit, moreover, Raphael makes it quite clear that he is also talking about reason and discourse itself; in fact, it is the hierarchy of epistemology and discourse (again, the two are not really distinguished) which he describes as being above but continuous with the scale of physical, substantial being. Reason discursive and intuitive differ "but in degree, of kind the same"; Raphael implies that although reason discursive (the entire realm of eloquence and rhetoric) is more *substantial* than the reason intuitive of Heaven, in the view of unfallen experience at least, the two modes of reason are essentially alike.

The passage is so striking that it is tempting to use it as a kind of key; here we have the poem's metaphoric ground, complementing the process which Milton makes more accessible throughout. Even if we miss the ambiguities in the speech itself, it seems essential to remember that Milton puts what Merritt Hughes has called "his most beautiful and crucial ontological passage" in the mouth of his "sociable spirit" Raphael. Indeed, though the narrator himself fills us in to an unusual degree as to the sources and status of *Paraise Lost* as a whole, it is primarily to Raphael that we owe our knowledge of the details of the poem's world. As the poem's expert on the world's original cosmology and on its discourse, Raphael clearly deserves careful attention.

To return to Raphael's caveat: if the difference between perfect human and angelic perception is one of degree and not of kind, as he has claimed, why does the angel's speech seem to allow for such a discontinuity? To be sure, his final question implies only that the web of analogical significances everywhere available in the unfallen Paradise—to be replaced after the Fall by the more remote "track Divine" (XI. 354)—is more immediately perceptible in Heaven. But despite the pressures of the "degree" speech a few lines earlier, these lines certainly seem to distinguish an intrinsic likeness sensed in the act of vision from the analogies thought, or even perhaps fabricated, at one or two removes on Earth. Milton is clearly using them, as in books I and II, both to undercut the realm (concrete, visual) to which simile will take us and to suggest the inadequacy of language to express his meaning: "though what if Earth / Be but the shadow of Heav'n, and things therein / Each to other like, more than on Earth is thought?" (v. 574–76).[5] If the tone of this is not downright ungentle, the phrase "is thought" suggests more intellectual community (and one of more limited capacity) than Paradise has yet to offer; and the Platonic attitude of the lines implies a more fallen earth than we might expect a strictly dramatic Raphael to intend. Milton's rhetorical questions throughout *Paradise Lost* are abundant and require careful treatment; Raphael's avoidance of "guarantee" here resembles his own cosmological discussion in book VIII in this respect (see especially *PL* VIII. 114 ff.). Certainly, things in Heaven *are* intrinsically more "like" than "on Earth is thought," and we know that in Paradise substance expresses spirit, even as the Son (divine similitude) expresses the Father. Only in a fallen world, of course, is likening necessary, in fact—that artificial argument, as it is called in the *Art of Logic,* which can function as one antidote to the chaotic "alter'd style" and the darkened perception of postlapsarian speech.[6] Thus, if Raphael's lines seem to ring with pessimistic overtones about the efficacy of fallen human vision and language when abstracted from their context, the ambiguous form of the angel's final caveat is Milton's concession to dramatic decorum. When viewed as a decorous dramatic utterance, at any rate, Raphael's hesitation cannot refer to the Platonic dissociation, necessarily one of "kind," that many readers have urged or assumed.[7]

In his helpful essay on the War in Heaven, Arnold Stein has

5. In addition to the annotated editions, see James H. Hanford, *A Milton Handbook* 4th ed. (New York: Appleton-Century-Crofts, 1946), p. 205; M. M. Mahood, *Poetry and Humanism* (New Haven: Yale University Press, 1950), p. 204; and Paul Shorey, *Platonism, Ancient and Modern* (Berkeley and Los Angeles: University of California Press, 1938), pp. 41–42, 184. On Milton's relation to Plato generally, see Irene Samuel, *Plato and Milton.* William Madsen argues persuasively against the Platonic interpretation in "Earth the Shadow of Heaven."

6. Milton's syntax in this passage describing Adam's fallen speech renders our grand sire's constraint: "From thus distemper'd breast, / Adam estrang'd in look and alter'd style, / Speech intermitted thus to Eve renew'd" (IX. 1131–33). The description of Adam at this point recalls Chaos, the "Anarch old" who speaks to Satan in book II "with falt'ring speech and visage incompos'd" (II. 989); in a sense Adam's "distemper'd breast" has partly assimilated the realm of Chaos, including the "thousand various mouths" (966). See also IX. 1119–31.

7. See Madsen, "Earth the Shadow of Heaven."

seen in the lines we have just considered the introduction of a "complex metaphor"; [8] but the passage encompasses much more. The War in Heaven is fully developed as narrative, as a series of incidents chronologically preceding the main action of the poem. Hence, unless we heed Raphael's choric guidance, it is especially easy on a first reading to ignore the fact that books v–vi, at any rate, consist largely in the delivery of an expanded trope of conventional Renaissance qualities—possessed, that is, of what Milton calls "aptitude for argument" (see above, chap. 5, p. 133). This particular figure is unusual for its mere size; but it is more than another instance of Waldock's minute flaw become a gulf.[9] For the commentary which frames it serves the function of keeping us in touch with decorum—that is, with the appropriate responses of the *prime* of men. As a dramatized audience, somewhat like Hamlet in the play scene, Adam must indeed find the substance of Raphael's narration to be "high matter and strange." For a strictly unfallen Adam, the War in Heaven is virtually incommunicable. But in responding to the wonders he has just heard, Adam is fair only to the unfallen point of view; the great difficulty of Raphael's task is not one in which the fallen reader is likely to participate: "Great things, and full of wonder in our ears, / Far differing from this World, thou has reveal'd / Divine Interpreter" (vii. 70–72). In *our* ears. What is emphasized here is an "unlike" which serves to remind Milton's reader of the still unfallen, "primitive" Eden. And, perhaps more immediately, it jars disturbingly with our own experience of Raphael's narrative, one of more or less immediate recognition. For the reader of *Paradise Lost,* the War in Heaven is nothing so remote. It is, in fact, continuous with what has been structured within the poem as his literary and historical memory, and Raphael's commentary points squarely at his own experience, as that has been shaped in

8. I am indebted in this discussion to Arnold Stein's essay on the war in *Answerable Style: Essays on "Paradise Lost"* (Minneapolis: University of Minnesota Press, 1953), pp. 17–37. I wish to be more precise than Stein, however, about the rhetorical significance of the war, which I view as essentially simile rather than as simply "metaphoric." That is, I wish to call attention to the function of the commentary and explication itself, which I believe works like an expanded "as when."

9. Waldock, *"Paradise Lost" and Its Critics,* p. 19.

part by the formal imagery of books I and II. The angel's remorse at "the ruin of so many glorious once / And perfet while they stood" (v. 567–68) both echoes and modifies Satan's horror at the wrecked appearance of the fallen Beelzebub (see I. 84 ff.). The "meaning" of the passage necessarily engages Milton's as well as Raphael's audience by recalling Satan's feelings after the original expulsion. On the whole, it seems more likely that the landscape and population of unfallen Eden, if not the entire action of *Paradise Lost*, is "high matter and strange" than that we will fail to recognize the landscape and speech of Hell, or the War in Heaven.

So neatly does the War in Heaven dovetail with the reader's experience in the first books of *Paradise Lost*—and so clearly does it figure an ultimate battle in the last days of our time as well—that the indecorousness and contradictions of Raphael's abundant comment can hardly be deemed gratuitous. He can perhaps best be seen as a projection into the narrative of the poet himself in his critical aspect: not Milton, but in effect the Attendant Spirit, at times the sociable opposite of that *anima conglobata* of the seventh Prolusion, at times "rapt above the Pole." This is clearly the figure described so fully in the invocations and in Milton's prose, autobiographical and otherwise. As well as any critique of the poem, in fact, the commentary of Raphael actually defines the position and suggests the problems of the Protestant epic, and prophetic, poet. We need only think of Milton's own great argument, rather than the War in Heaven, as the high matter.

In presenting Raphael's narration quite frankly as a measurement of heavenly by earthly things, then, Milton is clarifying the interplay he has deliberately created between two distinct audiences, the dramatic and the rhetorical audiences. Even as Raphael uses "likeness" in order to present a fabled heroic military action to a dramatized audience knowing only peace, that audience is itself being presented as a protagonist in another fable both archetypal and true—one which is supposed to involve us. Central to the artistic and normative mission of both speakers is the art of likening things spiritual to things corporal. At times, as we have seen, it is difficult to distinguish Raphael's dramatic voice from Milton's rhetorical or critical one. Where we can isolate the performance of Milton the public poet, however—in those moments when Milton may seem to us most "unpoetic"—we discover quite similar intentions. Generally speaking, Milton's own poetic language is the same sort of measuring as Raphael's more clearly explicated likening.[10] This is why the similes, long considered the prime receptacles of Milton's lyric genius, are such an ideal analytic focus for defining the intermixed function of poetry and rhetoric in *Paradise Lost.* But Milton invites the connection in other ways too. By echoing God's charge to Raphael (and we may recall the similar tenor of Milton's prose warnings in the 1640s [v. 233–45] and by forcing us to watch Eden become the scene of urban and literary commonplaces of the theatrical surfaces previously used only as the means of our verbal and logical access to Hell (see above, chap. 6), Milton makes his *own* fable a dire example. Most important of all, the personal invocations, and even the occasional invectives attacking royal welcomes or starved lovers, should be seen as integral parts of this poem's world. They provide the origination and perception of Milton's great argument and thus serve as the utmost isle of his poetic world. We should be especially careful in resisting the distinction to which *Paradise Lost* itself so frequently invites us, between subject and answerable object. The poem's achievement is actual, if its social results are not. The hypothetical *if* which so tenuously links the poem's first-person speaker and the style owned by the

10. The didactic intent of this technique is equally inescapable as he closes his account of the war (VI. 893–912). In speaking of his performance as a measurement, Raphael (and Milton) links it with the operation of the creating Logos, who "circumscribes" this universe in "the vast immeasurable Abyss" of Chaos with golden compasses (VII. 205–11). Elsewhere Milton uses the metaphor carefully to distinguish divine from human art. In his "wary" thirst to know "of things above his World," for example, Adam frames his speech to the archangel (v. 460). Paradise itself is distinguished from the realm of human art of measurement thus: "Nature here / Wanton'd as in her Prime, and play'd at will / Her Virgin Fancies, pouring forth more sweet, / Wild above Rule or Art, enormous bliss" (v. 294–97). As it provides the direct object, the last phrase, "enormous bliss" (with its literal meaning, bliss "beyond the measure of a mason's square"), dramatizes the energy of unfallen Nature. Like other details of the fable, for example the simile of Vallombrosa, the metaphor seems to fulfill Raphael's definitions.

Celestial Patroness is just one way in which Milton forces into the critical ken the *figure,* as it were, of the human poet, seeking thus "blamelessly" to express or to assert.

Task and Argument: The Invocations of Paradise Lost

In simplest terms, what we discover in the invocations is the conditions of the poem's achievement, a highly elaborate frame for the exaltation of poetry into vision. They can be said to offer a perspective even on that world of the simile which we have previously discussed as a kind of utmost reality in the poem; for they amplify the argumentative aspect of the poem's similes to the point of isolating, and even to an extent describing, the poet of *Paradise Lost.* As we have seen, the similes display him in moments of relative familiarity with the poem's audience. The invocations, on the other hand, imply some measure of alienation. In the most public-conscious of them, the poet prays for a safe return "to my Native Element" and for the kind of help appropriate to the difficulties of a poet partly reunited with society. From this point, "Standing on Earth, not rapt above the Pole," the poet sings "more safe . . . with mortal voice" (VII. 23 f.). It is at this point in the poem, just after Raphael's presentation of the War in Heaven, that his responsibilities are of a fundamentally social kind. He is working in evil days, and evil tongues still make the fate of an Orpheus possible at the hands of those who cannot (with the "fit . . . though few") understand the peculiar social function of the Christian bard:

> But drive farr off the barbarous dissonance
> Of *Bacchus* and his Revellers, the Race
> Of that wild Rout that tore the *Thracian* Bard
> In *Rhodope,* where Woods and Rocks had Ears
> To rapture, till the savage clamor drown'd
> Both Harp and Voice; nor could the Muse defend
> Her Son. So fail not thou, who thee implores;
> For thou art Heav'nly, shee an empty dream.
>
> [VII. 32–39]

Following Raphael's narration of the War in Heaven, the poet appears to muse specifically on the audience of rapture, that mode so frequent in *Paradise Lost* itself. Hence it is appropriate that in descending Milton should contrast his own heavenly guide with the mother of Orpheus, "an empty dream," and to indicate in similar terms that a failure in inspiration at this point—when appeals will be more rhetorical than visionary—would leave the poet, like Bellerophon, wandering in madness "on th'*Aleian* Field" (VII. 19).

In thus reverting to the myth on which he built an important section of *Lycidas,* Milton would seem to be breaking the poem's illusion in that apologetic manner so often lamented by post-Jamesian novelists and critics. But even in his lines on the evil times and tongues—"In darkness, and with dangers compast round, / And solitude" (VII. 27–28)—Milton refers not, for instance, to his personal danger at the Restoration but more immediately to a kind of inverse decorum, the paradox that such "outward circumstance," apparently more conducive to satire, is actually the necessary condition for epic. More characteristically, the conditions of the poem's achievement, as developed in the invocations, have less to do with the times—which we might also relate to the typological dimension of Raphael's similitude [11]—than with the more personal circumstances of the poet himself, whose raptures and dreams they serve to ballast with allusions to the menial level of his task. If the times are unlikely in book VII, in book IX it is the climate, age, and psyche of the poet changing his notes to tragic. His scruples connect this level of reference with the realm of study and mere technique, the "maistry" of epic machinery; but we should notice that his telling us so is in part the strategy of making the poem "hers." What is conveyed in the movement of such passages as the following, in other words, is the sensed problem of the poem's ownership:

> higher Argument
> Remains, sufficient of itself to raise
> That name, unless an age too late, or cold

11. These connections, at any rate, are demonstrable; see Madsen, "Earth the Shadow of Heaven," and my discussion at the beginning of this chapter.

> Climate, or Years damp my intended wing
> Deprest; and much they may, if all be mine,
> Not Hers who brings it nightly to my Ear.
>
> [IX. 42–47]

To an extent, all the invocations involve us in similar scruples. At the outset of book VII, the poet calls the "meaning not the name" of the divine voice he follows "above th'Olympian Hill." The poet's hesitancy here has hardly discouraged learned conjecture about Urania. He is helpful only to the extent of connecting the voice with Eternal Wisdom ("thy Sister") conversing and playing, like Adam and Eve, "in presence of th'Almighty Father, pleas'd / With thy Celestial Song" (VII. 11–12). Though she seems to be an archetypal figure of divine poetry, intimated in Milton's earlier prose discussions of this subject, the difficulties of precise identification have challenged Milton's exegetes almost as fiercely as the haemony of *A Mask* (see above, pp. 34–36). The point for our purposes here is that the poet, dealing as he must in names, includes the nominal possibilities which, taken together, will enable him to transcend them. At times he even explains his choice of metaphoric accesses. After summoning the Holy Light which is "offspring of Heav'n first-born" and here named "Bright effluence of bright essence increate," he continues: "Or hear'st thou rather pure Ethereal stream, / Whose Fountain who shall tell? before the Sun, / Before the Heavens thou wert" (III. 7–9). The opening invocation includes a version of this, appropriately literary in its emphasis:

> Sing Heav'nly Muse, that on the secret top
> Of *Oreb* or of *Sinai,* didst inspire
> That Shepherd . . .
> . . . Or if *Sion* Hill
> Delight thee more, and Siloa's Brook that flow'd
> Fast by the Oracle of God; I thence
> Invoke thy aid to my advent'rous Song,
> That with no middle flight intends to soar
> Above th' *Aonian* Mount, while it pursues
> Things unattempted yet in Prose or Rhyme.
>
> [I. 6–16]

Such distinctions apply even to the most pathetic of the invocations, in which the poet is himself dramatized and even located in a kind of landscape:

> thee I revisit safe,
> And feel thy sovran vital Lamp; but thou
> Revisit'st not these eyes, that roll in vain
> To find thy piercing ray, and find no dawn;
> So thick a drop serene hath quencht thir Orbs,
> Or dim suffusion veil'd.
>
> [III. 21–26]

It is passages like this which most severely try critical vocabularies, leading biographers (as theologians are led elsewhere) to conclude that the poem's reference is primary, that indeed the poem *is* a system of reference of one sort or another. Here, perhaps, the experience behind the poem need not worry us excessively, for the appeal *is* to experience of a particular and precisely medical kind: the drop serene, whose effects Milton describes at some length in the *Second Defence* (CPW, 4 : 583). If there is a trace of self-pity in the lack of reciprocal visits, however, it is lost when the object of the Lamp's visit is more and more alienated, distinguished from the *I* who does in fact successfully "feel" the "sovran vital Lamp." And indeed, we sense process in an extraordinary way in moving from "these eyes" to the kind of distance supplied by medical names and the metaphors which follow. With extraordinary immediacy and particularity, the whole experience of seeing has been placed and then substituted by another kind of visitation and sustenance. In midline, Milton builds the paradox which makes all such experience (and thus the poem's "circumstances," as revealed in other invocations) the necessary condition of his status as a prophetic poet. He does this so skillfully that he can end the invocation with perhaps the darkest passage emotionally in the poem, without losing its value as argument:

> Yet not the more
> Cease I to wander where the Muses haunt
> Clear Spring, or shady Grove, or Sunny Hill
> Smit with the love of sacred Song, but chief

> Thee *Sion,* and the flow'ry Brooks beneath
> That wash thy hallow'd feet, and warbling flow,
> Nightly I visit: nor sometimes forget
> Those other two equall'd with me in Fate,
> So were I equall'd with them in renown,
> Blind *Thamyris* and blind *Maeonides,*
> And *Tiresias* and *Phineus,* prophets old.
> Then feed on thoughts, that voluntary move
> Harmonious numbers; as the wakeful Bird
> Sings darkling, and in shadiest Covert hid
> Tunes her nocturnal Note. Thus with the Year
> Seasons return, but not to me returns
> Day, or the sweet approach of Ev'n, or Morn,
> Or sight of vernal bloom, or Summer's Rose,
> Or flocks, or herds, or human face divine;
> But clouds instead, and ever-during dark
> Surrounds me, from the cheerful ways of men
> Cut off, and for the Book of knowledge fair
> Presented with an Universal blanc
> Of Nature's works to me expung'd and ras'd,
> And wisdom at one entrance quite shut out.
>
> [III. 26–50]

The paradoxical nature of this argument emerges only gradually, from the involutions of the first double negative to the simplicity of the final three monosyllables, whose paradoxical content need no longer be spelled out. But although we are offered even the informality of the poet's visits and his nourishment on "thoughts," we hardly expect the confidence of the invocation's petition:

> So much the rather thou Celestial Light
> Shine inward, and the mind through all her powers
> Irradiate, there plant eyes, all mist from thence
> Purge and disperse, that I may see and tell
> Of things invisible to mortal sight.
>
> [III. 51–55]

The art of the entire passage is the way in which Milton converts his own alienation from elemental natural rhythms and from social and religious community into the necessary condition for the poet's prophetic authority. If this alienation is carefully juxtaposed with the events of the narrative—with *Satan's* relief at finding "the sacred influence / Of light" (II. 1034–35)—it is, nevertheless, unmistakably pathetic in its appeal. So completely are we given the poet's setting, and so physical is the portrayal of his blindness, that we think of the author's blindness instead of "corporeal vision," the poetic vocation instead of this poem. In short, this invocation in particular dramatizes the strategic *use* of the poem's sources, including the poet's experience, for the poem.

Although Milton is notable for the leeway he gives his reader in responding to his poetry, we are ultimately forced to connect the reality of an impression with the authority of a particular speaker or viewer—and the two activities seem inseparable in this poetry. Milton's speaker is remarkable in his flexibility, in the extent to which he ranges through the entire hierarchy of vision and discourse, as well as the particularity with which Milton describes him in the invocations. He has nearly the stylistic freedom of Adam and Eve, whose orisons in book v are duly paid, but paid in "various style":

> For neither various style
> Nor holy rapture wanted they to praise
> Thir Maker, in fit strains pronounct or sung
> Unmeditated, such prompt eloquence
> Flow'd from thir lips, in Prose or numerous Verse,
> More tuneable than needed Lute or Harp
> To add more sweetness
>
> [v. 146–52]

We have encountered this "various style" previously, including even the "holy rapture," in the uncouth swain's use of "various Quills"; and the "prompt eloquence" is available to the epic poet only when he is assisted by his Celestial Patroness.[12] But unlike his audience, he is by no means limited even to Adam and Eve's "level," and there is some evidence of his participation in the

12. Compare Milton's conception of Jesus' stylistic versatility in *AP, CPW,* 1 : 901.

vision of Heaven. Just after the worshiping angels cast down their crowns "inwove with Amarant and gold," we are reminded of our lost happiness and the fact that Paradise is now embedded in history:

> Immortal Amarant, a flow'r which once
> In Paradise, fast by the Tree of Life
> Began to bloom, but soon for man's offense
> To Heav'n remov'd where first it grew, there grows,
> And flow'rs aloft shading the Fount of Life.
> And where the river of Bliss through midst of Heav'n
> Rolls o'er Elysian Flow'rs her Amber stream;
> With these that never fade the Spirits elect
> Bind thir resplendent locks inwreath'd with beams,
> Now in loose Garlands thick thrown off, the bright
> Pavement that like a Sea of Jasper shone
> Impurpl'd with Celestial Roses smil'd.
>
> [III. 353–64]

Even better as an example of the poet's abandonment of explanation for rapture is the convergence of his voice with the angel chorus. After the Almighty's announcement of a new Paradise which he promises will spring from the ashes of the burning world (III. 333–35), we are told that the hosannas of response are loud "as from numbers without number" and "sweet / As from blest voices uttering joy" (III. 346–47): the music begins to invade the rhythms of the line, but the figurativeness of it all is still quite clear; we know where we are. At line 365, however, the poet appears to be caught up:

> their gold'n Harps they took,
> Harps ever tun'd, that glittering by thir side
> Like quivers hung, and with Preamble sweet
> Of charming symphony they introduce
> Thir sacred song, and waken raptures high;
> No voice exempt, no voice but well could join
> Melodious part, such concord is in Heav'n.
>
> [III. 365–71]

From this point, the poet's own voice, "rapt above the Pole," merges with the angel choir. It is a tone which the poet elsewhere contrasts with the more subdued accents proper for treating the events of the Fall, and one suitable for a speaker "fall'n on evil days . . . and evil tongues" (VII. 25–26). Until the phrase which restores the frame, "Thus they in Heav'n," there is no such accommodation as is indicated elsewhere by "thus spake" or "uttering thus"—or, for that matter, by an "as when." Instead the poetry works on us directly, itself celebrating first the Father, invisible and inaccessible, then the Son, divine similitude. When the song reaches the subject of the divine sacrifice, it is a singular angel (or the Bard as angel) who breaks into worshipful "naming," the sort of exclamation we get elsewhere from the Bard himself:

> O unexampl'd love
> Love nowhere to be found less than Divine!
> Hail Son of God, Savior of Men, thy Name
> Shall be the copious matter of my Song
> Henceforth, and never shall my Harp thy praise
> Forget, nor from thy Father's praise disjoin.
>
> [III. 410–15]

At this point, by no means unique in *Paradise Lost,* the private human voice is passionately fused with the public and celestial chorus. The convergence is more complete than the corresponding moment in *Lycidas,* where the "disappearance" of the poet is managed with somewhat finer detail.

Just as the ending of book I calls attention to the margins of fiction within the poem, by appealing to a definition beyond poetic description—in the formal context of simile—the poem as a whole may be said to include and finally to transcend the secular, chiefly in its invocations. These invocations act as the argument of simile writ large and appeal consistently to a world of meanings, not names, and thus to the poem's most real world, in which essences are not accessible, as in ordinary poetry (or the perception of other artificial phenomena), to our corporeal eyes. In general they serve to dramatize the presentation of the poem as speech (on the lowest level), just as the poem's narrative can be said to extend the material of simile. The way in which they engage with or frame the narrative, indeed, is the best index to the function of the poet, for whose vision, or mere words, the invocations indicate the source. More than perhaps any aspect of *Paradise Lost,* the invocations place the poem; by dramatizing the poet, of whose presence in the poem so many details remind us, by explicating as fully as possible the poem's several origins, they serve in part as what Robert Penn Warren calls "the context of composition." [13]

The phrase is a useful one. But when we ask just what the invocations of *Paradise Lost* add to the poem per se, it is clear that "impure" poetry in any Miltonic sense involves more than expressive considerations. Passages such as those we have just examined may strike us as especially immediate, or even autobiographical, I would suggest, because in them the poet is explicating the poem's causes—the causes, that is, of the poem he himself, in *Paradise Lost,* is merely pursuing, the poem he intends to write. What makes a poem true for Milton involves its emergence from the various sources, to be sure. But to dramatize that process was also to make the poem *work.* Milton's early and persistent preoccupation with the poem's success is reflected somewhat later in the first invocation. The poet appropriately prays for the illumination which precedes all technical accomplishment. Only then does he speak of the poem's effective result—omitting only that crucial "act" of the reader:

> And chiefly Thou, O Spirit, that dost prefer
> Before all Temples, th'upright heart and pure,
> Instruct me, for Thou know'st; Thou from the first
> Wast present, and with mighty wings outspread
> Dovelike sat'st brooding on the vast Abyss
> And mad'st it pregnant: what in mee is dark
> Illumine, what is low raise and support;
> That to the highth of this Great Argument
> I may assert Eternal Providence,
> And justify the ways of God to Men.
>
> [I. 17–26] [14]

13. In "Pure and Impure Poetry," *Selected Essays of Robert Penn Warren* (New York: Random House, 1943).

14. On the "act" which is the greatest decency, see above, pp. 78–79.

Milton here relies upon the irony that the poem's beginning pretends to *anticipate* the instruction, the access to the great argument; and it is significant that, although the poet elsewhere appears to cause divine motions, at this point he speaks of himself as recipient of divine wisdom and as only potentially a source of justification or illumination himself. In logical terms, the poet's plea at first seems confined to the matter of invention; poesis here is knowing and conception, without which a poem, like Pandemonium, is a structure raised from the darkness of some inner abyss and mere "disposition"; Milton here initiates the poetic world antithetic to the Muse's own, especially in the ambiguous possibilities of "prefer"—a world and an implied poem which *Paradise Lost* transcends most clearly at IX. 1. And yet, of course, the lines ultimately imply a fusion of the two provinces of logic, at least for this poem; for the great argument is already invented, in the real poem already *there,* something Milton had suggested in the prose of 1642. The Muse's support, that is to say, is crucial even in the merely technical matter of answering the argument.

More particularly, the invocations of *Paradise Lost* guarantee the "success" of this poem by allowing us to see its poet, in effect, as a spectacle, *in propria persona* and virtually outside the poem. Taken together, they suggest the discreteness, though not the separability, of poem and process. In *Lycidas* and *Paradise Lost* alike, narrative is made more than potentially answerable to the poet's song. But in *Paradise Lost* far more than *Lycidas,* Milton expands upon the poet's authority, uncouth or otherwise, and even upon the poem's form, making both kinds of self-consciousness into paradoxical conditions of success in answering the poem's great idea. The measure of this success is the way in which Milton's wondrous narrative joins with what we have called argument in these pages. (*Summons* might be a more appropriate word, since the narrative as a whole in *Paradise Lost* seems both to dramatize the responding Muse and to represent the providential ways.) To judge from book III, in particular, the articulation of the poem's origins with a definitive narrative *result* of the poet's words—corresponding to the *ottava rima* narrative confirming the poet's words in *Lycidas*—is a prime focus of Milton's art.

Milton's care in dovetailing what we have called poem and process is clear from the outset. Whoever speaks "Th'infernal Serpent; hee it was . . . ," the poetry of the lines that follow clearly implies an answer, perhaps in part misleading, to the speaker's original request to know the causes moving our grand parents. More often such answers are clearly designated, and even framed, in the manner of the passage describing Mulciber's fall. The lines following are unusual only in that they make explicit the quasimagical connection of words and action which works virtually throughout *Paradise Lost:*

> He spake; and to confirm his words, out-flew
> Millions of flaming swords, drawn from the thighs
> Of mighty Cherubim; the sudden blaze
> Far round illumin'd Hell.
>
> [I. 663–66]

In book III, Milton introduces another major segment of *Paradise Lost,* taking us with the poet—and with a much-relieved Satan—from the "obscure sojourn" of Hell to the realm of invisible light. It is primarily because of where we are going in the poem's voyage, and of where we have just been, that we here get the distinction between mortal, corporeal sight and the inspired insight of the prophet. As a whole the invocation serves to underline the visibility "to mortal sight" of the first two books of the poem; and it is in supporting his request to "express thee unblam'd" (III. 3; see above, pp. 234–43) that he fills in the details of his poet's own shadiest covert" with a glance, perhaps, at the pastoral beginnings of the epic poet's vocation. He does so, as we have seen, to suggest the human cost of his authority. Given the paradoxical context, the more pathetic the passage the better; the medical disability, imaging the poet in his most "creatural" aspect, works ultimately to put the seal of authenticity upon the narrative wonder that succeeds and confirms the poet's words:

> Now had th'Almighty Father from above
> From the pure Empyrean where he sits
> High Thron'd above all highth, bent down his eye,
> His own works and thir works at once to view:
> About him all the sanctities of Heaven

Stood thick as Stars, and from his sight receiv'd
Beatitude past utterance; on his right
The radiant image of his Glory sat,
His only Son

[III. 56–64] [15]

This speaker's importance seems most evident when we consider those points in the poem at which speech pulls away from action or experience, and most notably in Heaven. The speeches of the Father and the Son are obviously not meant to be natural or immediate; and probably no justification of their ways will ever satisfy readers who judge all literary discourse by the criterion of domestic colloquy. Lacking an instinct for appreciating these speeches, we may too easily insist on the likelihood of real difficulties on the part of Milton the man, without considering all that we are told *about* the speeches, and thus about discourse in Heaven, by the narrator's stage directions. What immediately precedes God's first speech, if indeed it does not provoke it, is the glimpse of Satan (with whom we have been virtually identified as readers for two books):

Him God beholding from his prospect high,
Wherein past, present, future he beholds,
Thus to his only Son foreseeing spake.

[III. 77–79]

The lines seem to imply that the entire action of the poem's episode, if not the poem as a whole, is, so to speak, contained in God's "prospect high." Furthermore, Milton actually involves God's discourse in the sensations which constitute the immediate experience of Heaven; if we are excluded from that experience, there is no missing the powerful sense of effortless communication and immediate, exotic, perception available to the "elect": [16]

Thus, while God spake, ambrosial fragrance fill'd
All Heav'n, and in the blessed Spirits elect
Sense of new joy ineffable diffus'd.

[III. 135–37]

15. Compare the "utterance" of the catalogue at I. 567 ff.
16. On sensation in Milton's verse, see W. B. C. Watkins, *An Anatomy of Milton's Verse* (Baton Rouge: Louisiana State University Press, 1955), pp. 3–41.

The new joy sensed by the blessed spirits—and implied in the energy informing Milton's latinate English—is then amplified and imaged independently in what follows, the appearance of the Son. And if the Son's speeches themselves do not delight us, again we may at least consider the way in which they are introduced; the important and joyous thing here, at any rate, is that the Son has actually, visibly appeared, like the form of Chastity to the Lady and—if Rosemond Tuve is right—to the audience of *A Mask* (see above, pp. 90). Given the metaphoric economy of his poem, Milton's choice of metaphor for the Incarnation makes a traditional Christian link between the realm of light or spirit and that of expression (of all kinds): the relation between Logos and God is that between flesh and spirit. If we go along with Milton's syntax, the Son's speech is the immediate and literal expression of measureless love and grace, just as his visible form expresses the divine attributes; as for us, the poet's poor accommodation is here clearly and frankly a substitute, a measuring:

> Beyond compare the Son of God was seen
> Most glorious, in him all his Father shone
> Substantially express'd, and in his Face
> Divine compassion visibly appear'd,
> Love without end, and without measure Grace,
> Which uttering thus he to his Father spake.
>
> [III. 138–43]

And again, at the end of the Son's first speech, the offer of intercession, as if refusing to allow us to miss the point, the poet reminds us of the lameness of his vehicle and of the Son's actual transcendence of words:

> His words here ended, but his meek aspect
> Silent, yet spake, and breath'd immortal life
> To mortal men, above which only shone
> Filial obedience.
>
> [III. 266–69]

Clearly in such passages the severity of the speech is contrasted with a wondrous narrative which only seems so distinct from it; we can respond only to the narrative and to the *assertion* of continuity between speech and aspect if the words themselves seem inadequate to the description.

If there is any single moment in the poem at which its status as a true poem is most clearly urged, it is in the invocation of book IX, where the poet turns strategically on conventional heroic poetry. In a satiric and apparently unpremeditated burst, Milton clearly signals the poem's opening out and, more particularly, its transcendence of the very world which early in *Paradise Lost* is portrayed as "our" world. Like the references to the poem in its lowest aspect—to the circumstances of composition—the formlessness of the attack makes this one of the poem's "spontaneous" moments, though we should not forget that once again we are in the midst of an elevating heroic device. We are very close here to Milton's satiric prose, for example, in *Of Reformation*. But more astonishing is the fact that he appears to be demolishing the very world of reference he has previously used to establish Hell and which he originates on the narrative level in the description of Chaos. In effect, this is the vehemence threatened by the Lady in the *Mask at Ludlow Castle* and indulged in the antiprelatical prose—the literary annihilation of "all thy magic structures":

> I now must change
> Those Notes to Tragic; foul distrust and breach
> Disloyal on the part of Man, revolt
> And disobedience: on the part of Heav'n
> Now alienated, distance and distaste,
> Anger and just rebuke, and judgment giv'n
> That brought into this World a world of woe,
> Sin and her shadow Death, and Misery
> Death's Harbinger: Sad task, yet argument
> Not less but more Heroic than the wrath
> Of stern *Achilles* on his Foe pursu'd
> Thrice Fugitive about *Troy* wall; or rage
> Of *Turnus* for *Lavinia* disespous'd,
> Or *Neptune's* ire or *Juno's,* that so long
> Perplex'd the *Greek* and *Cytherea's* Son;
> If answerable style I can obtain

Of my Celestial Patroness, who deigns
Her nightly visitation unimplor'd
And dictates to me slumb'ring, or inspires
Easy my unpremeditated Verse:
Since first this Subject for Heroic Song
Pleas'd me long choosing, and beginning late;
Not sedulous by Nature to indite
Wars, hitherto the only Argument
Heroic deem'd, chief maistry to dissect
With long and tedious havoc Fabl'd Knights
In Battles feign'd; the better fortitude
Of Patience and Heroic Martyrdom
Unsung; or to describe Races and Games,
Or tilting Furniture, emblazon'd Shields,
Impreses quaint, Caparisons and Steeds;
Bases and tinsel trappings, gorgeous Knights
At Joust and Tournament; then marshall'd Feast
Serv'd up in Hall with Sewers, and Seneschals;
The skill of Artifice or Office mean
Not that which justly gives Heroic name
To Person or to Poem. Mee of these
Nor skill'd nor studious, higher Argument
Remains, sufficient of itself to raise
That name, unless an age too late, or cold
Climate, or Years damp my intended wing
Depress; and much they may, if all be mine,
Not Hers who brings it nightly to my Ear.

[IX. 5–47] [17]

"Strategically" would seem just the wrong word for this passage, which along with other invocations may well strike us as agreeably intimate and "low"; surely, here again is the dissociation of which Eliot made so much in his reading of Milton—the blind poet's profound refusal to commit himself to his own greatest performance.

The passage gains in complexity and interest, however, the

17. "But now my Oat proceeds, / And listens to the Herald of the Sea" (*L*, 88–89).

moment we question any simple identity of the prominent *I* of these lines with Milton the man. Whatever the objective counterpart for that Celestial Patroness, for example, at least two points are demonstrable and relevant to the poem: She is probably the Urania—or the meaning if not the name of that sister of Wisdom mentioned in book VII who conversed and played "in presence of th'Almighty Father." [18] More immediately, she is to be distinguished from earthly sponsors of poetic performances, particularly no doubt those requiring such arguments as Tasso's (see Hughes, pp. 668B–69A, and above, p. 59). As we have seen, it is the internal distinctions which make such passages part of the poem. While the violent attack on conventional heroic arguments seems almost out of hand (it is closely related to Milton's political invectives), even touched off by the single word "Wars," Milton images the world of conventional "feigned" literature recognizably as the world of simile, inhabited and beheld by the reader and by the poem's pilots and belated peasants. It is more clearly "royalist," to be sure, and associated with the "troublesome disguises which we wear," but its basis in self-deception and outright dreams is clear enough. It is preeminently a world of *visible* objects as well, quite of the sort we find in Milton's own Hell. Milton juxtaposes all previous literary arguments with the gilt surfaces of various furniture, with menial servitude (like the "grooms besmear'd with gold" which set all crowds agape), and even with ceremonial eating. It is perhaps the most extensive *collection* of imagery in the poem; but clearly it is a collection of Milton's *own* imagery. The realm of "the better fortitude" involves a negation of this surface world; Milton would appear to insist that it is beyond aesthetics altogether. The passage's details refer most immediately to the visible details of *Paradise Lost* itself, including the War in Heaven. But even if we do not recall the blistering satire of *Eikonoklastes,* directed in part at the

18. See above, pp. 35–36. For two quite different but pertinent studies of wisdom see Frank M. Manley's introduction in *John Donne: The Anniversaries* (Baltimore: Johns Hopkins University Press, 1963), and M. Jack Suggs, *Wisdom, Christology, and Law in Matthew's Gospel* (Cambridge: Harvard University Press, 1970).

frontispiece of the forged *Eikon Basilike,* it is plain here that the "impreses quaint" are more than literary in their nature.[19]

Thus, in turning back on ordinary poetry, Milton turns back on the visible portions of his own poem, including many of the passages we have examined in some detail. If we are right in seeing a single world in those similes of *Paradise Lost,* then, the invocation refers both to the poem's outside and to the origins of that world in Chaos and in the human names of the catalogue.

We can be somewhat more particular, however, even if we hesitate to put such a burden on a casual outburst or to speak of a single world implied by the metaphoric clusters of the poem. For the very impression of the invocation's casualness—and this one is by no means unusual in this respect—is itself highly premeditated, if only we care to notice. While the attack we have just examined appears to burst spontaneously from the stimulus of war, it arises from a fundamental distinction in *Paradise Lost* between the argument of the poem, which already exists and antedates *Paradise Lost,* and the poem's mere style, potentially answerable to that idea but mediated through the poet / scribe. The style itself, we may notice, must be obtained from the Celestial Patroness—even the Ramists' "disposition" is not this poet's province. The subject only is available already, though it may not be universally pleasing. Thus, the poet's attack here is not on the knights or furniture per se; it merely distinguishes the normal technique or "maistry" of epic (a word significantly original in Milton's Chaos) from *heroic argument.* When Milton wrote "I now must change / Those Notes," he was thus calling attention to the poet in his lowest aspect, to the level of mere competence, at which the writer as it were at work, comments

19. For the fullest discussion of *Eikon Basilike* and *Eikonoklastes,* see *CPW,* 3 (ed. Merritt Y. Hughes) : 147–67, and the annotated text, 337–601. "How much their intent . . . drives to the . . . end of stirring up the people . . . appears both by the conceited portraiture before his Book, drawn out to the full measure of a Masking Scene, and set there to catch fools and silly gazers, and by those Latin words after the end . . . intimating, That what hee could not compass by Warr, he should atchieve by his Meditations. . . . But quaint Emblems and devices begg'd from the olde Pageantry of some Twelf-nights entertainment at *Whitehall,* will doe but ill to make a saint or Martyr" (*CPW,* 3 : 342–43).

forlornly on his "sad task." But "task" is by no means necessarily equivalent to the "argument" which follows two words later.[20] The argument exists objectively, as an archetype beyond any merely technical performance; "sufficient of itself to raise / That name" (heroic). The confusion of ends and means which produces conventional epic is precisely what "will" happen "if all be mine, / Not Hers who brings it nightly to my Ear."

It is thanks to the paradoxical tension between the poem's process of speech and its great argument that we break out of such analyses of "the poem itself" only to fall into fictions about "what will happen." At this point we part ways with the poet (if not, perhaps, with the author), who consistently connects the real poem only with the latter. Ultimately the invocations are related to internal aspects of *Paradise Lost,* to the poet's, but not the author's, mind and history. While they reveal very little about the act of composition or the biographical background of *Paradise Lost,* on the other hand, it seems useful to connect them with Milton's prose career and even the autobiographical prose of the 1640s. For in effect, they continue the half-theoretic, half-vocational discussion with which we began. As revelations of the poet's person and of the poem's situation (sometimes in references apparently "low"), they embody the literary strategy which can make poetry at once sincere (in the root meaning of "spotless") and true.

Coming to the poem from previous epics—not to mention Milton's earlier work in both prose and verse—we must be impressed not just with the burgeoning of the epic's "margins" but with the conversion, in effect, of conventional epic techniques into instruments of discourse and vision, into an apparatus of perception. If at times the poem seems abrupt or inelegant, the reason is usually artistic; it has more to do with the audience of Milton's epic than with its writer. The significance of this controlled participation of the speaker in the angel chorus is not that Milton is both "in" and "out" of such passages—a debatable and

20. Compare: "Courteous Reader, There was no Argument at first intended to the Book, but for the satisfaction of many that have desired it, I have procured it . . ." ("The Printer to the Reader," added during the printing of the first edition).

finally irrelevant question. It is at least clear that we are almost irrecoverably out of them—once we have read them, they leave us behind and below, as mere readers of poetry. The consistent fact in every such rhetorical violation of the dramatic frame for the poem's music is the pastness of the Fall and the irrecoverability of the original Paradise. The cause for the entire song—and the reason for any dramatic inconsistency in the merging of voices in these passages—is man's first disobedience. While we have not yet rehearsed the Fall in the poem's narrative, it is never absent as our implied history, as the poem's way of locating us—even when we momentarily join the angel chorus or enter Eden. This indeed would appear a compelling reason for distinguishing clearly between such terms as *structure* and *narrative*. Neither the chorus nor the epic as a whole is as incommunicable as the opaque, discrete image of postromantic poetry, although Milton often speaks "darkly," as Bard or Prophet.[21] At the very moments when poetic description approaches definition, he most frankly acknowledges the lameness of his vehicle. It has been pointed out, most often in complaint or apology, that there is an irreducible and carefully controlled mediateness about this art, in which the poet's language and tone of voice at times block and then urge our sympathy or participation, now dissociating us (or reminding us of our dissociation) from Paradise, now allowing us once again, quite imaginatively, to accompany the incursions of chaos, death, and history, into the poem's Garden.

21. See, for example, Kermode, *Romantic Image,* passim.

Index